Reading *Real Courage*, I find n
answers to the fears described ir
devotion, Thaddeus Barnum cor
answer to my fears by using these
— JW (

Incredibly rich with wisdom, insight, personal vulnerability, and severity, *Real Courage* is for every believer who desires a more honest relationship with Jesus. In this beautifully written devotional, Thaddeus Barnum takes us on a practical and, at times, painful journey into the depths of weakness and transformation through the lens of Jacob. Theologically rich and practically informed, *Real Courage* will challenge you to abandon a shallow understanding of brokenness, fear, shame, loss, and distress, and instead discover the joy of wholeness only discovered at the feet of Jesus. Let Jesus wrestle with you as you read. I highly recommend this book for anyone seeking a deeper, more personal, understanding of the love of Jesus in the midst of a broken world.

—JIMMY DODD, founder and president of PastorServe, author of *Survive or Thrive: 6 Relationships Every Pastor Needs* and *Pastors are People Too*

Thaddeus Barnum artfully connects the real-life fears with which the great patriarch Jacob wrestled, transparently connecting biblical truths to life through his own compelling story. For those tired of superficial calls to finding inner strength, this beautifully crafted book shines the light of Scripture into the darkest, most dreadful corners of life. Courage is the great need of this day and the only source is God himself.

—JO ANNE LYON, General Superintendent Emerita and ambassador for The Wesleyan Church

Real Courage is an excellent read. It dares to address our struggle with fear and faith. The story of the patriarch Jacob comes to life as his foibles serve as building blocks for our faith. Filled with Scripture and vulnerable personal experience, this book will enrich any disciple in our world ravaged by the monster "fear."

—MUTUA MAHIAINI, international president of The Navigators

When I face my own fears I know it's here I'll meet Jesus. *Real Courage* gives solid hope that peace is possible—that Jesus will meet, restore, strengthen, and encourage—no matter how dark the days seem. This book is discipleship—reorienting us and bringing the gospel practically and powerfully to bear.

—THE RT. REV. KEN ROSS, Anglican Bishop

Using the story of Jacob and Esau as his guide, Thaddeus Barnum helps us to see that courage is not simply an emotion that we can gather up on our own, but the result of deep wrestling—with our circumstances, with ourselves, and most importantly, with God himself. As always, Thaddeus' teaching is humble, gracious, and inspiring. I highly recommend this book to anyone struggling with anxiety or fear.

—REV. WINSTON T. SMITH, faculty at Christian Counseling
and Educational Foundation

Thaddeus Barnum is an incredible storyteller, and through this, he invites readers into his fears to show us that we are not alone. By mixing real-life stories with scriptural truth, this book will help you understand why God's Word is so important when battling fear. *Real Courage* will inspire you to wrestle with your fears, and with God, in order to give you the courage to stand filled with faith.

—MARK O. WILSON, pastor and author of
Purple Fish and *Filled Up, Poured Out* (WPH)

Thaddeus Barnum has written one of the most honest, vulnerable books about grappling with fear I have ever read. He acknowledges the power fear wields to distort the truth, especially for leaders in the church, and through illuminating meditations on Scripture, alongside gripping anecdotes from his life, *Real Courage* invites us into a robust, but never simplistic, faith to handle the day's most pressing crisis.

—REV. DR. JOHN W. YATES, II, Rector of The Falls Church in Falls Church, VA

REAL COURAGE

WHERE BIBLE AND LIFE MEET

THADDEUS BARNUM   9/23/17

Dear Andrew,
     What a happy day!
I'm so proud of you and
the man you have become.
Megan is a treasure and
so are you.
          Lots of love,
               Mom

wesleyan
PUBLISHING HOUSE
wphstore.com

Copyright © 2016 by Thaddeus Barnum
Published by Wesleyan Publishing House
Indianapolis, Indiana 46250
Printed in the United States of America
ISBN: 978-1-63257-167-0
ISBN (e-book): 978-1-63257-168-7

Library of Congress Cataloging-in-Publication Data

Barnum, Thaddeus, author.
Real courage : where Bible and life meet / Thaddeus Barnum.
Indianapolis : Wesleyan Publishing House, 2016.
LCCN 2016034778 | ISBN 9781632571670 (pbk.)
LCSH: Courage--Religious aspects--Christianity. | Jacob (Biblical
  patriarch)
LCC BV4647.C75 B37 2016 | DDC 242/.5--dc23 LC record available at
https://lccn.loc.gov/2016034778

To Erilynne—in the joy of our thirty-fifth anniversary

CONTENTS

Use *Real Courage* devotions to accompany
group Bible studies or preaching from Jacob's life.

Free shepherding resources are available at
www.wphresources.com/realcourage.

ACKNOWLEDGEMENTS

I remain indebted to my dear friend, Craig Bubeck. Thank you for editing this work, your patience when I was late with the manuscript, and for always surprising me with encouragement as a writer. Thank you, also, to Rachael Stevenson (editor) and Lyn Rayn (cover and interior design). Wayne MacBeth, thank you for your faithful witness of Jesus to me.

Thank you to the board and staff at www.call2disciple.com. It's a joy to be on team with you.

Thank you also to ministries like CCEF (Christian Counseling and Educational Foundation: www.ccef.org) that bring the heart of biblical faith to those of us who need godly counsel.

Erilynne and I get overwhelmed sometimes by family, friends, and countless people who come alongside to love us, pray for us, support us, and cheer us on—especially when the nights are long and the wrestling never seems to end. You know who you are and you have our thanks, our love. We pray we are there for you too.

To God always be the praise, honor, and glory.

INTRODUCTION

What do we do when we're really afraid? Where do we go? Who do we talk to? Does it surprise or annoy you that Christians suffer from fear and anxiety too? Shouldn't faith inform fear? What happens when it doesn't?

To the secular mind, all we need is courage to face our fears. We "man up." We access the power within us. We overcome because we can. When it gets really bad, we try anything—Eastern meditation, medication, music therapy—whatever. Desperation needs answers, real answers.

The simple fact is: Nothing out there works. Nothing lasts. The Bible is different. It introduces us to "El." He is a real person. *El*, in Hebrew, is the short version of God's name, Elohim. It's a most personal, intimate name for the Lord. When we're terrified, nothing compares to Him. If you want five easy steps to stop panic attacks, El's not for you. He demands a real encounter with you.

Worse, He wants control. The more we fight, the more He fights back. And that's the story of this devotional. I want you to meet El: He's the real wrestler, the One who met a terrified Jacob at the Jabbok River and wrestled him all night long. And when it was over, when El did what He came to do, something wonderful happened to Jacob.

Real courage came.

It can happen for you and me too. You see, the secular mind is wrong. Real courage doesn't come from within. It comes from above. It's the gift God gives. He's the One— "perfect love"—who "casts out fear" (1 John 4:18).

I know this personally. I am a fellow sufferer from the torments of fear. And, if you'd let me, I'd like to take you to the Jabbok River, introduce you to El, and let the wrestler do what only He can do. No matter what you're facing, you'll find in Him real courage like you've never known.

PART 1

WHY WON'T
FAITH COME?

1

WHEN FEAR ENTERS THE SOUL

*And the messengers returned to Jacob, saying,
"We came to your brother Esau, and he is coming to
meet you, and there are four hundred men with him."
Then Jacob was greatly afraid and distressed.*

—GENESIS 32:6–7 ESV

On the day it happened, Jacob was standing at the river Jabbok. This river, descending some fifty miles down "deep-cut canyons," fed straight into the Jordan.[1] At this spot began the highway home to the land God had promised to his grandfather Abraham, to his father Isaac, and now to him and his children forever.

Still, it would take time to get home. His slow-moving flocks stretched across the land for as far as the eye could see. It was lambing season with nursing ewes and newborns that could not be driven hard (Gen. 33:13). How different than the last time he stood at this river. Back then, he crossed the ford of the Jabbok alone, as he often said, "with my staff only" (32:10). But now, he was a man with family, abundant flocks, and great wealth. His years of slavery under his tormenting uncle Laban were finally over.

Of all days, this one should have filled his heart with joy.

Instead, one thing captured his mind—the one story written deep into the fabric of his soul, one that dated back even to his mother's womb. The two of them, twins. Wrestling even there.

Esau.

It had been twenty years since Jacob had seen his brother. On that parting day, their father had made it sound like he was sending Jacob to Mesopotamia, back to his mother's family, to find a wife (28:1–2). Truth be told, Jacob was running from Esau and his fury (27:43–45; 35:1).

Was Esau different now? Had his anger subsided?

Jacob had to find out. He crafted a carefully worded message announcing his return (32:4–5). He sent messengers to get a read on Esau. He had to know how Esau would react when they met. Would he extend favor and kindness? Would he be indifferent? Or worse, would he somehow oppose him, threaten him?

Soon enough, the messengers returned.

But their report was more than confusing. "We came to your brother Esau," they said. But they carried no letter from him. They had no words to report, no message. They provided no indication of how Esau received them or how he reacted when the news first hit his ears. All they said was, "He is coming to meet you." And then, "Four hundred men are with him."

At the sound of these words, fear entered Jacob's soul.

The Message *phrases it this way: "Jacob was scared. Very scared. Panicked . . ." (32:7). It was, in every way, a declaration of war. An army was coming against him. And what did he have? Farmhands! Eleven sons and a daughter all under the age of fourteen! No doubt he only had weaponry enough to fight off wild beasts and looters. Not this. Not an army of four hundred. Not under the command of Esau and old, bitter rage.*

Here at the Jabbok, Jacob "was greatly afraid and distressed" (32:7).

What can I say? Sometimes fear wins.

I lose balance and perspective. I try to reason things out but I can't. I can't think straight. Like someone kicked me in the stomach so hard I can barely breathe. Like someone tossed me out of the boat in a storm, and I'm doing everything I can to keep my head above water.

On this particular night, I can't sleep. I wonder why it's harder at night.

I go to our guest room in the early morning hours. I gather my Bible, my journal, and a pen—old, trusted friends. I kneel at the side of the bed and stare out the window at the streetlamp. My heart races. My mind spins, the scene of the previous afternoon playing over and over again in my head, all out of proportion—like me. I know to come here. On my knees. Before the Lord. There's nowhere else to go.

Why does it hurt so much?

Just hours before, I was in a meeting. One of the men, a man of influence, well-respected in secular and Christian communities, lashed out at me. In front of others. It wasn't his first time. We all know his temperament. He's a complicated man—brilliant, affable, funny at times. But cross him and out comes a self-centered, oppressive bully who dominates people with his anger.

I handled the moment, by God's grace, when it happened.

But not tonight. All I can feel is fear coursing through my veins. I can't stop my heart from pounding. My palms are wet. There's dryness in my mouth and a cry to God deep in my soul that is begging for help.

Fear—as far back as I can remember. Why is it always fear?

I think of all the people like me tonight. People living in fear because somebody dominates them—a drunken family member, an abusive boss, an obsessed friend, a caretaker forgetting us in our old age—anybody with power to enslave the soul.

I think of people halfway around the world where war rages in their streets. Where the government steals any hope of finding security, peace, and basic human dignity.

I think of children trying to sleep in homes where fear reigns.

Some years ago, as a young clergyman, I sat at the bedside of a dying saint in his late eighties. He had long served the Lord. He'd known Him since the days of his youth. He'd spent years in the Scriptures. He knew them. He taught them.

But there, in his final days, I saw what I didn't want to see. He was afraid, almost panicked, and I didn't understand it. How could a man so full of faith be so full of fear?

It made me wonder if I'd ever be free of it.

Now I look at the clock radio beside the bed—2:32. Hours to go before daybreak. I flick on the light and open my Bible and journal. For some time, I've sensed that the Lord wants me at the Jabbok with Jacob, this man after God's heart, to pitch my tent, settle in, and let this narrative in Genesis 32 wash over my soul—slowly, deliberately.

For here Jacob, like me, wrestles with fear bigger than himself.

This exercise is the first of my disciplines. When fear attacks, I come to Scripture and prayer. I know, by His design, the Father has given us access to himself by His Spirit through His Son (Eph. 2:18). Here I can be with Him. I can pray. I can cry. I am not alone. This, of all privileges known to the human race, is the highest.

But I know, too, I'm not to go it alone. I know this about fear—I can't handle it. Fleshly pride mixed with the Devil's counsel always urges us to keep up our image. Be strong. Be courageous. Say, "I'm fine!" when I'm not. But the Lord designed us to be in community—His community. I won't go it alone. Come morning, I will talk about this with my wife. I will tell trusted friends in Christ.

But for now, tonight, I come to Genesis 32. With all my heart, I believe that "man does not live by bread alone, but man lives by everything that proceeds out of the mouth of the LORD" (Deut. 8:3; see Matt. 4:4). I need His Word, by His Holy Spirit, to comfort and feed my soul.

I will make this my study over the weeks ahead. I will ask the Lord to help me engage this text so that what happened to Jacob in this passage can—and will—happen to me. Fear will not have my soul. Real courage will rise. Faith will come, sent from heaven above, to give everything I need to face all that is soon to come.

I believe that. So here I am. At the Jabbok. On this night like no other night.

The wrestler and me.

Weeping may last for the night,
but a shout of joy *comes* in the morning.

—PSALM 30:5

QUESTIONS FOR REFLECTION*

What were the circumstances the last time fear entered your soul? Can you name your "four hundred"? What makes you feel pushed into places of distress and panic?

What do you do when you're afraid? What disciplines do you engage? Do you run to the Lord? Do you try to handle it on your own? Are there friends in Christ to help?

NOTE

1. Victor P. Hamilton, *The Book of Genesis: Chapters 18–50* (Grand Rapids, MI: Eerdmans Publishing Co., 1995), 328.

* *The reflection questions at the end of each devotion are designed to encourage prayer, journaling, and conversation in small group settings. It's easy to read and go on. It's better to read, stop, and engage in dialogue and prayer.*

2

THE CAMP OF ANGELS

Now as Jacob went on his way, the angels of God met him.
Jacob said when he saw them, "This is God's camp."
So he named that place Mahanaim [Two Camps].

—GENESIS 32:1–2

But why was Jacob "greatly afraid and distressed"? It makes no sense.

Before the news ever hit his ear about Esau and the four hundred men, God gave Jacob everything he needed. Nothing held back. If we "walk by faith, not by sight" (2 Cor. 5:7) then Jacob was blessed; he was granted something more than faith—much more. He was given sight. He saw the spectacular, the magnificent.

The heavens opened up before him.

Here at the beginning of Genesis 32, as Jacob entered the Promised Land, "the angels of God met him." There is no mention that it was a dream. The dream had happened years ago, back when he was running from Esau. Back then, Jacob was at Bethel. He fell fast asleep, and in his dreams he beheld "the angels of God" (Gen. 28:12). But that's not the story now.

The writer told us "the angels of God met him" and Jacob "saw them." They were real, physical, and face-to-face. How close were they? What distinguished them? Did he recognize them from his dream at Bethel? All we're told is that Jacob knew they were angels, something different than him. Last time, he reacted. He was "afraid" (28:17). This time, he simply exclaimed, "This is God's camp" (32:2), or, "This is God's army!" (RSV). Which meant it wasn't just one angel—although, wouldn't that have been enough?—or even a dozen.

Jacob had an army on his side. He had a military escort, and he knew it.

Immediately, he named the place (as he did at Bethel in 28:19). He called it "Two Camps." Why? Did one camp belong to Jacob and the other to the angels? Or had the angels assembled in two camps, one in front and one in back, as a theologian once asserted saying, Jacob was "everywhere surrounded and fortified by celestial troops"?[1]

Either way, Jacob was given an extraordinary gift.

He knew—he saw—what a prophet would later put into words; "Do not fear, for those who are with us are more than those who are with them" (2 Kings 6:16). And again, an apostle would say, "If God is for us, who is against us?" (Rom. 8:31). So why, I wonder, didn't Jacob laugh at the news that Esau was coming with an army of only four hundred? Why did he care? How could fear capture his soul and rob him of any remembrance that "legions of angels" (Matt. 26:53) stood at his side? Since when did fear wield that kind of power?

Fear bigger than faith. Fear bigger than sight.[2]

There I sit, a young pastor at the bedside of a dying saint. I must say, of all the people I've known down through the years, only a handful have ever told me they'd seen angels and were aware of it.

But that is his testimony.

He had served as a pilot in the military. One day, returning from a routine mission, on final approach, his plane went into catastrophic failure. The plane rolled, the nose angled down, and he lost control of the aircraft. There were three on board. He and his copilot did everything they could to right the plane. They were headed straight into the ground when, suddenly, the nose pulled up.

He glanced out the window—off to the right, then to the left—and saw angels under the wings. One on each side. As real as the sun in the sky. There one minute, gone the next, but visible long enough for both pilots to see.

That's his story.

He's spent the rest of his life telling it. He's had a singular passion to win men to Christ. "I shouldn't be here," he tells them. "But I recommitted my life to Jesus Christ that day. He rescued my plane. He rescued me. He can do the same for you." A simple message that won the hearts of many. There is something about this man that makes us feel safe—like there is nothing to dread. Not with God on our side. Not with His angels "sent out to render service for" those who put their trust in Him (Heb. 1:14).

So why doesn't he feel safe now? Why is he so plagued by fear?

He confides in me about a month before he dies. He is in the hospital. I can tell something is wrong. Panic sparks in his eyes. He is uncharacteristically fidgety. "My doctors have given up on me," he complains. "Who's fighting for me now?" I can tell he still sits in the pilot's seat. His body has gone into catastrophic failure. One last nosedive, and he is fighting for control.

"I'm afraid," he admits bluntly.

He asks if I'd come around more often—which I do. One day when he is back home, about ten days before he dies, I open my Bible and read from 2 Kings 6. I want him to hear the story of the mighty prophet Elisha and that epic moment when the king of Syria came against him. The king sent "a great army," with horses and chariots, to seize one man. They came by night. They "surrounded the city." At first light of dawn, Elisha's servant saw them and panicked.

"What shall we do?" his servant said (v. 15).

Elisha answered, "Do not fear, for those who are with us are more than those who are with them." And then the prophet prayed that God would open his servant's eyes to see the vast angelic army "full of horses and chariots of fire all around Elisha" (vv. 16–17).

I look at my old friend and say, "You've been given the same gift. You've seen angels." He nods, but I can tell it gives him no relief.

"Maybe we should pray for the Lord to open your eyes again so you don't fear the coming days. What do you think?" I ask.

"Two nights ago," he replies, "I was having a fitful sleep. Too much pain in my body and too much anxiety in my soul. At some point, in the early morning hours, I fell back asleep, and in my dream I saw them again. Clear as day. Like it was sixty years ago."

"Saw who again?"

"Same angels. Same faces. Same look in their eyes. But this time, there was no plane. They'd come for me like they'd been appointed by God to take me safely to His heavenly kingdom (2 Tim. 4:18). For a brief moment, fear left my body and faith filled me. I got to feel that old feeling again—the one I had when our wheels hit the runway. We laughed, we cried, with joy I'd never known before."

For the first time in weeks, I see that joy—that faith—light up his face. And then, just as fast, it disappears. As if it had never been there. Fear returns in force, and he is spiraling back into a nosedive. Nothing I say, nothing I do, can recover him.

Not even now? Not even after the angels appeared to him a second time? What could be more comforting, more convincing, than that? I try to reassure him that God speaks to us through dreams: "Didn't the prophets say, 'your old men shall dream dreams'" (Joel 2:28; Acts 2:17)? But he can't hear me. Not now. His eyes dart back and forth in frenzy. As if none of it ever happened.

As if the angels never came at all.

The angel of the LORD encamps around those
who fear Him, and rescues them.

—PSALM 34:7

QUESTIONS FOR REFLECTION

In 2 Kings 6:16–17, seeing the angelic army dissipated the servant's fear. Why didn't the same thing happen for Jacob? Why did fear have power over him (see 1 John 4:4)?

Why does fear make us forget what the Lord has done in our lives? Does it happen to you? Does His faithfulness in the past help you in the present when you're scared?

NOTES

1. John Calvin, *Calvin's Commentaries: The First Book of Moses Called Genesis*, vol. 1 (Grand Rapids, MI: Baker Books, 2005), 185. Calvin wrote, "Much more probable, that angels were distributed in two camps on different sides of Jacob."

2. It's almost unthinkable that this angelic meeting is recorded in two brief verses. Shouldn't it occupy as much space as the Bethel story in Genesis 28? Instead, Jacob's reaction to Esau dominates Genesis 32. The reader is left to conclude that fear overwhelmed any remembrance that the angels ever came.

3

MOM AND DAD

~~~

Two nations are in your womb; and two
peoples will be separated from your body;
and one people shall be stronger than the other;
and the older shall serve the younger.

—Genesis 25:23

Do God's promises help us when we're afraid?

Jacob's first promise from God came through his mom. It happened during the days of Rebekah's troubled pregnancy. For twenty years, she had suffered with childlessness. Isaac had married her at forty and would not hold the twins until he was sixty (Gen. 25:20, 26). He prayed all those years in between, and finally "the Lord granted his prayer" (v. 21 ESV). But the pregnancy wasn't easy.

The boys wrestled in her womb.

Rebekah didn't understand it, so she went to the Lord in prayer and asked why. We're not told how He spoke to her; but He did, and He told her, "The older shall serve the younger" (v. 23)—the complete opposite of their culture and Jewish tradition. But this was God's promise, His purpose, His choice, and His call on Jacob and his offspring (Rom. 9:10–13).

Is it possible this was why "Rebekah loved Jacob" while "Isaac loved Esau" (Gen. 25:28)?

Did Isaac know about the promise? Did he believe it? Was it ever spoken out loud to Esau? What about Jacob? Did Mom whisper it to him as a baby? Is it possible the promise burrowed deep in his soul from his earliest days so he knew—always knew—that he was special to God? And his brother, poor Esau, would have to bend low and serve him?

How did this promise shape Jacob—this gift from his mom?

Jacob had a bigger gift from Dad.

Forget how he got it for the moment. Fact is, he got it—the coveted blessing of Abraham—passed down to his father, Isaac, and then to him. It was irrevocable—that's the beauty of it. It was a legal transaction, signed and sealed by God himself. When Esau heard Jacob had stolen it, he "cried out with an exceedingly great and bitter cry" (27:34). But his father could not reverse it (v. 33). The blessing had passed, forever.

And with it, all the promises God gave to Abraham.

Of course, one promise, though in fine print, stood out: Jacob would forever dominate Esau. Isaac told Jacob in no uncertain terms, "Be lord over your brothers, and may your mother's sons bow down to you" (v. 29 ESV). Isaac repeated it to Esau: "Behold, I have made him lord over you," and "you shall serve your brother" (vv. 37, 40 ESV).

Exactly what Rebekah had said.

By God's edict, Esau would never prevail. Not then. Not now at the Jabbok. Jacob had no reason to fear this great army of four hundred marching toward him. He had God's irrevocable promises given through his mom and dad. All he had to do was remember. Believe. Then watch every fear vanish into thin air.

From childhood, my old friend had something I didn't have growing up. He had the promises of God from Scripture written on his heart. You see, he was raised in a Christian home. His parents nurtured him and his siblings in the knowledge and love of the Lord.

"I can still hear my mom singing the great hymns of the church," he said to me one day. "And every night, we'd read the Bible and pray together as a family. Whenever I suffered from bouts of fear, there was never a shortage of family, friends, and people at church I could run to for prayer and comfort."

I didn't have that.

When I was afraid, all I could do was remember a song my mom taught me:

> Whenever I feel afraid I hold my head erect
> And whistle a happy tune so no one will suspect
> I'm afraid

> When shivering in my shoes I strike a careless pose
> And whistle a happy tune and no one ever knows
> I'm afraid

The song goes on to say, "Make believe you're brave, and the trick will take you far. You may be as brave as you make believe you are."[1] Mom never sang that part. But I found it was true. Whistling didn't work. It was all make-believe.

If only Mom and Dad had given me the gift my old friend had been given.

As a child, I imagined fear as a monster.

At night, alone in bed, I'd leave a light on. That way, I could always look around and make sure he, that monster, wasn't around. I didn't like him. I didn't like the way he made me feel. Like one time when my family went shopping. I was maybe four or five. At one point, I reached up for my dad's hand and it wasn't my dad. This stranger looked down at me and scared me. I looked everywhere for my family and couldn't find them. I screamed as loud as I could.

Fear made me feel unsafe. Unprotected. Alone and far from home.

My first day at school was a disaster. I'd seen my older brother and sister get through it. But it was hard for me. I had the worst case of homesickness imaginable.

Not long after, my dad got a new job. We moved from Detroit to Lakeland, Florida. On the day we finished packing and piled into the car to leave, we stopped at my grandparents' house to say goodbye. My grandfather hugged me so hard it hurt. He was a giant of a man. I still remember the day my mom took me to his office in downtown Detroit. As we ascended to this big office, way up high in a giant building, I was starry-eyed.

Great men like my grandpa don't cry, right?

But he did. On the day we moved to Florida, I saw his tears. I felt his sobs. I heard him try to speak, but he couldn't. It broke his heart for us to leave.

And I knew then—it never goes away. Homesickness would be with me for the rest of my life. It's simple, isn't it? We are not supposed to be far from home, far from those we love. That's where we are safe, secure, and protected. No monsters. No fear.

"You'll grow out of it," a camp counselor advised me when I was twelve. It was my first summer away from home. With my face red and swollen from crying, embarrassed by my peers who called me names, I assured him he was wrong.

I tell this story to my old, dying friend.

"It would've been different if I'd been raised like you—knowing the promises of God in my heart," I say.

"Yes and no," he says back.

The stories come quite freely as he testifies of times the Lord met him in his fears. "I've always had people around me who've known Jesus and His promises. They've prayed and strengthened me when I had no strength. I've always had a home with my brothers and sisters in Christ."

But then he shakes his head, and I ask why.

"I miss her," he says sadly.

And somehow, in this moment, I realize why his fears have come back with such a vengeance. All those years, since his early twenties, he had his wife at his side. She knew like no one else how to bring her husband to Jesus and speak His promises to his heart—calming him, comforting him. She was gone now. Three years, I think.

"You're right," he says. "It never leaves us. We're home-sick all the days of our lives until He brings us safely to His heavenly home."[2]

"I wish she was here for you," I whisper.

And, gently, he nods his head.

He has granted to us His precious and
magnificent promises, so that by them you may
become partakers of *the* divine nature.

—2 PETER 1:4

QUESTIONS FOR REFLECTION

How have the promises of God in Scripture shaped your life? Are they in your heart? Do you believe them? Are there people in your life who speak them to you regularly?

What impact do these "precious and magnificent prom-ises" have on you in times of fear, crisis, and suffering? When have they comforted you? When have they not?

NOTES

1. Oscar Hammerstein and Richard Rodgers, "I Whistle a Happy Tune," *The King and I* (New York: Rodgers and Hammerstein Organization, 1951).

2. Iain H. Murray, *David Martyn Lloyd-Jones: The First Forty Years 1899–1939* (Carlisle, PA: The Banner of Truth Trust, 1982), 23–24. According to one biography, Martyn Lloyd-Jones, while recalling his childhood, said, "I suffered at the same time from a far greater sickness, and a more painful one, which has remained with me all along life's path—and that was . . . [homesickness]." He also said, "I believe that I shall never totally recover from this until I reach the country where we shall meet never to part anymore." Iain H. Murray, *David Martyn Lloyd-Jones: The Fight of Faith 1939–1981* (Carlisle, PA: The Banner of Truth Trust, 1990), 51.

4

BETHEL

He had a dream, and behold, a ladder was set
on the earth with its top reaching to heaven; and behold,
the angels of God were ascending and descending
on it. And behold, the LORD stood above it.

—GENESIS 28:12–13

*What about the stone pillar in Bethel? Why didn't it help
Jacob as he waited for Esau?*

*Twenty years back, while first running from Esau and still in
the land of Israel, Jacob got to the city of Luz at dusk. As he fell
asleep that night something wonderful happened. Jacob fell into
a dream that was more than a dream.*

He was in God's presence.

*He saw a ladder, a real ladder, stretching into heaven with
angels on it, real angels, with everything focused on the One atop
the ladder. There He stood, capturing center stage, real and in
the flesh. Standing as a man stands. Jacob would later testify,
"God Almighty appeared to me at Luz" (Gen. 48:3).[1]*

How does God do that? How does He appear to man as man?

*It wasn't the first time. Maybe Jacob already knew that. Maybe
he'd heard the stories of Eden with "the Lord God walking . . .
in the cool of the day" (3:8). Surely he'd heard the story of his
grandfather Abraham, before Sodom was destroyed, when God
appeared and spoke to him as a man speaks to his friend (18:1, 22).*

But this was Jacob's first time. He saw Him. He heard Him say, "I am the Lord, the God of your father Abraham and the God of Isaac." With that, the Lord confirmed to Jacob that he was, and always would be, the recipient of the promises given to Abraham just as his father Isaac had said (28:13–14). But that wasn't all.

The Lord made a personal commitment to Jacob, saying, "I am with you and will keep you wherever you go, and will bring you back to this land; for I will not leave you until I have done what I have promised you" (28:15). In response, all Jacob could do when he woke in the morning was to worship Him. Yes "he was afraid," but it wasn't the panic fear he knew so well. It was the reverent, holy fear that comes from being in the Lord's presence.

Jacob knew he was standing on holy ground. He immediately changed the city's name from Luz *to* Bethel *(meaning "house of God") and made a personal vow of commitment, pledging himself and his tithe to the Lord (28:20–22).*

At the same time, he erected a stone pillar as a witness—as if it had heard all the words the Lord promised Jacob (Josh. 24:27). It shouted good news: "Jacob, never fear! The Lord is with you. The Lord will protect you. You will never be forsaken. You will come back to this land in safety."

Now, at the Jabbok before Esau arrived—now Jacob needed that good news. If he could just remember his direct encounter with God Almighty. He had seen His face. He'd heard His voice. He knew His promises. That stone pillar—why didn't it help him now?

"You've got to know the Lord for yourself," my old friend used to say. He loved to teach men the Bible. "Growing up in a Christian home won't save you. Being married to a Christian woman won't save you. You've got to meet Him yourself."

And then he'd tell us his story.

During one of our last times together, I told him I'd heard his story so many times I could recite it verbatim. And I began, imitating his voice as best as I could: "I was sixteen years old, handsome, and the fastest kid in our state. I held more records than—"

He laughed.

Of course, he picked up where I left off. He had a full college scholarship as a high school track star before he and his friends got into a car accident. Three survived, one didn't, and my friend broke his leg so severely he never competed again. He told it all, every detail, and especially the part where Jesus Christ met him in his darkest hour.

"There are times," he said to me, "when I tell my story, and it's like I'm there again. Back in His presence. Feeling the rush of faith and joy come into my soul, and it's everything to me. Why can't I feel it now?" he asked, his eyes moist with tears. He tried to remember. He wanted to remember. But it all felt distant and old.

He looked at me and groaned, "Stupid monster."

I agreed with him. He prodded me to tell my own story again; so I did, starting with the good part. "I came to faith in Christ when I was nineteen."

"Not so fast," he snapped. "Last time we talked, you were twelve and wrestling with fear and homesickness. Did it get better or worse?"

"Worse," I responded.

"Start there," he insisted.

"Sand castles," I blurted. "I learned it doesn't matter if the walls are thick and the moats deep. The ocean's tide always comes in and washes it away. That's my story. I was fourteen when Mom and Dad separated and later divorced. My brother graduated high school and moved out. Dad got a job in another city. I couldn't stop the tide."

"I know," my old friend sighed.

"We even lost our dog. I can't tell you how much that scared me. We had a fenced-in backyard. One minute she was there, the next she was gone. We looked everywhere. The police said somebody probably stole her, and that image stuck in my head. I couldn't bear the thought of her feeling alone. Stuck with strangers. Scared. No idea what happened to her. No way home."[2]

I paused. The memory still a little too raw.

"That's what happened to you, isn't it?"

"Yeah," I nodded. "Not long after, Mom went in for gallbladder surgery. They found cancer everywhere."

"So you went to live with your dad?"

"No," I said. "His job took him to Europe. My family found a boarding school for me about an hour from my grandmother."

My old friend got that panicked look again. He turned his head away and slowly began to repeat my words back to me: "Feeling alone. Stuck with strangers. Scared. No idea what happened to her. No way home."

I tried to change the subject.

"Not so fast," he repeated. "Were you there when she died?"

"Kind of," I said. "I got to her bedside at the hospital a few hours before. Enough time to tell her I loved her. But I couldn't stay with her. I wanted to, but I wasn't strong enough. Too young, too scared. I've always regretted it. My sister stayed with her. She was there when Mom died. I am forever grateful for that. In those days, my sister had already come to know Jesus and could pray for Mom like no one else."

"But not you?"

I shook my head. "Not yet. But I knew about Him. I could see something different in my sister Kate, my aunt Barbie—and also my dad. They were the first whisper in my ear that a real encounter with the Lord Jesus Christ was possible."

"What happened next? Right after the funeral?"

I looked at him, not wanting to answer. He saw my hesitancy and jumped in. "I bet you went back to the boarding school alone. Stuck with strangers. No idea what had happened to you. No way home—home was gone—and you were scared."

"The tide came in," I said. "The monster roared."

He grabbed my hand and squeezed it as hard as he could. Somehow our stories were strangely linked. Mine then, his now. And that somehow made him feel safe enough to confide his heart to me: "Stupid monster. Why won't he leave us alone?"

For he has said, "I will never leave you nor forsake
you." So we can confidently say, "The Lord is my
helper; I will not fear; what can man do to me?"
—HEBREWS 13:5–6 ESV

QUESTIONS FOR REFLECTION

Where are the "stone pillars" in your life when Jesus
Christ made himself real to you? What good news do they
shout? How does that good news help you today?

Can you talk about times when fear won't leave you
alone? When the story of your "stone pillar" feels distant and
old? When you feel disconnected from Hebrews 13:5–6?

NOTES

1. Victor P. Hamilton, *The Book of Genesis: Chapters 18–50*
(Grand Rapids, MI: Eerdmans Publishing Co., 1995), 241.
Hamilton stated: "Here in 28:13 Yahweh and Jacob are near each
other. . . . Jacob says a few verses later (v. 16), 'Surely, Yahweh
is in this place,' presupposes Yahweh's immediate presence in the
place."

2. Thaddeus Barnum, "Undistracted Eyes," in *Real Identity*
(Indianapolis, IN: Wesleyan Publishing House, 2013), 343–347.

5

TAKING HIS LEAD

Then the LORD said to Jacob,
"Return to the land of your fathers and to your
relatives, and I will be with you."

—GENESIS 31:3

The last time Jacob stood at the Jabbok, circumstance led him there. Esau was in control. He wanted to kill Jacob. Their mother, knowing this, urged Jacob to leave. She made sure her husband, Isaac, agreed and gave his blessing (Gen. 27:42—28:5).

That was then. This was now.

Circumstance still played a part. Jacob had lost favor with his uncle Laban. Even though Laban admitted "the Lord has blessed me because of you" (30:27 ESV), the tension between them was real (31:1). It was time for Jacob to go (30:25). They both knew it. Together, they worked out a financial settlement (30:33–34). But, truth be told, that's not what drove Jacob to leave when he did.

God was in control.

The Lord took the lead. He spoke to Jacob, though we don't know how. We only know that He who spoke to our fathers "in many portions and in many ways" (Heb. 1:1) spoke directly to Jacob (Gen. 31:3) and told him to "return to the land of your fathers." And then He promised the Bethel promise once again: "I am with you and will keep you" (28:15).

Then, to reassure him, the Lord spoke again. This time, in a dream, an angel called Jacob by name and said he knew about the injustice Jacob suffered under Laban. He announced, as God's messenger, "I am the God of Bethel, where you anointed a pillar, where you made a vow to Me." Same God, same promises, with a simple message: "Arise, leave this land, and return to the land of your birth" (31:11–13).

Not once but twice, Jacob received direct, God-given guidance to go home.

In response, Jacob called his family together. He told them all that was on his heart. Remarkably, Leah and Rachel, two rival sisters always at odds with each other, spoke with one voice and said, "Do whatever God has said to you" (31:16).

They wanted Jacob to follow God's lead.

And he did. Because he knew the Lord, "who has been my shepherd all my life" (48:15), was being his shepherd now. God was in charge, leading the way. Not Jacob. Not circumstance. Not human reasoning. This was the Lord's doing. And with it came God's promise of divine protection: "I will be with you."

If ever there was an antidote against fear, this was it. So why didn't it work? Why did Jacob let fear steal the reins of his heart and suddenly take the lead?

"I'm not leaving until I tell you the good part," I insisted.

I hated seeing him like this. My friend's body was tired, ravaged by disease and old age, his face pale and drawn, his soul not at peace. I could see his torment and, as a young pastor, I felt inadequate, not knowing how to comfort him.

"Don't sugarcoat it," he instructed, his voice still strong.

"At boarding school, they gave me a single room," I began. "My advisor pushed me to stay busy—classes, sports, social events, that kind of thing. But night always came. I had to go to my room, close the door, and face being alone. Sometimes I'd put headphones on, play music from my childhood, and pretend none of it happened."

"Never works," he grunted.

"No," I agreed. "Some nights got really bad. I'd lie in bed and all I could think about was the funeral, the hospital room, my family, scenes from the past—all of it—and I'd start to panic. This wail would come out of me, loud—too loud. I was afraid somebody might hear. So I'd leave. I'd prop open the back door of the dorm and head out into the night for as long as it took for the wailing to stop. Till I was too tired to cry anymore. Eventually I'd find my way back and fall into bed.

"That lasted until one night I got caught. A dorm advisor saw me leave and decided to follow me. He and his wife had an apartment on the top floor of the dorm."

"Got in trouble, huh?"

"I thought I would, but no," I replied. "When he came up alongside me that night, I was so embarrassed he'd heard me crying. I tried to explain, but he just put his arms around me and told me never to go out alone again. 'You knock on my door,' he said, 'and we'll walk the streets together. That's how we deal with matters of the heart. You got that?' And from that point on, he watched out for me.

"It made a big difference," I told my old friend. "This man never led me to Jesus. But he knew the monster's first principle of tactical assault."

"Get us alone," he said quickly.

"My advisor was a gift to me. He lived a simple message: 'I'm here. You're not going through this without me.'" I let the words hang in the air. My friend had the same gift, and he knew it. Many of us refused to leave him alone — especially now, in these last days. But all I got back was a slight nod of his head and a deep sigh.

"Go on," he muttered.

"After that, I did what I thought my dad would do. I got my act together, graduated high school, went to college, and set my sights on graduate work. I raced through those years, stuffing grief down, pushing fear away.

"But one night, in my last year at college, a pastor and his wife invited me for dinner. They were old friends of our family. He'd actually been at my mom's bedside a day or two before she died."

"I know where this is going," he mused.

"The pastor saw right through me. He didn't buy my act for one minute. Halfway through dinner, he looked at me and said, 'I know those eyes. I had those eyes once, a long time ago. So full of sadness, so full of fear. It's not easy, is it, holding it all in?' Just those simple words and it was like his scalpel had scraped the scab off my heart; and that wail, that old, miserable wail, started again.

"I had to excuse myself from the table. I had no control over it. I went outside, like I always did, and there he was right beside me, refusing to let me go it alone."

"But this time it was different, wasn't it?" the old man sparred.

"Yeah, this time was different. The pastor had lost his wife and baby daughter in a car accident when he was in his twenties. He knew grief. He knew the monster. He knew Jesus. And he knew how to help me know Jesus, too."

My old friend turned his head away.

I knew enough even in those days not to fill the silence between us with words. I sat back and waited. A frown formed on his brow. "I do know this," he said. "The Lord sends us people at just the right time. He knows us. He knows how to lead us. It's what He does. It's your story, but it's mine, too."

He got that professorial look on his face that I loved.

"And it's always the same message, isn't it?" he reflected. "I will never leave you. You never have to go through what you're going through alone. I will be there; I will see you through."

I sat there quietly, watching him. He did know. He did believe. Surely this would bring him comfort. But it didn't. I could see it—the torment still there. The fear still in control, still in the lead.

And me, not knowing what else to say.

Trust in the Lord with all your heart and do not lean on your own understanding. In all your ways acknowledge Him, and He will make your paths straight. Do not be wise in your own eyes; fear the Lord and turn away from evil.

—Proverbs 3:5–7

QUESTIONS FOR REFLECTION

Is the Lord in control of your life today—not you, not circumstance, not fear? How have you known His guidance? What needs to change for Him to take the lead?

Have you experienced the monster's first principle of attack: to get us alone? When has it worked? When hasn't it? When have you refused to let others go it alone?

6

HIS WATCHING

~~~

Then Jacob became angry and . . .
said to Laban. . . . "God saw my affliction and
the labor of my hands and rebuked you last night."

—GENESIS 31:36, 42 ESV

Esau wasn't the first to mount an attack against Jacob.

Uncle Laban struck first. When he heard Jacob had left him, he felt tricked (31:26). He "hotly pursued" Jacob with every intent to harm him (v. 36). Jacob anticipated this. It was why he fled in secret (v. 21). He was afraid. He was fully convinced Laban would steal his family "by force" (v. 31).

He knew that Laban wasn't in his right mind.

This was Jacob's family. Leah and Rachel were his. He'd served Laban fourteen years for that right. The children were his. All the flocks were his—they'd agreed upon that together. But Laban turned on Jacob. In Laban's own pompous, arrogant mind, he declared, "The daughters are my daughters, and the children are my children, and the flocks are my flocks, and all that you see is mine" (v. 43).

It was a lie. None of it was Laban's. But Jacob had to face facts: His uncle had become his enemy. Laban, his sons, and all his men were coming to attack him. And it would have happened if God hadn't intervened.

God was watching.

He came to Laban in a dream and said, "Be careful that you do not speak to Jacob either good or bad" (31:24). These words ended Laban's plans. He had power to destroy Jacob and told him so: "It is in my power to do you harm, but the God of your father spoke to me last night" (v. 29).

God stood between them.

This fact gave Jacob courage to speak boldly to Laban (vv. 36–42). And why not? The Lord had seen Jacob's affliction and defended him. He'd protected him, just as He'd promised (28:15). Laban's power over him was no power at all.

In response, Laban forced Jacob to enter into a covenant with him. He insisted they erect a pillar and a heap of stones as a physical witness that neither man would pass by them to harm the other (31:52). In this way, the Lord would "watch between you and me when we are absent one from the other" (v. 49).

Jacob had no need of this covenant. The Lord was already standing watch. But for Laban's sake, he went along with it. He let the heap and pillar be named: "Witness" and "Mizpah," meaning "watchpost." But what did these pillars mean to Jacob? The Lord was his Mizpah, the watcher who stood guard over his soul. Nothing could harm him. Not then. Not ever. This was the simple fact—Jacob knew it in his soul.

It should have given him courage as Esau approached. Why didn't it? If his Mizpah was watching before, wouldn't He be watching now?

I stood up to go. I promised my friend I'd return in the morning.

He reached for a notebook on his bedside table, opened it, and flipped through the pages. He told me it was the journal he had kept while his wife was dying.

"I was sitting where you're sitting now when I wrote this," he said quietly. He found the page he was looking for and handed it to me. "Mind staying a few more minutes? Won't take long."

I took the notebook, sat back down, and started to read.

"Out loud, please," he instructed.

The first entry I saw was dated March ninth. "Ellie's asleep now for the night," I read, "and it has been a relatively good day. Hospice came twice. Our daughters were here most of the day. A few family and friends visited, all nicely spread out, none staying too long. She slept a good deal. In snippets, we kept writing our story little by little."

I stopped, not understanding. "What story?" I asked.

"Our last few months together, we reminisced. I wrote some of it down and read it back to her. She loved it. She'd make a comment here and there, adding details I'd missed. In her last days, it's all she wanted me to do. Just read the stories to her. It soothed her somehow."

He pointed to the top of the next page and told me to keep going.

"March tenth," I said. "I'm still bothered by our last conversation. Just before she slept last night, she looked at me with those piercing eyes and said, 'You know this isn't the way I planned it?'

"'I do,' I tell her, and I know what's coming next. We've had this talk before.

"'I wanted it the other way around.' She shrugs.

"I nod. I tell her I want her better. 'I feel so helpless, Ellie. I wish I could protect you from all this, and I can't.'

It's as honest as I can be. I am scared for her, scared for me. I don't want this to happen, and I know it will. I sit here with death's army near, circling around my wife's bedside, and I can do nothing about it, nothing at all.

"'You always change the subject,' she tells me.

"'Yes, I do,' I admit.

"'Who's going to sit with you when your time comes? Answer me that.'

"I can't. She knows I can't. I mutter something stupid like, 'I'll be fine,' but it annoys her.

"'No, you won't,' she says sharply. 'It's going to be harder for you.' She pauses. Then she makes me remember my last time in the hospital. My raging fears. Her countless efforts to calm me. She knows how to do it. She knows no one else can.

"'Why is it different for you?' I ask.

"She's not afraid of the question. I've asked it so many times before in different ways, under different circumstances. Usually when I'm at my worst, I beg her to tell me her secret. Sometimes, in response, she reads Scripture to me. Sometimes she prays. Sometimes she brings Christian friends around. And sometimes she simply sings a quiet hymn of praise. But nowadays, all she does is reach for my hand and hold it tight.

"That's what she does now. And I take it, as I always have.

"She doesn't need to say more. In times past, she's said, 'When we're in the valley of the shadow of death, we have nothing to fear. I imagine our hands on His staff and His hands over ours. He has in His control what we do not.'

"Other times she's said, 'He's our Mizpah, our Watchman. He's the stone pillar we can put our hands on. Nobody can harm us now,' and then she'd squeeze my hand as if, somehow, it's hers, and mine, and His—all bound together as one.

"I feel the squeeze of her hand again.

"'I'll be OK,' I assure her. I want to say, though I don't, 'I wish I knew Jesus like you.' But she hates when I say that. She always replies, 'That's not true. You're too much in your head, that's all. You have to help your heart know what you already know.'

"I can see she's impatient. 'Now answer my question,' she insists. 'Who's going to sit there when your time comes? I don't want you alone.'

"I feel the tears, warm against my cheek. I squeeze her hand back. She knows I can't answer her. 'Today is my day,' I finally reply. 'I get to do what you always do for me. It's my turn to put your hands in His.' The faintest smile stretches over her face. She knows I'm right and gently nods her head.

"I ache inside. I want to tell her, 'I have loved you too much. You have been my stone pillar, my watchman, my Mizpah.' But I don't. She wouldn't like it. She'd tell me Jesus is all that and infinitely more. And she's right, I know. But still, I don't want to let go of her hand. And yet slowly, gently, she pulls it away.

"And I'm left feeling scared and alone."

The LORD is your keeper; The LORD is your shade on your
right hand. The sun will not smite you by day, nor the moon
by night. The LORD will protect you from all evil; He will
keep your soul. The LORD will guard your going out and
your coming in from this time forth and forever.

—PSALM 121:5–8

QUESTIONS FOR REFLECTION

Do you see the Lord as your watchman, your Mizpah?
In Psalm 121, He is our helper, our keeper, our protector. How
has this proven true in your past? How is it real for you now?

Who points you to Jesus? Who reminds you, in your
times of greatest fear, that you have a Mizpah watching
over you? What comfort does it bring? Do you do this for
others? How?

7

GOD ON MY SIDE

If the God of my father, the God of Abraham
and the Fear of Isaac, had not been on my side . . .

—GENESIS 31:42 ESV

For Jacob, the conflict with Laban proved helpful. It gave him a chance to look back over the years and reflect on God's faithfulness in his life. Amid all the tension, Jacob could say with confidence, "The God of my father has been with me" (Gen. 31:5).

But the subsequent years clearly affected him.

"I have served your father with all my strength" (v. 6), he told Leah and Rachel. This, no doubt, changed him physically. Growing up, Esau was the outdoorsman. Not Jacob. He was "a quiet man preferring life indoors" (25:27 MSG). But under Laban, he'd become a man of the field. Now he was likely strong and powerful like his brother Esau. As a shepherd, he'd learned to suffer in the heat of day, and in "the frost by night" when sleep "fled from [his] eyes" (31:40). And what gift did Laban give in return?

Laban cheated him. Ten times he altered Jacob's contracted wages (vv. 7, 41). He even cheated his own daughters (v. 15). But every time he tried to harm Jacob, his efforts failed. Jacob could look back over twenty years and reach the same conclusion: "God did not allow him to hurt me" (v. 7).

The Lord was on his side.

But it wasn't easy. He was constantly tested. When, for example, a wild beast killed one of the animals, Jacob was forced to bear the loss himself. If an animal was stolen, as Jacob reminded Laban, "You made me pay whether it was my fault or not" (v. 39 MSG). When sorely tempted to take one of the flock to feed his own family, Jacob never gave in (v. 38). For him, honor and integrity mattered.

"My honesty will answer for me," he told his uncle (30:33 ESV).

Through it all, the Lord blessed Jacob. "The little you had when I arrived," he reported to Laban, "has increased greatly; everything I did resulted in blessings for you" (v. 30 MSG). Even in their last days together, Jacob's flocks kept multiplying and strengthening. Laban's grew weaker (v. 42), which provoked his anger. If he could, if it had been in his power, he'd have sent Jacob away with nothing.

Jacob confronted him with this fact: "If the God of my father, the God of Abraham and the Fear of Isaac, had not been on my side, surely now you would have sent me away empty-handed" (31:42 ESV).

But that's the whole point: God was on his side, and Jacob knew it.

He could review the years and know the Lord had been faithful to him, always faithful. At the Jabbok, his prayer testified he knew this (32:9–12) even though Esau was coming to attack him. Even though fear filled his heart. Yet he had confidence.

God was on his side!

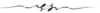

Early the next morning, a hospice nurse called. My old friend had a setback during the night. She'd called his children, who both lived out of state, and they were on their way. "If it's possible," she asked, "could you come this morning?"

I didn't know it then. But it would be the last time my friend and I would sit together. Just the two of us.

At first sight, I almost didn't recognize him. He lay in bed, on his side, hair disheveled, glasses off, a frown set deep on his brow, and eyes darting here and there like I'd seen before. I called out his name but got no response.

I'm not sure he knew I was there.

For a while, I knelt beside him, put my hand on his shoulder, and prayed the Lord Jesus Christ would attend his fearful heart. On the night of His resurrection, Jesus said, "Peace be with you" (John 20:19), and then He breathed on His disciples the gift of the Holy Spirit. I prayed for that breath to fill my old friend now.

On his bedside table, I saw a notebook much like the one I'd read from the day before. I reached for it and saw the words "Our Story" on the front. "Is this it?" I asked him. "Is this the story you wrote with Ellie?"

He didn't respond.

I pulled the chair next to his bed closer so I could rest my hand on his arm. It was my turn, I realized. Just as he'd read to Ellie, I could now read to him. I opened the journal and, to be honest, what I found surprised me. I was sure this would be their love story. How they met. How they fell in love. Names, places, phrases in a language all their own, that—just the sound of them—could transport them back in time.

Instead, I read on the top of the page, "For our children, their children, and their children to come. Always remember, 'God is faithful, and he will not let you be tempted beyond your strength' (1 Cor. 10:13 RSV)."

I flipped through the pages.

This told the story of three, not two. In their last hours together, all they could do was sing the Lord's praise. He had been with them. His mercy and His faithfulness were inextricably woven into the fabric of their everyday life. This was His story in their story. A few pages in, I saw an entry and decided to read it out loud to my friend.

"The Toy Vacuum," I said, reading the title.

"'Tell about Eva,' Ellie says, and I know which story she means. 'You want to see me cry,' I tease her. Eva's story always had that effect on me.

"'Maybe.' She smirks, but I can tell she wants to hear it again.

"We were still living on Westfield Road. Our first house. Barely enough pennies to rub together after the bills were paid. Little Eva seemed all grown up at the ripe old age of four. Kathryn was a year and a half. And all Eva wanted in life was a toy vacuum.

"'She wanted to help me clean house,' Ellie smiles.

"It broke my heart to say no to her. But we had no choice in those days. We couldn't afford it. So at night, when we prayed together, Eva started asking God for it. I told her that our heavenly Father knows what's best for us and some-times He says no, too. But that didn't stop her prayers night after night!

"'That's when you started looking for it,' Ellie recalls.

"'I called everywhere. There wasn't a store in the country that had one. I finally had to sit Eva down and quietly tell her that little toy vacuums didn't exist. It didn't faze her one bit. She kept right on praying, absolutely sure she'd get one.'

"'Our sweet little girl,' Ellie says with a sigh.

"'A few weeks later, the Wilkersons, from Chicago, moved in next door with three kids a little older than ours. We went over one night to introduce ourselves and bring a meal. Sam Wilkerson took one look at Eva and said, 'I bet I know what you want!' A minute later, he held in his hand a lime green toy vacuum cleaner. Our little girl squealed with delight! Do you remember the expression on her face, Ellie?'

"'I remember yours more,' she says. 'You were beside yourself.'

"'I still am. I still can't believe her heavenly Father knew her that well and loved her that much.'

"'You never let her forget.'

"I shake my head and wipe the tears from my eyes. Ellie says quietly, 'He hasn't changed, you know. He knows *us* that well, too. He loves *us* that much.'

"'Yes, He does,' I say and look into her soft, beautiful eyes. And somehow we both know 'The Toy Vacuum' is the story of our lives. Always has been. Always will be."

The journal entry ended.

I looked at my old friend and saw he was calmer. He was looking at me like he knew I was there. He didn't say anything, but there was the tiniest impression of a smile on his face. These memories had soothed him somehow. So I turned the page and kept on reading. Just like he'd read for Ellie. A love story not of two, but of three.

So that Eva and Kathryn, their children and grandchildren, never forget.

———

Bless the LORD, O my soul, and forget none of His benefits;
Who pardons all your iniquities,
Who heals all your diseases;
Who redeems your life from the pit,
Who crowns you with lovingkindness and compassion;
Who satisfies your years with good things,
So *that* your youth is renewed like the eagle.

—PSALM 103:2–5

———

QUESTIONS FOR REFLECTION

———

Are you able to recall God's faithfulness in your life (Ps. 103:2–5)? Even in conflict, when fears assault you, can you see God on your side and trust Him? What makes this easy or difficult?

Have you got "toy vacuum" stories in your life? Is there a regular discipline built into your family life of remembering the Lord's goodness to you? If not, why not? What can you do to begin one?

8

ANTICIPATING FAITH

*"We came to your brother Esau, and furthermore
he is coming to meet you, and four hundred men are with
him." Then Jacob was greatly afraid and distressed.*

—GENESIS 32:6–7

Jacob

*There are obvious similarities between the lives of Jacob and
Moses. Both men were called by God to face their enemies. Both
decided the best approach was to send spies ahead of them. For
Jacob, it was the only way to assess his brother's heart.*

Moses

*Moses' reasoning was similar. He sent twelve spies to assess
his enemies in the Promised Land. They returned with a factual
report: "The people who live in the land are strong, and the cities
are fortified and very large" (Num. 13:28).*

But these words sparked fear in the people's hearts.

*Making things worse, ten of the spies fanned that fear into
flame. They lifted their voices and said, "We can't attack those
people; they're way stronger than we are" and "they looked down
on us as if we were grasshoppers" (Num. 13:31, 33 MSG). The
people's hearts melted (Deut. 1:28; Josh. 14:8).*

But thank God for Caleb and Joshua! These two spies rose up with strong faith and said, "Do not be afraid of the people of the land, because we will devour them. Their protection is gone, but the Lord is with us. Do not be afraid of them" (Num. 14:9 NIV).

Moses said the exact same thing: "Do not be terrified; do not be afraid of them. The Lord your God, who is going before you, will fight for you, as he did for you in Egypt" (Deut. 1:29–30 NIV).

We know faith comes by hearing (Rom. 10:17), but this news "did not meet with faith in the hearers" (Heb. 4:2 RSV).[1] They chose to embrace fear instead. And they acted on it. They wept. They grumbled. They cried out for a new leader who'd take them back to the slave camps of Egypt. They were done with Moses and done with God (Num. 14:1–4, 10). Because of it, their hearts hardened and unbelief took root (Heb. 3:12–19). The Lord, in disgust, responded, "How long will [these people] refuse to believe in me, in spite of all the signs I have performed among them?" (Num. 14:11 NIV).

Jacob

Jacob faced the same choice.

Fear struck his heart at the messengers' report. How would he respond to the fear? Would he embrace it? Would he let it turn his heart hard and his soul to unbelief? Or would he let faith come? Would he remember he had angels on his side? Or that he had the promises that were given to his mom and dad? Would he remember that the Lord met him in Bethel—and again, more recently—and promised him safe passage home? Would he remember that the Lord protected him from Laban and that God was on his side?

What would Jacob choose—the reign of faith or the tyranny of fear?

At the reception following my friend's funeral, I had a chance to speak to his wife's younger sister, Connie. She'd spent the most time with him in recent months.

"I've got a lot of questions," I said after we found a place to sit.

"That doesn't surprise me," she said quietly.

"He didn't die peacefully, did he?"

"No, he didn't," she revealed. "He was restless, thrashing really, almost to the end. Even when he went into a coma, that frown was still set deep in his brow—like he was still wrestling with God."

"I'm not sure why, though," I admitted.

"It's simple. He wasn't in control," she said. "He gave the impression he was. Always taking charge. Always making sure everything went well. Never afraid. It's not a bad trait, really. But impressions can be deceiving."

She looked at me, hoping I'd understand. "Very few people knew the truth about him," she confessed. "He constantly battled fear. He rarely felt in control."

I nodded my head. I told her I knew.

"It didn't matter the circumstance. When fear set in, he'd panic. He'd do everything he could to fix the problem. If it wasn't fixable, he'd blame himself. He'd say there was some unconfessed sin in his life. Or maybe he hadn't followed Jesus closely enough and that's why God allowed the Devil to torment him. The more his fears escalated, the harder he'd fight against it."

She shook her head, still frustrated by him.

"He knew better," she said sternly. "He knew to go to Jesus, say he was helpless in the situation, and ask Him to take control of it. That's exactly how he counseled others. He'd say, 'The Lord doesn't rescue us by what we do, but by what He does.' But fear is a horrible thing. When it took over, he lost all reason."

"Yes, I know," I wanted to say, but didn't.

"He even blamed himself for dying. I kept telling him, 'This sickness isn't about you. It's not about some secret sin in your past. It's about your body. It's old and tired. Just accept it, put your eyes on Jesus Christ, and let Him care for you.'"

"I'm guessing that didn't help," I said.

"No, and it made me miss Ellie. She knew exactly what to do." Connie turned her head away at the mention of her sister. She was quiet for a minute before she said, "He used to do the same thing to her, you know."

I didn't understand and asked what she meant.

"Ellie got sick a lot."

"And that scared him?" I guessed.

She nodded her head. She said, "It became more about him than her. If he couldn't fix her, he'd make her feel like it was her fault she was sick. She'd call me in tears, feeling guilty she'd done something wrong. Do you know what that feels like?" I actually do.

"But I'm confused," I told her. "He let me read some of the journal they wrote together when she was dying. The dialogue between them was beautiful. He wrote as if he'd accepted what was happening to her."

"That's Ellie." Connie smiled. "A month or so before she died, she had a good long talk with him. He was fine after that."

"If I remember right, she wanted him to go first," I said.

"She knew he'd die like this—fighting death till the bitter end. She wanted to help him, that's all. She wanted to bring him to Jesus. The only consolation she had was her confidence in him. She knew he never blamed God. No matter how bad the fear got. He refused to go down the path of unbelief."

"That's why he blamed himself?"

"Exactly," she said. "I only wish I had Ellie's gift. I've known him nearly all my life. We loved debate. We loved to argue politics, theology, you name it. It energized us. But when he succumbed to fear, he wanted nothing to do with me. He pushed me away. Nothing I said helped."

"Fear is like that," I commented.

"A few days before he died," she recalled, "he looked straight at me and said, 'You know there are two kinds of faith, don't you? Faith that comes and saves us—you and I have that. We have faith in Jesus Christ that no one else can take from us.'

"So I asked him, 'What's the other faith?'

"'Faith to handle the present crisis,' he said. 'Faith for the battle at hand. When I have it, fear has no power over me. When I don't, it does.'

"'What are you talking about?' I asked him.

"'I just have to accept it, Connie,' he said. 'Sometimes fear wins.'"

The LORD is my light and my salvation;
Whom shall I fear?
The LORD is the defense of my life;
Whom shall I dread? . . .
Though a host encamp against me,
My heart will not fear;
Though war rise against me,
In *spite of* this I shall be confident.

—PSALM 27:1, 3

QUESTIONS FOR REFLECTION

When fear strikes our heart, what do we do with it? Read the story of Numbers 13–14 and its commentary in Hebrews 3:12—4:2. How do we let faith come into our hearts?

Is it true that sometimes fear wins? Can we have saving faith in Jesus and not have the gift of faith for the present crisis?

NOTE

1. Philip Edgcumbe Hughes, *A Commentary on the Epistle to the Hebrews* (Grand Rapids, MI: Eerdmans Publishing Co., 1977), 156. Hughes also noted F. F. Bruce's comment on this verse: "The good news had to be appropriated or assimilated by faith if it was to bring benefit to the hearers" (p. 158, footnote 62).

PART 2

THROUGH THE LENS OF FEAR

9

DISTORTIONS

—⁓✐⁓—

*Thus you shall say to my lord Esau: "Thus says your
servant Jacob, 'I have sojourned with Laban, and stayed
until now; I have oxen and donkeys and flocks and
male and female servants; and I have sent to tell
my lord, that I may find favor in your sight.'"*

—Genesis 32:4–5

Everything distorts when we look through the lens of fear.

We look back on our past—people, conversations, events—
and it all changes. All gets reinterpreted. The longer we keep the
lens on, the more it affects how we think, how we feel, how we
act and react in everyday life. It affects how we see ourselves.
Eventually, fear defines us. It defines everything.

It did for Jacob. Did you notice his message to his brother?

It's confusing at best. Why did he choose those words? He
knew they were wrong. He knew the Lord had spoken to his
mother and said, "The older shall serve the younger" (Gen.
25:23). He knew his father had blessed him with similar words:
"Be lord over your brothers." And he knew Esau was fully aware
of it, for Isaac told Esau, "I have made him lord over you . . . and
you shall serve your brother" (27:29, 37, 40 ESV).

Those words were the right words.

But for Jacob, it was all distorted. He chose to rewrite history
as if what happened never happened. As if he never received Esau's
birthright or Abraham's covenant blessing. He denied it—all of it.

He told the messengers, "Thus you shall say to my lord Esau: 'Thus says your servant Jacob'" (Gen 32:4).

It wasn't true. It was backward. He should've said, "Thus you shall say to my servant Esau: 'Thus says your lord Jacob.'" That's the right order. It honors history. It honors his father who gave the blessing and God who stood by it. But instead, he turned his back on it as if his position before God meant little to him.[1]

And why? Why was he driven by this need to find favor with Esau? Why did he turn the clock back to their childhood days and say to Esau, in effect, "You're older. You have the birthright and the blessing. You're my 'lord' and I'm your 'servant,'" not the other way around?

Why tell Esau what he thought Esau wanted to hear? Why this great push to make peace with him? Why take a humble posture and deny the past?

Could it be that he needed control of his brother so he wouldn't fear him? That was the whole point, wasn't it? Jacob was afraid of Esau's anger. It was why he ran before. It was why he was doing what he was doing and saying what he was saying at that moment—security at any cost.

Even if it meant dishonoring what God had said to him.

Jacob was seeing through the lens of fear. He had the wrong glasses on.

I was grateful for what my old friend had told Connie.

"There are two kinds of faith," he said. These simple words tell my story. I was in college when saving faith finally came. All these years later I remember it as if it were yesterday. It was Palm Sunday night. I was in church. The words of the Bible and the sound of the preacher's voice pierced through my heart: "I am with you always, even to the end of the age" (Matt. 28:20). And that night it all became real.

I wasn't alone anymore. I wasn't forgotten or abandoned.

As I walked home that night, everything felt different. Somehow I was certain that Jesus, my Lord, had spoken those words to me. I don't know how I knew it, but I did. My heart had strangely healed a little. I felt clean inside. I felt loved with a love I'd never known before, and it made me feel safe again.

Like I was home.

After my family life shattered, I never dreamed I'd feel like that again. And if I did, why would I trust that feeling? If it could be taken from me once, it could be taken from me twice. And I didn't want that to happen again.

But that night surprised me.

Faith had entered my heart. I believed in Jesus. I knew He died for me. I knew He was alive and Lord of my life. He'd brought me into His family, His home, and promised, "I am with you always"; and I believed Him.

My old friend was right. There is a faith that "comes and saves us . . . that no one else can take from us." And somehow, at nineteen, that saving faith had come to me.

The other faith? I didn't know about it. Not then.

I got the first inkling that I needed it from a man at church. He was a few years older than me. I was confident of his faith in Jesus as I spent time with him. But he confused me. I saw him wrestling with the monster. He fought fear and anxiety. He wasn't sleeping at night. He said he needed prayer.

I didn't understand it. From the moment faith came into my life, the monster had been gone. "Perfect love," I'd read in the Bible, "casts out fear" (1 John 4:18); so I reasoned the monster was gone for good, and he'd never trouble me again. Yet why was this believer so tormented by him? It made no sense to me. If Jesus is always with us, how can the monster be anywhere near?

It wasn't long after that I boarded a plane for New York's LaGuardia Airport. As we descended, the pilot told us there was a storm over the airport and the ride would be bumpy. As the plane tossed here and there, all the old feelings came back—adrenaline pumping, hands sweating, heart racing. I prayed. I pleaded. I wanted the plane to break through the clouds so I could see land.

We kept descending. No visibility.

Then suddenly the engines roared, the nose pulled up, and we rose back into the air, climbing. For a brief second, I thought I glimpsed the runway below us.

"What happened?" I asked the flight attendant seated nearby. She shook her head, said she didn't know, and then she said the strangest thing to me—calmly, eerily—"You know, we all have to die sometime."

Those words shot fear straight to my heart. I turned to the window. We were still tossing. The pilot simply announced, "We missed the runway. We're going to try again."

Did he say "try"?

I pressed my nose against the window and knew the monster was back. Fear had come in full force and with it the sound of mockery: Are you really a Christian? Are you sure Jesus is real? How could He be? If He promised to be with you, where is He?

The old glasses were back on.

I started seeing everything through the lens of fear again. I didn't know my old friend's distinction yet. There's faith that will not be taken from us. And there's faith that comes to handle the present crisis—faith that fights today's battle, deals with today's storms, and meets the monster head on with unexplainable courage.[2]

I needed that "present crisis" faith then. I didn't have it. I didn't know about it. And without it, on the plane, in the storm, I started questioning the faith I did have. Was it really real? Did what happened to me actually happen? Had Jesus Christ truly saved me?

The monster was back, and everything was distorted.

Simon, Simon, Satan has asked to sift all of you as wheat.
But I have prayed for you, Simon, that your faith may not fail.
And when you have turned back, strengthen your brothers.

—LUKE 22:31–32 NIV

QUESTIONS FOR REFLECTION

What does life look like through the lens of fear? How do things distort for you? Has fear ever controlled you to the point of turning your back on God and His promises?

Has fear ever made you question whether you're a Christian or not? Reflect on Luke 22:31–32. How do our Lord's words, "But I have prayed for you," make a difference?

NOTES

1. Allen P. Ross, *Creation and Blessing: A Guide to the Study and Exposition of the Book of Genesis* (Grand Rapids, MI: Baker Book House, 1988), 542. Ross wrote that Jacob's use of language here appears "to be an attempt to minimize the blessing that Jacob had received from his father" and therefore appears "to be relinquishing what the blessing had given him."

2. Consider, for example, 1 Corinthians 13:2. The apostle Paul discussed the gift of faith given by the Holy Spirit "so as to remove mountains." Again, in Ephesians 6:16, we in the faith are to take up the "shield of faith" in withstanding the Evil One. Faith during dire circumstances is distinct from faith that saves.

10

TRAUMA

*So Esau bore a grudge against Jacob because
of the blessing with which his father had blessed him;
and Esau said to himself, "The days of mourning for my
father are near; then I will kill my brother Jacob."*

—GENESIS 27:41

*Jacob's message didn't work. Esau was now fully in control.
What Jacob feared most was about to come upon him. It begs
the question: When did it all start for Jacob? When did fear start
plaguing his soul?*

*Was it from birth? Was it part of his inherent personality? Had
he acquired fear from his family or friends? Did it come out of
insecurity in the world around him? For so many children today, that's
their story. They live in the scariest of conditions—little food, no clean
water, gunshots in the streets, violence and death everywhere. And
then, worse, something happens to them. A trauma of some kind.
And when it does, fear comes with it. Fear stays. Fear never leaves.*

What's Jacob's story?

*The Bible doesn't tell us everything. To guess would brand
Jacob unfairly. But we do know this: twenty years before their
encounter near the Jabbok River an event happened. Jacob
deceived his father and stole the blessing of Abraham that wasn't
his. It belonged to Esau. That one act had the power to break
Jacob's relationship with his brother.*

Esau was enraged.

He "cried out with an exceedingly great and bitter cry" (Gen. 27:34). He "sobbed inconsolably," he "seethed in anger" (vv. 38, 41 MSG), and he began to plan Jacob's death. His mother caught wind of it and warned Jacob, "Your brother Esau is plotting vengeance against you. He's going to kill you. Son, listen to me. Get out of here. Run for your life" (vv. 42–43 MSG).

And Jacob ran. The intent was to stay away for a few days until Esau's fury subsided (v. 44). A few days turned into twenty years, and all that time Jacob lived with his brother's last words ringing in his ears: "I will kill my brother Jacob."

Is this it? Is this when fear took root in Jacob's soul?

So many years later, we know Jacob was still living in fear of his brother. We see it in that odd, distorted message he sent him in which he clearly anticipated that Esau's anger had never subsided. He knew those words, "I will kill my brother Jacob," could be just as alive now as they were then.

The trauma of the past would be nothing compared to the trauma yet to come. He had run before. But he couldn't run from Esau and his army now—not with children under the age of fourteen. Not with a multitude of flocks in his possession. Jacob was seemingly out of options and completely out of control.

Fear—no matter when or how it started—was back in full force.

As years passed, I grew in confidence. No matter how often the monster roared, or how overwhelmed I felt, I knew I was a Christian. I knew to run to the Lord with the cry that belongs to the children of God: "Abba! Father!" (Rom. 8:15).

My old friend had given me courage. Win or lose, I could face fear in Christ.

I soon learned this wasn't true for everyone. I saw people, seemingly strong in the Lord, "fall away" (Mark 4:17). They'd suffer some kind of trauma—job loss, cancer, the sudden death of a child, divorce, division and betrayal in the church—and it would shake them to the core. Rather than running to Him, they ran from Him.

They were tested, just as Jesus taught in the parable of the sower.

So, as a young pastor, I knew my job was to do everything I could to bring people to saving faith in Jesus Christ. That way, I thought, when the monster ambushed them, they'd be ready. They wouldn't fall away. And we'd do what my old friend said to do: We'd ask the Lord for faith—real and strong—to deal with today's battle.

It's what Christians do.

We come alongside those who wrestle with fear and anxiety. It's everywhere, isn't it? It's common language nowadays to talk about "panic attacks" and antianxiety medications like Xanax and Prozac—even for our children and pets. Most say it's because we're too stressed in life. Too pressured to perform. Too busy.

Some say 9/11 is to blame. We're not safe anymore.

Regardless, what I want to know is this: What's your story? When did it all begin? When did fear start plaguing your soul? I remember a ten-year-old boy once answered the question by saying, "Since birth."

"Really?" I asked, wondering how he knew.

"I was adopted late," he stated matter-of-factly. "I didn't have parents until I was two. My counselor says it's an attachment disorder." And then he smiled and said with a confidence I wish I always had, "I just need Jesus to help me, that's all."

He knew his story. I find most people know their story. Our church works with men and women in recovery from drug and alcohol addiction. They easily testify they know when and how it began, and too often it goes back to a broken home where fear was all they'd known. It was what got them hooked. It was how they coped.

But, I find, fear shows no partiality.

We see it in single moms holding jobs, juggling day care, and trying to make ends meet. It's real in teens who struggle with the social pressure to be perfect in everything. It's how seniors feel who find themselves alone and pushed aside. It has little to do with education, title, wealth, or appearance. Anxiety is simply a way of life nowadays.

It's everywhere.

I mostly counsel men. Some quite honestly admit they have a fearful, cautious personality. Some wrestle with post-traumatic stress. Some can't handle relational or emotional issues at home or work. Some deal with long periods of unemployment or health issues or the fear of feeling insignificant. Others have lived life like the horse who "laughs at fear" and is "afraid of nothing" (Job 39:22 NIV). That is, until the monster comes. And then, like little boys, they shake with fear just like me.

"Go deeper," Luka once said to me.

Luka was a member of the church I pastored in my early thirties. He was about my age, married with two children, and a design engineer by trade. He was a gentle, kind man with a quiet personality but was cheerful, encouraging, and always genuinely seeking the welfare of others. Our church family loved and trusted him.

One day he came to see me.

"I'm here because, frankly, I can't handle my fears," he announced.

But he surprised me. He didn't talk about some presenting issue in his life. He didn't even go back to some event in his past. Instead, he took out his Bible and opened it to Genesis 3. "My story," he began, "is a lot like Adam's. We're not so different."

He read Genesis 3:10 out loud and then commented, "After Adam sinned, he hid from his wife. Then, hearing the Lord walking toward him, he hid from Him too. He was honest. It's the first time in the Bible we hear the words, 'I was afraid.'"

Luka looked at me with sad, tired eyes. "He was afraid because he was naked. He was scared of being seen. He didn't want the shame of being exposed, so he hid."

He closed his Bible and released a long sigh. "Me too," he confessed. "I feel that shame. I've felt it since I was a child. I can tell you the whole story if you want. I learned to hide—and I hide really well. But why do I do it? I still think everybody sees me. My peers, teachers, bosses. Even God. I feel vulnerable and exposed and afraid."

And that's when he said it.

"All of us have stories. We've had traumatic things happen to us. But the challenge is to go deeper and ask, 'How real is it? What kind of power does it have over us?'"

"If you don't mind," he asked, "could we start there?"

Yet You are He who brought me forth from the womb;
You made me trust *when* upon my mother's breasts.
Upon You I was cast from birth;
You have been my God from my mother's womb.
Be not far from me, for trouble is near;
For there is none to help.

—Psalm 22:9–11

QUESTIONS FOR REFLECTION

What's your personal journey with fear? Has it been with you since birth? Did you acquire it from others? Have you experienced traumatic events that shaped you? What were they?

What do you learn about the power of fear and shame in Adam's first words after he fell into sin? What kind of power do fear and shame have in your past and present?

11

WHAT'S YOUR NAME?

Esau said, "Not for nothing was he named Jacob, the Heel. Twice now he's tricked me: first he took my birthright and now he's taken my blessing."

—GENESIS 27:36 MSG

If only the messengers had returned to Jacob and said, "Esau's thrilled. He can't wait to see you. He's coming with his family. He wants you to know that all is well." But all wasn't well. By all appearances, Esau was coming to do what he'd promised: "I will kill my brother Jacob."

Esau—how did he say Jacob's name? Did he spit it out like a cuss word? All these years later, could Jacob still hear the sound of his brother's voice as he said it?

"You named him rightly!" Esau said in effect to his father.

It made sense to Esau. On the day he and his brother were born, Isaac and Rebekah saw their first-born son and named him after his appearance. He "came forth red, all over like a hairy garment; and they named him Esau" (Gen. 25:25). They saw their second son and named him based on his actions. He was holding his brother's heel (v. 26). That's the exact meaning of Jacob's name: "the grabbing of the 'heel.'"[1]

But that's not how Esau saw it. Not since Jacob deceived his father and tricked, cheated, and robbed Esau of his blessing. In his anger, Esau could now convincingly tell his father that Jacob *grabbed his heel at birth—just as he'd done now—for the purpose of tripping him up.*

"You named him rightly—Jacob, the Heel!"

Esau had all the proof he needed. He could now spin Jacob's name in the negative with meanings like: Deceiver! Trickster! Supplanter! And who could argue? Jacob was those things. He had done exactly what he was accused of.

But was Esau right about his parents' motivation? Is it possible Isaac and Rebekah held their little baby and named him "Heel"? Or "Deceiver"? Or "Supplanter"? Or "Tripper-upper"? What parent would do that? Isn't it more likely they named him Jacob simply to "commemorate the unusual event, the grabbing of the 'heel'"? Nothing more than an affectionate term.[2]

But to Esau, it wasn't an affectionate term at all. The name was nothing less than a prophetic utterance by his parents speaking forth Jacob's true nature. He wasn't just a "heel-grabber." He was a "heel-swiper." He was a cunning, deceptive man who would come from behind and swat the back of the heel to make his victims fall so he can supplant and conquer.

That was Jacob—the real Jacob.

Could Jacob still hear Esau spit out his name? Could he hear the tone in Esau's voice express what he really meant to say: "You contemptible, despicable heel!" And was Esau right? Was that really him? Down deep, was that how his father still thought of him? Was it how God thought of him? And—truth be told— was it how he saw himself?

Luka loves to take walks.

"It's what I did as a kid. I'd have a hard day at school and take the long way home. Through the woods. By myself. I found it quite peaceful," he explains.

So Luka and I meet at the local park and roam the trails through the woods. He feels comfortable there. Even on this, our first visit, he asks if we can take a walk. He has things to share. He's having troubles at work.

Out we go—like two old friends enjoying the day.

"Every few months at work," he starts, "we have a week-long seminar. It's the only way to keep up with the industry. Things change fast in the technology world. If we don't keep up, we'll lose our competitive edge.

"Weeks before, I start getting anxious," he says. "I don't sleep at night. I get a short fuse with my wife and children over little things, stupid things, that don't mean anything. But to me, at that moment, they do. I'm all wound up inside."

He's animated. I watch his hands frantically tighten an imaginary spring.

"I never do well in those seminars. My bosses like my work. They tell me how valuable I am to them and the company. But I have no proof they mean it. For eight years, I've held the same position. Everybody around me gets promoted. Me, never. They pass over me every time."

He turns toward me, walking sideways. "It's all because of these seminars."

I listen but don't understand. "Why the seminars?" I ask.

Luka tries to answer but can't. He looks at me surprised, like I should know. Finally, he blurts, "Because I'm stupid, that's why." Luka's cheeks blush red. I still don't understand; but I can tell that, whatever it is, it runs deep in his soul, like it's been there a long time.

I press in and ask, "Who says you're stupid?"

"Who doesn't?" he snaps back and then quickly apologizes. "It's a complicated story," he laments.

I tell him I want to hear it.

"I don't process information the same as everybody else," Luka begins. "In elementary school, we had two types of kids: those who could follow the teacher and pass the tests, and those who couldn't and were categorized as 'special needs' kids. That was me. You see, there were no alternative ways of learning. You either fit in or you didn't."

"And you didn't," I say, stating the obvious.

"No. My classmates called me 'stupid,' 'idiot,' and 'Luka-da-lose-ah' like I was a freak of some kind. My parents hired a tutor so I could keep up with my class. And I did. Some years, I scored higher than anybody else. It didn't change things. They still made fun of me. They'd see me squirm every time the teacher called on me to answer a question and I couldn't—not right away. They'd all laugh at me."

He picks up the pace. He says, almost under his breath, "I hated school."

"It sounds like it never got better."

He shakes his head and says, "Nobody knew what to do with me. Nobody knew how to teach me in a way I could understand. So I grew up thinking my peers were right—I was stupid. It's why I had to have a tutor and work harder than anybody else. It was very lonely and humiliating."

He puts his hands on his heart.

"It's like I had a placard across my chest that said, 'Hey everybody! I'm Luka-da-lose-ah!' I felt stark naked, stupid, and worth nothing. I tried to tell my parents how ashamed

I felt and how frightened I was to go to school. I begged them to let me stay home."

He shakes his head, frustrated. All these years later and it feels as though his frustration is as real as it was when he was a child. The story hasn't changed. The placard still remains. It makes me wonder if he thinks I see him the same way. What about his bosses? Is that why he gets anxious before the seminars? Is that why he's never promoted? Still naked and exposed. Still stupid and worth nothing.

I risk the question. "It's still happening at work, isn't it?"

"Yeah," he says with a deep, dark sigh.

"But times have changed, haven't they? We know people process differently. Can't you tell your bosses?"

"I'm afraid they wouldn't understand. I might lose my job."

"So do you believe it?" I ask.

"Believe what?"

"Your name," I say. "The one written on the placard."

He doesn't answer. He just wants to walk. So we do. With an ease that surprises me, he changes the subject and talks about other things. As much as I want to circle back and ask more questions, I don't. It makes me wonder if we'll ever talk about it again and whether, in time, the placard will finally—forever—come off.

For this reason I remind you to fan into flame the gift of God,
which is in you through the laying on of my hands, for God gave
us a spirit not of fear but of power and love and self-control.

—2 TIMOTHY 1:6–7 ESV

QUESTIONS FOR REFLECTION

Esau interpreted the meaning of Jacob's name in Genesis
27:36 through his own experience. How important is your
name? Does it matter how others see us or what they call us?
How has it shaped you?

If you have a placard around your neck, what does it say?
Is it the same one from childhood? From ten years ago?
What names have the most power over you today?

NOTES

1. Allen P. Ross, *Creation and Blessing: A Guide to the Study and Exposition of the Book of Genesis* (Grand Rapids, MI: Baker Book House, 1988), 441.

2. Ibid. Ross wrote, "Because the name sounded like the word for heel, the parents chose it to commemorate the unusual event, the grabbing of the 'heel.'" Again, "the seizing of the heel would have conveyed an affectionate thought." And lastly, "It is quite unlikely, however, the parents would have named a baby . . . 'deceiver.'"

12

IN SELF-DEFENSE

Esau said, "Isn't he rightly named Jacob? This is the second time he has taken advantage of me: He took my birthright, and now he's taken my blessing!"

—GENESIS 27:36 NIV

Through Esau's lens, Jacob was a deceiver and conniver. He grabbed heels and tripped up his victims so he could prevail. That's what he did. That's who he was. But Esau was wrong. He complained to his father, Isaac, "He has deceived me these two times." What two times? What does he mean, by deception and trickery he "took my birthright"?

It was a lie. That's not what happened.

Esau, the "skillful hunter," had worked all day in the field, come home, and was starving. It was just the two of them together, the brothers. Jacob had cooked a meal. Esau wanted some. He told Jacob he was famished (Gen. 25:29). Jacob, the businessman, was willing to negotiate. He set the price for the meal: "First sell me your birthright" (v. 31).

Straightforward.

Nothing deceptive. No tricks. Business is business. Esau could have said no. He could have prized his birthright more than his own life. His name, his honor, should have meant everything to him. Instead, he complained he was "about to die" of hunger.

That's why he told Jacob, "What use then is the birthright to me?" (v. 32).

He had a choice. He wasn't being forced. He could have said no.

For Jacob, the deal was closed when Esau gave his word. He had to swear to the sale—that was how legal transactions were done. "First swear to me," Jacob said. He needed Esau to say it out loud to him. To God. And Esau did.

Esau swore—he sold his birthright—by his own choice.

With the price paid, Jacob gave him the meal. Esau ate and drank. And when he was done he rose and went on his way (so was he really at the brink of death?). Never is it recorded in the annals of history that Jacob deceived Esau for the birthright. He didn't sneak up behind him and steal it. The biblical account says Esau "despised his birthright" (25:34). Esau—the "immoral," the "godless"—"sold his own birthright for a single meal" (Heb. 12:16).

Jacob got it by fair agreement. He then held the title of "firstborn" in his family and before God as the legal owner. It's why he had the firstborn's right to inherit the blessing of Abraham and Isaac. When Esau declared, "And now he's taken my blessing!" he was wrong. It wasn't his blessing anymore. The blessing belonged to the firstborn. And who was that?

Jacob—by Esau's choice. In exchange for a single meal. Jacob had unfairly been called "deceiver" and "conniver." That was Esau's spin. Jacob did nothing wrong regarding the birthright. For Esau did what should never have been done: he despised what should have been honored.

"I need to know something," Luka says on our second walk. "I need to know what's written on your placard."

I thought about that a lot since our last time together. So much of our identity is wrapped up in how others see us, what they call us, and how deeply it takes root in our soul. But sometimes it's more complicated than that.

"Never good enough," I say quickly.

He looks at me, intrigued. I explain, "Growing up, I had the sense my mom was never good enough for my grandfather. He adored her. But he'd call her 'too fat' when she wasn't. Or 'not pretty enough.' 'Not smart enough.' My parents never did that with me. But I felt it as a young boy anyway. Still do."

I can tell he's surprised. "Nobody made you feel that way?" he asks.

"Not really. I think a lot of it was self-imposed. I was convinced that no matter what I did, no matter how hard I tried, I'd mess up. I'd miss some invisible mark maybe nobody set but me. It's why I always felt guilty—like it was my fault for not reaching it. And fearful—because I was afraid I was disappointing everybody."

Luka looks relieved. He says, "Even now?" I guess he means, "Even now, as an adult, a Christian, and a pastor?" I nod my head. I admit, "What I have written across my chest is actually true. I never will be good enough. I've sinned and fallen short of God's glory [Rom. 3:23]. I know that. I know it's why I needed Jesus to save me. But these feelings run deep. They go back as far as I can remember."

"Thank you," Luka says. "You make me feel like I'm not alone."

We walk for a while. I can tell Luka is processing what we've said, but I ache for him. His placard is not true. All

his life — in school, at work — he's been called a loser when
he's not. He's been treated unfairly. He's experienced shame
and isolation. I wonder if the church is a safe place for him.
Is he afraid that if he tells his story, his brothers and sisters
in Christ will treat him the same way?

"My dad has always been my hero," he says matter-of-
factly.

"In what way?" I ask.

"He never wanted me to defend myself in school. He said
if I tried, it'd only make things worse. They'd see me react and
continue to provoke me. 'Don't let them,' he'd say. 'Stay quiet
and to yourself.' So I did, for the most part. I do the same at
work. I put on a mask so nobody can see how hurt I am inside."

I could see the hurt right then — in his eyes, on his face.

"But what my dad did was ingenious. He knew I
processed things differently. I think he could relate. I think
we're a lot alike. So he'd ask me, 'Do you think your Father
in heaven calls you "Luka-da-lose-ah"? Do you think He
thinks of you like that?'

"I'd say no, but I wasn't sure.

"He'd say, 'Well, what does He call you?' When I said I
didn't know, he said he'd teach me. Every night before bed
he'd read from the Bible, and he'd say things like, 'See, you're
a child of God. He is your shield and defense. He is your shepherd and protector. He has become your Savior. All you need
to do is ask, and He will give you all the wisdom you need.
Jesus is our wisdom. He's the source of all knowledge.'"

Luka turns toward me, smiles, and proclaims, "He taught
me how to talk to myself."[1]

"I'm not sure what you mean," I respond.

"In the Psalms, it says, 'Why are you in despair, O my soul? And why have you become disturbed within me? Hope in God, for I shall again praise Him' (Ps. 42:5). My dad said, 'You see! The psalmist is talking to himself. And if he can do it, you can do it! Learn from him. Say, 'Hey, soul! What's going on with you? You need to get with the program. Stop being so miserable—hope in God!'"

Luka laughs out loud, delighting in the memory of his dad.

"Did it work?" I ask.

"Sometimes."

"Are you still doing it?"

"I have to," he admits. "It keeps happening. I mean, nobody at work calls me names. I haven't been called 'Luka-da-lose-ah' since I was a teenager. But I still hear it in my head every time we have a seminar or I'm passed over for a promotion. It's how people see me. Sometimes I think it's how the Lord sees me."

"You know that's a lie," I say.

"Yes, but like you said, the feelings run deep. They go back as far as I can remember, too. I still feel shame. I still feel pushed aside."

"Hey, soul!" I say, loving the idea of talking to myself. "What's going on with you?" I stretch out my hand, and Luka meets it with a firm clasp. "Yeah soul," he says, "defend yourself! Why do you believe all those lies? Aren't you supposed to hope in God?" And he makes me smile.

Luka and I are not so different and I find him surprisingly comforting.

"Thank you," I say, just like he said to me. "You make me feel like I'm not alone."

———

> Why, my soul, are you downcast? Why so
> disturbed within me? Put your hope in God, for I
> will yet praise him, my Savior and my God.
> —PSALM 42:11 NIV

———

QUESTIONS FOR REFLECTION

Have you carefully examined what people have named you? Are they right? If not, why not?

Are there lies that have taken root in your soul? What are they? Are you still struggling with them as a Christian?

Have you ever practiced the discipline of talking to yourself (Ps. 42:11)? What would you say to yourself now?

NOTE

1. D. Martyn Lloyd-Jones, in his extraordinary sermons on spiritual depression, said, "You have to take yourself in hand . . . preach to yourself, question yourself. You must say to your soul: 'Why are thou cast down?'" D. Martyn Lloyd-Jones, *Spiritual Depression: Its Causes and Cure* (Grand Rapids, MI: Eerdmans Publishing Co., 1965), 21.

13

ON THE DARK SIDE

*And [Isaac] said, "Your brother came
deceitfully and has taken away your blessing."*

—GENESIS 27:35

*Was it true? Did Jacob's name really mean "trickster,"
"deceiver"? No. Not in terms of the birthright. Esau was wrong
about that. It was a business deal, a fair transaction. But in terms
of the blessing, was he right? Was Jacob a thief and a cheat?*

Maybe.

*The family was divided. Rebekah believed that Jacob, with
the birthright, was legal heir to the blessing. Isaac didn't. He
believed the blessing belonged to Esau. Why? Was Isaac unaware
Esau had sold his birthright? Or did he know and choose to ignore
it? And why was Esau expecting to receive it? Had he convinced
himself the transaction between him and his brother meant
nothing? Not to his father? Not to God?*

Rebekah reacted.

*She knew what to do. Her husband was blind. She could
easily transform Jacob into Esau and force the issue. But Jacob
pushed back. He said, "My brother is a hairy man and I am a
smooth man" (Gen. 27:11). He feared his father would find out
and curse him.*

His mother prevailed. She dressed him in Esau's best clothes. Ingeniously, she made his hands hairy like Esau's. She gave Jacob the best of meals. And then she sent him—Jacob, the pretender—to his father.

Isaac reacted.

At the sound of Jacob's voice, he knew something was wrong. "Who are you, my son?" he asked. Jacob was suddenly faced with a hard reality: Would he lie to his father?

"I am Esau your firstborn," he testified. "I have done as you told me" (vv. 18–19).

Isaac wasn't sure. He felt his son's hands, but it confused him: "The voice is the voice of Jacob, but the hands are the hands of Esau" (v. 22). So he asked his son again, "Are you really my son Esau?" (v. 24).

"I am," he stated, lying for a second time.

It was almost enough for Isaac. He ate the meal. But still he felt uneasy. He made his son come and kiss him. It was all Isaac needed. As Jacob drew near, his father smelled the smell of Esau, the mighty outdoorsman. Isaac was sure now. He was able to give with confidence to his firstborn son the blessing of his father Abraham (vv. 26–29).

Jacob the consummate actor was now Jacob the blessed.

It didn't take long for Isaac to learn he'd been tricked. When he did, he "trembled violently" (v. 33). "Your brother," he told Esau, "came deceitfully and has taken away your blessing."

That's the story. His father knew he was a deceiver. Esau knew it and declared that his name, Jacob, had always meant deceiver.

Always? Was that true? Was Esau right?

Jacob, there was a dark side to him—his deceit, his lies. Maybe it was why he feared Esau's wrath. He knew better than anyone that Esau wasn't all wrong.

Luka calls one day and says, "Any chance we could meet soon?" Urgency sounds in his voice.

"What's going on?" I ask, as we start our usual walk.

"Do you ever feel like it's true—you're not good enough?" His face looks tired and sad.

I'm guessing he doesn't mean the question in the obvious sense, but that's how I answer him: "Yeah, of course. I've spent most of my life believing it's true."

"No," he says, shaking his head. "I mean, is it really true—to God?"

We walk for a while. I ponder how much I should say. I know it's hard for Luka to talk about himself. He doesn't like it. It's easier if I start. I've found if I open up a little, it often gives him courage. But this time I don't want to. It's odd how selfish I feel.

"I went to an older pastor for help with that," I admit. "I was concerned I was doing more for the praise of men than the praise of God. It's like every book I read, every pastors' meeting I go to, every time I'm with the elders of our church, I walk away feeling completely inadequate— like I'm not doing enough. If I just worked harder, the church would grow. If I preached like the guy across town, more people would come to know Jesus. It's my fault when these things don't happen."

"What did the pastor say?" Luka jumps in, like he wants some magical answer.

"He made it simple. He taught me to examine my heart."

Luka looks puzzled and asks me to explain.

"He said there's nothing wrong with feeling inadequate. In fact, it can be a good thing. It makes us rely on the Lord. We work, we strive, according to His power, not ours (see 1 Cor. 15:58 and Col. 1:29). But if our heart isn't right, he explained, we lose perspective. And for me, that's where I fall short. When I feel inadequate, all the old guilty feelings come back, and I react. I do everything I can to make things right."

"In your strength?" Luka presses.

"I have a dark side," I say.

"So do I," Luka replies. "When I examine my mind, I'd say I know what's been said about me is a lie. But not when I examine my heart. I'm still afraid people will see me for who I am and call me names."

We walk for a while. Luka grows quiet, as if he doesn't know how to talk about this.

"It's easier to stay quiet and to myself," he says, his voice shaky. "That way, I minimize the fear of being exposed and feeling ashamed."

I see anguish in his eyes. I decide to ask what he asked me. "So is it really true—to God? Are you a loser?"

"It's more about my wife," he responds quickly. I watch him take out a handkerchief and wipe his eyes. "Every time we argue, she tells me the same thing. She says she doesn't know me. She says I'm guarded like I'm hiding something. Every time she gets too close, she can feel me pushing her away."

Luka stops walking. He presses the handkerchief against his eyes like he wants the tears to stop. He confesses, "It's true. I do that."

"Intentionally?" I ask.

"It's how I've survived all these years."

"But your wife knows your story, right?"

"She knows everything. She's seen me with our friends. She knows I'm an actor. I get along with most everybody—cheerful, happy-go-lucky me. Until somebody gets too close. I protect myself; she knows that. She sees it. She doesn't even mind—except with her. That's where she draws the line. She can't stand it." He tells me they have a good marriage. The kids are happy. He and his wife don't fight often, but they did a few nights ago. He tells me things are better again, "back to normal."

"I know why I do it," he states bluntly and then starts walking again.

"Why?" I ask.

"I think, deep in my soul, I believe it's true."

I think I understand, but I'm not sure. "You're afraid she'll find out it's true too," I say. "You don't want that, so you push her away—is that it?"

"Yeah," he sighs. "Right now, we both agree—what I've been told all my life is a lie. But when we fight, I start to doubt. I get scared she's going to see the real me and when she does, it'll be over. I'll lose her. So I shut down, which only makes things worse between us."

"You want to keep the dark side hidden," I say.

"But I want to let her in—I really do. I should have that kind of intimacy and trust in our relationship. I owe it to her. But I don't know how, and just the thought of it makes me anxious. I don't know how else to say . . ."

His voice trails off. I realize we are very different men with different stories, but we have at least one thing in common: we're both terribly inadequate. And realizing that, my old pastor friend counseled, can actually be a good thing.

If You, LORD, should mark iniquities, O Lord, who could stand?
But there is forgiveness with You,
That You may be feared.
I wait for the LORD, my soul does wait,
And in His word do I hope.
—PSALM 130:3–5

QUESTIONS FOR REFLECTION

What if what's been said about you in the past is partly right, partly wrong? How do you discern what is true? How do you confront your dark side with the Lord's help?

In what areas of your life do you feel inadequate? Do you try, in your own strength, to make things right? How would your behavior change if you relied on the Lord?

14

IS IT TRUE—TO GOD?

Isaac said to his son, "How is it that you have it *so quickly, my son?" And he said, "Because the* LORD *your God caused* it *to happen to me."*

—GENESIS 27:20

Fear remembers everything. It goes back to the past, analyzes every detail with utter precision—even the "what ifs" and "maybes"—so it can build its case, substantiate its cause, and justify its power over the soul. Through the lens of fear, we remember.

He lied to his father—twice.

No, three times. And what if the third time wasn't forgivable by God?

It happened just after he walked in with the meal. His father was surprised. He'd told Esau to go hunt, bring back the kill, and prepare a gourmet meal so he could bless him. All of that takes time—time to hunt, time to butcher the meat, time to cook the meal properly. How could he have done it all so quickly?

Isaac asked.

Jacob—playing Esau—could have said, "Lucky, I guess" or "It happens every once in a while." Instead, he did the unthinkable. He told his father, "The Lord your God caused it to happen to me" (Gen. 27:20).

God did not. That was a lie.

Unless Jacob wanted to argue, "Well, it's true. Mom got it and prepared it. But ultimately, the Lord provided it, right?"

No.

Jacob invoked the Lord's name, as if He stood with Jacob in his lies when He did not. It was slander, blasphemy. If the Lord wanted Jacob to receive the blessing and not Esau, He would have done it His way. This was not His way. Jacob, standing in front of his father, was also standing in the presence of God. Saying what should never be said.

"The Lord . . . caused it to happen to me."

And yet it worked. Jacob got the blessing. As he'd grabbed Esau's heel and tripped him up, had he also grabbed God's heel and tripped Him up too? It begs the question: Was it true—to God? Did Jacob's name really mean deceiver, trickster, in His eyes?

Sometime later, his uncle Laban did the same thing to Jacob. He tricked him. Laban knew Jacob adored his daughter Rachel. But on their wedding night, Laban sneaked in his oldest daughter Leah instead. It wasn't until morning that Jacob found out he'd been deceived (29:21–27). Why did God allow this to happen to him? Was it justice? Payback?

And was this why Esau and his four hundred men were coming now? Was it God's judgment on him for invoking His name wrongly all those years ago? If so, how could Jacob take courage, call on the Lord, and trust that He, according to the promises of the blessing procured by lies and deceit, would now defend him?

Jacob "was beside himself with fear."[1]

Perhaps the reason was simple. Fear remembers. It always remembers.

I remember Luka telling me after church one Sunday that he'd agreed to give his testimony at a luncheon for young professionals in his office building. "I never like doing this," he confided. "I'm too private a person."

He wrote out his talk and asked if I'd review it. All these years later, I still have it. I'm still struck by his honesty. He titled it, "Shame: Have You Ever Experienced It?"

Yes, I have. And maybe that's why I reread it from time to time. Especially this opening excerpt:

May 20, 1989

Good afternoon, everybody. I must start by telling you I need Jesus today more than ever.

Growing up, I didn't know anything was wrong with me. My parents, even my siblings, loved me the way I am. I didn't know I was different. Home was a safe place for me. But that changed as I started interacting with my peers. I could tell something wasn't right, though I didn't know what it was.

It made me afraid to go to school.

You see, I don't think like everybody else. I process things differently. My fear was that my classmates would find out and make fun of me—and they did. I was called "stupid" and "loser" all through elementary and middle school. It didn't matter if I changed schools. It still happened. I was always the outcast. From my earliest days I knew what fear and shame felt like.

It was like being seen completely naked and hearing everybody laugh. I'd try to run and hide, but there was nowhere to go. So I'd stand there and try not to cry.

When I was a teenager, my parents sent me to Christian camp in the summers. It was the first time outside my home I felt accepted and loved. I came to know God cares for the outcast. It's there I accepted Jesus Christ as my Savior and became a Christian.

I'd hoped it would change things for me.

But the problem persisted. In college, I became more of a recluse. I wasn't called names, but I'd come to believe everybody was right. I saw myself as they saw me. I had little or no value, no dignity as a person also made in the image of God.

So I was quite shocked when I met the woman who'd be my wife. She refused to do what everybody else did. She believed in me. She accepted me for who I am. I felt safe with her like I did growing up in my family. But honestly, in my heart, I was torn in two. I had lived with shame for too long.

You see, it's still happening. It hasn't stopped.

At work, my bosses tell me they love what I do. But in truth, they treat me differently than the rest of my colleagues. They don't confide in me. When it's time for promotions, they pass over me. Why? Is my work no good? Are they telling me lies? I'm constantly afraid there'll be job cuts, and I'll be the first to go.

With all my heart, I try to put my confidence in Jesus every day.

We go to church. We love it there. I think most people like me. They see my cheerful face and, over the years, they've come to trust me as a person. I help out—volunteering whenever I can. Though I must say, I don't let anyone get too close.

A few months ago, the pastor asked me to serve as a leader in the church. I told him no, I'd rather not. But he insisted I pray about it, so I did. But the more I did, the more anxious I became. If what happens at work were to happen at church, I'd lose the one place outside my family where I feel welcomed and loved.

I told the pastor, "I've prayed. The Lord doesn't want me as a leader right now."

He said, "Are you sure?"

I said, quite confidently, "Yes, I'm sure."

I went home and told my wife what I'd done. Her reaction shocked me. She said, "Why did you lie to the pastor? And why did you use God's name to lie?"

"I did not!" I said back.

"Be honest. It's because you're afraid."

And she was right. I was protecting myself. I told her, "I don't want to feel shame anymore. I don't want the people at church to see me."

"But Jesus knows shame," she said. "Jesus knows what it's like to be treated like you've been treated. He's the One who has borne your shame on the cross. You have to trust Him." When she said that, I got down on my knees and asked the Lord to forgive me. For my lies. For my fears. For not trusting Him as I should.

The next day, I called my pastor. I wanted him to know what I'd done, why I'd done it, and to confess, "I can't handle my fears." He wasn't put off. He didn't look down on me. In fact, he gave me a gift I hope I give to you today.

He said I wasn't alone. He knew this kind of fear too. And maybe together we could help each other take it to Jesus.

Create in me a clean heart, O God,
And renew a steadfast spirit within me.
Do not cast me away from Your presence
And do not take Your Holy Spirit from me.
Restore to me the joy of Your salvation
And sustain me with a willing spirit.

—PSALM 51:10–12

QUESTIONS FOR REFLECTION

Have you ever done what Jacob did? Can you look back at wrong choices in the past when you convinced yourself, and others, that the Lord was on your side and in support of your decision? What led to those times?

Do fear and shame control your prayers? How can we discern the Lord's will in our life if we're afraid of where He might lead us? Is it possible we, too, have lied to God?

NOTE

1. Victor P. Hamilton, *The Book of Genesis: Chapters 18–50* (Grand Rapids, MI: Eerdmans Publishing Co., 1995), 319. Hamilton's translation of Genesis 32:7 is quoted here.

15

SURVIVAL

In his anxiety he divided the people with him,
plus his flocks, herds, and camels, into two camps.
"If Esau should attack one camp and overrun it," he
reasoned, "the other camp may yet be left for escape."[1]

—Genesis 32:7–8

How do we stand firm when the ground beneath us is shaking? How do we stay in control when we've lost control? How can we help others, protect them, when we can't even help and protect ourselves?

What was Jacob supposed to do?

Emotion flooded his heart—he was afraid. He was anxious. He was going to die. His children, his family, all his people, were going to die; and there was nothing he could do about it. He couldn't win this one. But how could he just stand there and do nothing?

He had to do something.

He reacted. He reasoned. He assessed his situation. Like an army commander, he flew into motion. He knew Esau had declared war. He was coming to attack. His mission was to overrun and destroy. Jacob also knew instinctively he had no military power, in personnel or weaponry, to plan a counterattack.

Survival—was there any way possible?

He couldn't save all, but could he save some? Was there any way to outsmart Esau so that some would escape his fury? But *how? He thought. He strategized. He devised a plan that was "purely a military maneuver in an effort to save 50 percent" of his family and herds.[2] He concluded that the safest option was to divide everything he had into two camps. That way, if he went with the lead camp straight at Esau and sent the other in a completely opposite direction, maybe that camp would survive.*

It was possible.

It was the best he could do in his own strength. Esau would see Jacob. He'd see his camp and attack. He'd think that was all Jacob had—nothing more. And when he was done, Esau would go home thinking he'd won. He'd have no idea that Jacob, in part, had won too.

His plan would have worked. Half might survive. It was possible.

Jacob met with his family and the people with him. He told them he was dividing them into two camps. Did he explain why? Did he tell them they were going to war? That some would die? Or did he leave that part out? We don't know. It's not clear. All we know is that in Jacob's "anxiety, he divided the people with him."

Everybody got into motion.

And there he stood. By his quick, wise thinking, he was able to do something for half his family. But that was it. That was the limit of his strength, his mind, his ability. He couldn't save the rest. He couldn't save himself. There was nothing more he could do on his own.

He wouldn't survive. Half his family wouldn't survive.

Anxiety—it fills the soul and steals the breath away.

I started this book with a story of a man who'd lashed out at me in his anger in front of others. I had learned over the years—as a Christian and as a pastor—not to fight back at times like that and to do my best, in the Lord's strength, to respond with kindness.

It doesn't always work. It did that time, though.

I also learned I had to find ways—with trusted friends and counselors—to care for myself when I got hurt. It would have been far easier had this man not been part of our church family. I had, as his pastor, responsibility to care for him. This proved more than difficult.

As I said before, he was a bully. He had a deadly combination of wealth, good looks, a strong personality, and a high-profile job in our town. But as a Christian man, he had one trait no Christian should ever have.

He was immune to correction.

When he wronged others, he had no ability whatsoever to apologize.

I made it my practice to approach him privately every time he had an outburst at church. "It's got to stop," I'd tell him. But he wouldn't hear it. In fact, he'd argue with me. He'd state that, for reasons he couldn't fathom, he believed I didn't like him. He'd say, "I'll prove it to you. Answer me this: why do you prevent me from becoming a leader in our church?"

I'd answer as plainly as I could: "Not until these outbursts stop."

They didn't.

He kept asserting himself, politicking behind the scenes and in public. At one point, he came uninvited to one of our committee meetings. He said he had a certain issue that concerned him. He stated his case. He urged our support. He threatened to withdraw his funding if we didn't comply. And then, like before—but more gently, more graciously— he vented his anger.

At me. In front of everybody. Again.

This time Luka was there to witness it. The moment it happened, I saw him put his head down. Of all people, he knows what it's like to be humiliated in front of others. Then to feel the blush of shame wash over you as people look and stare. He knows the taste of fear that dries the mouth when we're threatened by someone stronger than us.

I sat there frozen in my seat, unable to speak. Selfishly, I wanted to vent my anger right back at him in self-defense. But more, I wanted to confront him for trying to manipulate the committee with his money. Instead, I sat there paralyzed until somebody finally spoke, breaking the awkward silence.

The man, the bully, immediately stood to leave. He took one last look at me as a smile, smug and barely noticeable, etched his face. He'd won. He knew he'd won. And there was little I could do about it.

Two days later, Luka poked his head into my office.

"Got a few minutes? I want to show you something," he announced. As he came in, I saw a slim package under his arm. I watched as he put it on the coffee table and sat down.

"Are you OK?" he asked.

I shrugged my shoulders and sighed. "Getting there, I suppose."

We went back over the meeting, assessing the story. It hadn't taken long for us, or the committee, to realize this man had given an ultimatum. We either complied or suffered the consequences. As we pondered this, Luka and I concluded this meant more than withholding money from the church.

"He'll leave, you know," Luka observed.

"Not just him," I replied. "I'm sure he'll persuade many to go with him." Just the thought made me nauseous. Luka nodded and said gently, "We're not going to win this one. You know that, right?" I didn't. I still believed I could appeal to his reason as a Christian man and convince him not to divide our church family.

Luka shifted to the edge of his chair. "You're not in control here," he said pointedly. "You've got to let Jesus Christ take control. He will help you bless this man—and all who leave with him—in a way that honors God and His church. Run to Jesus and you'll lose far less than you think."

"I don't know how to do that," I admitted.

Luka handed me the package that was on the coffee table. "Maybe this will help," he said. I opened it and saw a framed drawing of Mary, the mother of Jesus, kneeling. Her head bowed, her hands lifted in quiet surrender. "Be it unto me," the caption read underneath, "according to thy word. Luke 1:38" (KJV). It was signed by Luka.

"What she's doing—it's how we survive," he commented wisely.

I stared at the drawing and knew he was right. Even now, years later, I still stare at the drawing and wonder why— every time I'm anxious, every time I've lost control—I can't surrender like that. It makes me wish Luka was here. I need

him to show me how to do it again—how to run to Jesus
and let Him take control.

> My heart is in anguish within me,
> And the terrors of death have fallen upon me.
> Fear and trembling come upon me,
> And horror has overwhelmed me.
> I said, "Oh, that I had wings like a dove!
> I would fly away and be at rest.
> Behold, I would wander far away,
> I would lodge in the wilderness."
>
> —PSALM 55:4–7

QUESTIONS FOR REFLECTION

Jacob, filled with fear at the news of Esau's coming, had
to act. He had to do something. Are you like that? Do you
go into survival mode? How does that work out?

What happens when it doesn't work and you've lost
control? Do you want to "fly away and be at rest" (Ps. 55:6)?
Or, like Mary in Luke 1:38, can you surrender to God?

NOTES

1. Victor P. Hamilton, *The Book of Genesis: Chapters 18–50* (Grand Rapids, MI: Eerdmans Publishing Co., 1995), 319. This is Hamilton's translation. Hamilton commented on his rendering, saying, "'It became straight/narrow for him,' i.e., 'he was anxious, he was in straits/distress.'"

2. Ibid., 342–343.

PART 3

PRAYER AND DESPERATION

16

SPRINTING HEAVENWARD

———

Then Jacob prayed.

—Genesis 32:9 niv

We act. We react. We do what we can in crisis.

But when it's bigger than us, when we find ourselves at the end of ourselves, when nothing we can do is enough; what then? Where do we go? What do we do?

Jacob knew. Jacob shows us.

The second he divided his family into two camps, he ran to God (v. 9). There was no space, no words, no time passing between his acting and his praying. Jacob was suddenly, immediately, in his Lord's presence.

We're not given specific details. Was he alone? Did he kneel in reverence (Ps. 95:6) by his bed in the quiet of the night? Did he go to some special place and set up an altar like his father and grandfather did in the past (Gen. 12:8; 26:25)? Or did he run to the banks of the Jabbok, which he names in his prayer "this Jordan,"[1] and pace back and forth, crisscrossing from shore to shore?

Whatever he did, whatever his routine, he'd done it before.

This prayer—recorded for all time—reveals the heart of a man who knew his God. They'd talked before, a thousand times and more. He was not a stranger. He was not a secular man, panicked by distress, crying out to an "Unknown God" (Acts 17:23). Isn't that what most people do? They find themselves in dire straits. They toss prayers skyward—to any god who'll listen. They don't care who. They're desperate. They need help.

Not Jacob. He knew the one and only, the faithful and true God.

He'd spent a lifetime conversing with Him. He knew he had access to Him. He knew how to approach Him, speak to Him, and cry out to Him from a heart filled with fear and pain. His words, filled with honor, intimacy, and familiarity, are no different than the common language of a son talking to his father.

Like they'd always done. And that's their story.

In times past, the Lord initiated conversation. He came to Jacob in dreams and visions. Sometimes directly, sometimes indirectly—He spoke to him "in many portions, and in many ways" (Heb. 1:1). This time, Jacob initiated. He knew the Lord would hear him. He knew He would answer him. He knew he could say it all, hold nothing back, and be honest. Be real. He'd done it in times of blessing. He'd done it in times of distress. He'd do it again right then.

He sprinted heavenward.

He needed God to do what he could not do. He needed the Lord to stand with him, hear him, and act at once on his behalf. He was afraid. He was at the end of himself, helpless—he could not save his family. He could not save himself. He'd come to the only place that mattered most. His words—without preparation or rehearsal—came spontaneously.

And why not? He'd had a lifetime of practice.

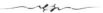

Ed Welch, a Christian counselor, psychologist, and professor outside Philadelphia, asked in his book *Running*

Scared, "What is, by far, God's most frequent command?" His insight surprises me. He wrote, "The actual answer is 'Do not be afraid.'" He added that there are "over three hundred occurrences" in the Bible.[2]

Clearly, the Lord knows us. He knows our adversary.

As for me, I'm not a counselor by training. I'm a pastor. When people come to my office to see me, I'm not sure they always know the difference. A trusted Christian counselor brings invaluable disciplines and perspectives I do not have. They are trained to deal with relational and emotional complexities—short term and long term. I know this. I've needed it in my life.

But as a pastor, I bring a more general discipline. My job is to bring people to Jesus, let the Bible wash over their souls, and pray for the Holy Spirit to do a work in their heart that grows them in Christ. It doesn't usually take me long to discern whether a person needs a counselor at their side or a pastor—or both.

It can be confusing though. Our jobs can look the same.

Early on in ministry, it seemed I had a sign over my head: "Troubles with the monster? Me too; let's talk!" I didn't post it there. But somehow people wrestling with anxiety, fear, worry, and shame found their way to me wanting— begging—for the Lord to step into their story and find, as I always say, "where Bible and life meet."

Here's the hard part: few wanted me distant and removed. They didn't want me polished and fixed, healed (past tense), and wearing a "survivor" T-shirt. Just the opposite. Most—how odd is this?—needed to know I still suffered and would be as willing to risk my story and my heart with them as they would with me.

Not always an easy choice.

What amazed me was that Luka and I weren't in the extreme minority. I quickly learned that fear is an epidemic. All it takes is for the proud and confident to suffer job loss, financial strain, a health threat, some cavalier sin that's suddenly—surprisingly—exposed to those we love, the death of someone close, or old-fashioned emotional burnout. And guess what?

He appears—the monster. Stronger than us. Terrifying us.

I made it my practice to keep Luka's framed drawing of Mary in my office. I also made sure all who came to see me saw it. Not as a quick fix. But to make it clear: This is why we're here. We're running to the Lord. We've raised our hands up in surrender. We need Jesus to come into our story. He's the One, the only One, who can deal with the monster; say to our frightened hearts, "Do not be afraid"; and calm the storm.

The phone rang one day.

I looked at the caller ID and saw it was Joshua—a pastor friend in the Midwest. I answered but found him already talking. I didn't recognize his voice. It was high pitched, loud, and frenzied. I said, "Hello?" but he didn't answer me. He was crying, sobbing with the wails of a troubled soul. I tried to understand him, but couldn't. Not at first.

Then it dawned on me. He wasn't talking to me. He was talking to the Lord. It felt as though, wherever he was, nobody else was there. Just the two of them. This was a man in prayer to God. I'd catch a word, a phrase, here and there. But I couldn't understand whole sentences. I had no idea what had happened to him.

"Joshua, what's going on?" I said loudly.

He didn't hear me. He didn't stop. I cupped my other ear to block the sounds around me, trying to listen more intently. As I did, I found what I heard captivating. It was like a psalm in the Bible had suddenly come to life. I could tell something had gone catastrophically wrong, and yet there he was—one minute full of praises, declaring the goodness, gentleness, and kindness of the Lord to him now and in the past. The next minute—he was panicked, begging the Lord for help.

I caught phrases: "I don't know what to do. . . . I can't. I can't. I can't. . . . I've got to go. I can't stay. I won't stay. . . . It's all empty and cold. What's happening to me?"

Most of it was garbled.

Then it hit me. He didn't know I was there. He must have called me by accident. I was an intruder. I had somehow entered the most intimate of places. Between two intimate friends. In the most intimate of conversations. Joshua was talking to Jesus his Lord, and I was listening in when I shouldn't be. An uninvited, unwanted guest.

At once, I hung up. Of course, I prayed for him—for his wife Cindy; his two boys, Sean and Carson. But how awkward. How confusing. What was I supposed to do next? Should I call him back later? Should I tell him what happened?

The phone rang again.

"Don't go," he said.

"I won't. I'm right here," I replied, and said nothing more.
And for the moment, neither did he.

———

With my voice I cry out to the LORD; with my voice I
plead for mercy to the LORD. I pour out my complaint
before him; I tell my trouble before him. When my spirit
faints within me, you know my way! In the path where I walk
they have hidden a trap for me. . . . I cry to you, O LORD.

—PSALM 142:1–3, 5 ESV

———

QUESTIONS FOR REFLECTION

What is your common, regular discipline of prayer and
conversation with the Lord? Does it come naturally, easily?
How has it strengthened you in times of distress?

What friend do you go to in crisis? Who is safe, trustworthy,
and reliable? Do you find them easy to talk to? How do they
strengthen your relationship with Jesus?

NOTES

1. See Genesis 32:10. The Jabbok feeds into the Jordan and
they are considered one and the same.

2. Edward T. Welch, *Running Scared: Fear, Worry, and the God
of Rest* (Greensboro, NC: New Growth Press, 2007), 59.

17

A LAMP TO MY FEET

*Jacob said, "O God of my father Abraham and
God of my father Isaac, O LORD, who said to me, 'Return
to your country and to your relatives, and I will prosper you.'"*

—GENESIS 32:9

Jacob's first word to the Lord, according to most translators, was O. In this single utterance, we hear Jacob's first cry.

But he was not a child. Children run to their parents, and all they can talk about is what ails them—their needs, their pains, their hurts. Not so with grown children. They know how to approach their parents as adults. This was Jacob. His prayer shows he was not a child. He was a mature man of faith. He knew how to approach his Lord.

"O God of my father Abraham and God of my father Isaac, O Lord . . ."

Jacob started with God's name. He remembered the dream at Bethel, twenty years back, when the Lord said to him, "I am the Lord, the God of your father Abraham and the God of Isaac" (Gen. 28:13). It's the perfect beginning. Not with an urgent petition. But by properly invoking the name the Lord revealed to Jacob at Bethel.

This name—no doubt it transported Jacob back in time.

It brought to mind all the stories of his grandfather Abraham and father, Isaac, in their "walk" with the Lord (17:1). They knew

Him. They called on Him when faced with insurmountable troubles, and He answered. He stood with them. He did great and wonderful things. His steadfast love, mercy, and faithfulness always prevailed.

That was what Jacob knew to do: call on Him!

And it's what we, as God's children, do when storms bear down on our souls, when we're in crisis, afraid, disoriented, and have no control. As the psalmist would later write, "Your word is a lamp to my feet" (Ps. 119:105). It's how we hear who God is, remember His saving works in the past, and embrace His promises in the present to all who fear Him.

"O Lord, who said to me . . ."

It was Jacob's turn now. The God of his fathers had also been his God. At Bethel, the Lord promised him, "Behold, I am with you and will keep you wherever you go, and will bring you back to this land" (Gen. 28:15). Again, more recently, He instructed, "Return to the land of your fathers and to your relatives" (31:3).

With those promises and directions came a guarantee: "I will be with you" (31:3). For Jacob, this meant, "I will prosper you."[1] That was God's word to him, and now he was clinging to it. A storm of terrifying power was about to descend upon him. All Jacob could do was run to God in prayer, call on His name, remember God's word, and hold His promises close to his heart.

Jacob made no mention—not yet—of the urgent need of his heart.

Instead he trusted that God's word was, as always, "faithful and true" (Rev. 21:5).

"He has said, 'I will never leave you nor forsake you'" (Heb. 13:5 ESV). Joshua's voice on the phone calms. But I can tell he's still crying.

"Yeah," I whisper back.

"Job didn't sin with his lips. He never blamed God for what happened to him. He said, 'Blessed be the name of the LORD,' [Job 1:21–22]. I've got to make the same choice. 'For the LORD is good; His lovingkindness is everlasting' [Ps. 100:5]. 'His mercy endures forever' [Ps. 136:1 NKJV]."

"Yes, it does," I say.

"And '[He] causes all things to work together for good to those who love [Him]' [Rom. 8:28]. He's going to work this for good. All of it," he assures me. "Because He 'is compassionate and gracious, slow to anger and abounding in lovingkindness' [Ps. 103:8]. 'His anger is but for a moment, His favor is for a lifetime; Weeping may last for the night, but a shout of joy comes in the morning'" [Ps. 30:5].

"I agree," I respond.

He keeps going, stringing together a long series of Scripture verses quoted from memory. Every once in a while he comments on them, applying them to his present troubles. Just as often, he slips back into prayer; and I feel myself to be, again, an intruder eavesdropping on an intimate conversation. I still don't know any details. I only know he's clutching to Scripture like a drowning man clinging to a buoy in the worst of storms, the roughest seas.

I listen. I don't interrupt.

"God the Father—He chose me from 'the foundation of the world' [Eph. 1:4]. He transferred me 'to the kingdom of His beloved Son' [Col. 1:13]. I have 'redemption through His blood' not because of anything I've done to deserve it. But 'according to the riches of His grace which He lavished on' me [Eph. 1:7–8]."

He continues for a while and then pauses, like he is doing everything he can to believe what he is saying. Then he asks, in desperation, "Why is this happening to me?"

"What?"

He starts his answer by saying something is wrong with him physically. His hands began shaking a few weeks ago—involuntarily. He says he always feels wired, like he's getting massive doses of caffeine 24/7. He can't sleep. He hasn't slept for weeks—not good sleep, not deep sleep. As a result, he's constantly on edge. Constantly anxious. Always feeling like he's either going to burst into tears or explode in anger.

"Have you seen a doctor?" I ask.

"Yeah, he ran some tests. He sent me to a cardiologist, not sure why. Tests came back normal."

"That's it?"

"Both doctors said the same thing. It's all psychological—stress related. I got a script for antianxiety meds and a referral to a psychiatrist."

"Do you think they're right?"

"I don't know," he says, frustrated. He tells me he's exhausted. Too much going on at church. Too much pressure to perform—in the pulpit, in pastoral crises, in endless meetings. He shares that he officiated five funerals in the past month. One a child. Another a suicide. Just too many people with too many demands on him. It's been like that for months. It never seems to stop. He says he barely sees his family. He never gets adequate time to prepare his sermons. Never time alone with Jesus.

"A few weeks ago I got so angry in a meeting—I tried to hide it, but at one point, I just got up and left. I didn't trust myself. Later that night, one of the guys in the meeting called me. He'd seen my hands shaking and the agitation in my face. He knew something was wrong. He told me I had to get away—take time off with my family."

"Did you?" I ask.

"Yeah, the church leaders met and agreed to it. So we did. Friends let us use their vacation home in the mountains." And then Joshua starts crying again. Just as quickly, he begins praying, and with every prayer he'd quote one passage of the Bible after the other and latch onto them with all his might.

"He 'disciplines us for our good,'" Joshua says at one point, "because I'm His son [see Heb. 12:7–10]. Because 'all who are being led by the Spirit of God, these are sons of God'—which means we can cry out, 'Abba! Father!'" [Rom. 8:14–15]. And he repeats it over and over, "Abba! Father!" as anguish pours out of his weary soul.

"We got back from the mountains," he begins. Suddenly he stops.

The pause is longer than I expect. I realize there is more bad news.

"Our house was broken into. A ton of stuff stolen. Every room ransacked," he says. "We're devastated." He tells me they discovered it just days ago. "I feel violated," he says and then it begins again. The prayers. The Scriptures. The loud weeping as Joshua, the best of pastors and my good friend, holds on for dear life.

I am losing all hope; I am paralyzed with fear.
I remember the days of old. I ponder all your great works
And think about what you have done. I lift my hands to
you in prayer. I thirst for you as parched land thirsts for rain.
Come quickly, LORD, and answer me, for my depression
deepens. Don't turn away from me, or I will die. Let me
hear of your unfailing love each morning, for I am trusting
you. Show me where to walk, for I give myself to you.
Rescue me from my enemies, LORD; I run to you to hide me.

—PSALM 143:4–9 NLT

QUESTIONS FOR REFLECTION

When you are in crisis, what are your first words to the
Lord in prayer? Is it your regular practice to call on His name,
cling to His Word, and recite His promises to Him?

Have you, like Joshua, stored Scriptures up in your heart?
Reflect on Psalm 143:4–9 and compare it to your own prayer
life. How does God's Word comfort you in trials?

NOTE

1. Victor P. Hamilton, *The Book of Genesis: Chapters 18–50*
(Grand Rapids, MI: Eerdmans Publishing Co., 1995), 323. Hamilton wrote, "Jacob has revised 'I will be with you,' a statement of
divine presence, into 'I will treat you well,' a statement of divine
treatment."

18

I AM LITTLE

*I am unworthy of all the lovingkindness and of all
the faithfulness which You have shown to Your servant;
for with my staff* only *I crossed this Jordan,
and now I have become two companies.*

—GENESIS 32:10

Jacob didn't cry out for help. Not yet. He had one more thing to say.

It had nothing to do with Esau or the impending attack. It was not about their past or present or who's right or who's wrong. Nor did Jacob seem to have any interest whatsoever in defending himself or arguing his case.

Something else had captured his heart.

He was in the presence of almighty God. He was standing where he had stood twenty years before—at the exact same spot, at this river bank, under these skies. But he was different now. He had become a vastly wealthy man. He just divided his family and flocks into two companies. Not like the first time he was here. He had nothing in those days. No possessions. No flocks. No wife. No children. It was just him. He said it out loud in prayer: "For with my staff only I crossed this Jordan, and now I have become two companies" (Gen. 32:10).

Jacob then, Jacob now.

The contrast profoundly moved him. He knew this was not his doing. It wasn't the brilliance of his mind, or the physical strength *of his body, or the determined effort on his part to live a pure, holy, and godly life that got him all he had. No, it was the Lord's doing. He showered Jacob with His "chesedh," His unconditional love; mercy; and lovingkindness. God stood by him in covenant faithfulness. He blessed him out of the abundant riches of His grace, and Jacob was suddenly overwhelmed by it all.*

He was loved by God.

In the Lord's presence, Jacob felt his own smallness. Who was he that the Lord had extended to him all this blessing and favor? This, too, he said out loud in prayer: "I am unworthy [undeserving] of all the lovingkindness and of all the faithfulness which You have shown to Your servant" (32:10).

In his Hebrew language, this sense of unworthiness is better translated, "I am little . . . I am less than all."[1] He now knew what his grandfather Abraham meant when he stood in the presence of almighty God and said, "Now behold, I have ventured to speak to the Lord, although I am but dust and ashes" (18:27).

"I am little."

I am "servant." This was his posture before the Lord. It was not like his message to Esau. He also told Esau he was his servant. But he said it to win his favor (32:4–5). That was not the story now. This was Jacob's real heart. No games. No disguises. No deceptions.

"I am little."

And if he was unworthy to receive all the blessings of the past, how much more in the present? Who was he for the Lord to hear, let alone grant, the cry of his heart?

"I've got to get out of here," Joshua says. I can hear the frenzy in his voice. "Maybe I'll go back to the mountains for a few days. Cindy and the boys will be fine. I need time to figure things out."

He knows he can't. His family is living in a hotel paid for by their insurance company until the police finish their investigation and his home is repaired. It'll be two weeks at least. Plus, his boys are scared. They don't want to live in that house again. They're afraid the robbers will come back.

Joshua is frustrated. He tells me there's an urge inside him: "I want to run. Get in the car and go. I don't care where. And never come back."

I try to understand, but can't.

Some call it the "perfect storm." Three major life events all at once. Maybe, in our own strength, we can handle one. But two tends to push us to our limit. Three, more times than not, pushes us off the cliff.

Joshua is exhausted by his workload. He displays all the classic signs of a burned-out pastor. Add to that his physical issues—he's scared. He has no idea what's wrong with him. Then add the violation he feels with the house.

He wants to run.

He tells me they've already decided to sell the house. "We can live with Cindy's mom for a while," he says. I ask if she lives close by. He says no. She lives on the West Coast. He realizes it'll be hard on the boys to leave their friends at school and start up somewhere new in the middle of the year. "They'll be OK," he assures me. "Kids are resilient."

"What about your job?" I ask, confused.

"I'm quitting," he announces, adding he has already written his resignation letter.

"Have you sent it?"

"No, I have a few phone calls to make first," he replies. "I've been here a long time. I can't just send a letter. They need to hear my voice."

I'm now convinced Joshua's spinning out of control. Talking on the phone frustrates me. I can't see his face. I can't look into his eyes. I beg him not to make those phone calls or send the resignation letter. Not now.

"Why?" he pushes back.

"It's impulsive. You've got to wait."

He grows quiet.

I ask, "Have you got people around you—confidants, close Christian friends?" He throws out a few names. He tells me they only know bits and pieces. He blames himself, saying, "It's my fault. I've made it sound like we're all right when we're not." He tells me Cindy's got support—two close Christian friends she talks to and trusts.

"It's harder for me," he admits. "I don't know how to be pastor and friend. Not at church. And who has time to develop friendships outside church?"

He pauses. He tells me it's lonely. He admits he's scared.

"I'm worth nothing," he says quietly.

"That's not true," I blurt out. I tell him it's common for people to blame themselves when something bad happens to them. "In my experience," I say, "it's easy to think we deserve it. We think God's mad at us. He's punishing us. We forget He loves us. Maybe He's the cause of our troubles, maybe He's not. When He is, when He disciplines us, He does it in love. He does it for our good. Not so with the

Devil. He is the 'accuser' (Rev. 12:10) always ripping us apart. Always making us feel like we're a piece of trash with no worth, no value, before God."

"That's not what I mean," he interrupts.

He starts to cry again.

"I have the most beautiful wife," he says. "Two incredible boys—both healthy. They make me so happy. My mom's still alive. Two brothers and a sister. There were a lot of rough patches growing up. We never went to church. Never talked about God or prayed together. It wasn't until high school that I even met a Christian. I wasn't interested at first, but after Dad died I didn't know what to do."

He tells me how he met Christ and gave his life to Him in college. He shares how a college pastor mentored him and how he knew he was to be a pastor, too. One story after the other, he recounts all the ways the Lord showered blessing on his family and the churches he's served.

"Maybe I deserve what's happening to me, or maybe not," he says. "All I know is I look back on my life and see I am the richest man in the world. The Lord has done so much for me. I don't deserve it. I'm not worthy of it."

He pauses. He wants to know if I understand now.

I tell him I do.

"Then explain to me," he says, his voice small like a beggar quietly asking for food, "who am I to ask Him for more?"

For thus says the high and exalted One who lives forever,
whose name is Holy, "I dwell *on* a high and holy place, and
also with the contrite and lowly of spirit in order to revive
the spirit of the lowly and to revive the heart of the contrite."

—ISAIAH 57:15

QUESTIONS FOR REFLECTION

Take time to reflect on "all the lovingkindness" and on
"all the faithfulness" the Lord has lavished on you. What
does it mean to feel "unworthy" and "little" before God?

Has the Devil ever made you feel small and worthless in
God's eyes? Has he blamed you when bad things happen?
How is being "contrite and lowly in spirit" different?

NOTE

1. Victor P. Hamilton, *The Book of Genesis: Chapters 18–50*
(Grand Rapids, MI: Eerdmans Publishing Co., 1995), 323.
Hamilton explained, "To be 'little' describes one who lacks legal
credentials to make a claim for himself, or a person who is totally
dependent on another for his welfare."

19

RESCUE ME

—✒—

Deliver me, I pray, from the hand of my
brother, from the hand of Esau.

—Genesis 32:11

It was time.

Jacob had prayed from his heart, unrehearsed. This new sound was different. He held it back. He chose first to speak out God's name. He knew Him. They'd walked together all those years. He had received from His hand blessings, too many to count.

He knew himself.

He was not worthy—not before God—to receive any of it. He was man, small and finite, and God is God. He was sinful man. Very likely tucked deep inside the word unworthy rests a quiet but real confession of his past wrongs. He had come in humility, his posture bent low, not as a child deserving his father's help, but as a servant who doesn't.

Yet even a servant has access to Him. He has permission to speak.

It was time.

This new sound out of his mouth—was it quiet or loud? Was he composed or had he lost all composure? Was he standing, able to lift his head to the heavens, or had anguish seized him and thrust him to the ground? Still, it came, a cry simple and true: "Deliver me. . . . Rescue me [NLT]. . . . Save me [NIV] from the hand of my brother." He said it once, then twice: "from the hand of Esau" who now had the upper hand of power.

Jacob did not. He was powerless. His circumstances were too big for him.

This cry—"Rescue me"—was why he was here.

Too often, this plea is the hardest of all sounds. The proud can't say it. The independent can't speak it. The in-control can't release control, surrendering their will to another. Yet three well-tested principles are all embodied in this one single sound:

Powerlessness. Dependence. Surrender.[1]

Jacob was done with Jacob. He was putting his full trust in the Lord who had rescued in the past. Would He not rescue now? Did He not save Noah and his family from the flood? Did He not save Lot and his daughters from the judgment of Sodom and Gomorrah? Did He not save Jacob when his uncle Laban came against him? He had rescued before. Would He not rescue now?

And yet what about Abel? Why wasn't he rescued from the hand of his brother Cain? Why did the Lord allow him to die? Could Jacob's story be like Abel's story?

"Rescue me!"

It was the sound of every generation since our exile from Eden. "O Lord," wrote the psalmist centuries later, "in You I have taken refuge; save me from all those who pursue me, and deliver me, or he will tear my soul like a lion, dragging me away, while there is none to deliver" (Ps. 7:1–2).[2]

We are powerless. We are dependent. We surrender our lives to His care.

At least for now, this is Jacob's heart, Jacob's cry.

I call Joshua the next day. He tells me his wife is "amazing." She got the boys back in school and in a regular routine. She plans most of the day for him, too—bringing order and surprising rhythm to their upside-down, chaotic life.

"She's far more together than I am," he muses.

She's handling calls from family and friends, coordinating work at the house, plus doing what she can to protect him from unexpected visitors. "A lot of people from church are stopping by the hotel with meals, flowers, and things for the boys," he says. "The elders, too—they're insisting I take as much time off as I need."

Order with structure somehow eases the fearful heart.

I tell him he sounds a little better to me. He admits he's not. He talks me through his house, room by room, describing in detail what the robbers did. His voice rises in indignation one minute and then collapses into aching sadness in the next. With the following breath, he's thinking about all the work piling up at church. He tells me he should be there. He's missing meetings. There are people in crisis he promised to help. He feels guilty. He also says he's tired. He wonders how Jonah slept on board a ship tossed by storm-enraged seas (Jon. 1:4–5).

Without sleep, he knows he gets disoriented, quickly falling prey to worry. Panic sets in and he's again fighting the urge to get in his car and flee.

"Lord Jesus," he prays softly, "I need Your help."

I start praying for him out loud. He starts crying again. He joins in the prayer. He tells the Lord the tremors in his hands are worse today. He feels more anxious than ever—wired and hyper, like he's about to jump out of his skin. He asks for mercy.

I wonder why he isn't pursuing other doctors. After our prayer, I ask him.

He says his wife's friends want him to see an endocrinologist. "They think it may be related to my thyroid, hormones, glands, that kind of thing." One doctor in particular came highly recommended. "I have her number," he tells me.

I ask why he hasn't called. He says he will, but I can tell he needs a push. I ask him to call now, get an appointment, then call me back. He agrees and ten minutes later tells me he'll see the doctor in a few days. I hear reluctance in his voice.

"She'll tell me I need a psychiatrist," he tries to joke.

Then he changes the subject. His thoughts return to the house — wandering through the rooms again. This prompts memories from his childhood. Times he felt unsafe. He briefly mentions his parents' divorce. A fire in the basement. His grandmother's death. Older kids at summer camp hanging him on a peg by his underpants. Times he was left alone in the house with no one there. No one but him and his dog.

He feels unsafe again.

The robbery has cut deep and ripped off old scar tissue. Past wounds reopen, shockingly fresh and sore to the touch. I want to talk to him about it. I want to push him like I did with the doctor appointment, but he changes the subject again.

"Early mornings are hardest," he confesses. "I can't turn my head off. Anxiety goes off the charts. I have no strength to combat it. As fast as I can, I make coffee and go to my desk. All I want to do is read the Psalms. It's like they know me. They know what I'm going through. They force my eyes off my crazy world and focus them on the Lord. I can trust Him. He is safe. He rescues. He protects. No one else."

He pauses. "I can't describe it," he finally says. "But I feel the difference. Everything inside me calms, and I can jump into my regular devotions."

I ask him what he means.

Every morning, every day of his life, he spends time with the Lord—reading through the Bible, worshiping, and interceding for those the Lord has given him. It is his routine, a rhythm well established before everything around him collapsed.

"It's saving my life," he says confidently. "I know He's with me. I know He's infusing my soul with enough strength, enough grace, to get through today, just today. If I didn't have the daily discipline of being in prayer, in His Word, and in the community of His church, I'd be on a ton of medications right now."

He amazes me. One minute, he begs Jesus for help. He feels anxious, lost, and out of control, powerless to get out of the mess he's in. The next minute, he tells me that help has already arrived.

"I mean it," he says. "I know He's here with me."

And I believe him.

LORD, there is no one besides You to help *in the battle*
between the powerful and those who have no strength;
so help us, O LORD our God, for we trust in You, and in
Your name have come against this multitude. O LORD,
You are our God; let not man prevail against You.

—2 CHRONICLES 14:11–12

(Prayer of King Asa as he faced an army of a million men.)

QUESTIONS FOR REFLECTION

How often do you come to the Lord in humility, your
posture bent low, and cry for help? What does it take to admit
you're powerless, dependent, and surrendered?

What disciplines of devotion do you keep on a regular
basis? Have you experienced His help, His grace, and His
presence even when the storm around you is at its worst?

NOTES

1. Compare these three principles with the first three steps of
"The Twelve Steps of Alcoholics Anonymous": admission of
powerlessness, belief that God can restore, and turning self over
to God. Also see 2 Chronicles 20:12.

2. The word *deliver* used in Psalm 7:1 is the same Hebrew word
Jacob used in his prayer. The word *save* is also used, synonymously,
and is the word from which comes the ancient cry, "hosanna."

20

I AM AFRAID

For I fear him, that he will come and attack
["slay us all" RSV] me and *the mothers with the children.*

—GENESIS 32:11

Why say more?

Doesn't "Rescue me! Help me!" say it all? When the heart is desperate, this cry, this need of our heart, tends to be everything. It's our surrender. It's our confession. It hands our lives into the hands of almighty God. Why say more?

But Jacob did.

He was not done. He had yet to reach the height and the depth of his prayer to God. His next words did that. For behind his heart's cry for rescue was the condition of that heart. He knew what was happening to him. He felt it. He was able to say it.

"I am afraid" (Gen. 32:11 NLT).

Who does this? When emotion overwhelms us, we feel it in our gut. We hear it in our voice. We may try to deny it. We may try to control it. We may try to hide it from others. But it's there. It's real and bigger than life. But who stops to listen to it? Who puts it into clear, simple words? Who's that honest with themselves? And who has courage to admit it to someone else, let alone to God? Who's that vulnerable, that exposed, that known?

"I fear him."

Jacob was called the deceiver, the trickster. But that wasn't him, not here. This was the real Jacob. He felt fear. He knew fear. He didn't mince words. It wasn't some vague feeling he couldn't get his mind around. No, he had it: fear. And it had him. It was far bigger than a passing emotion. It had power.

It held him captive, paralyzed, no doubt breathless.

For this fear has focus. There are panic attacks that come for no reason at all. But this wasn't that. Jacob had reason to fear. Esau's knife was at his throat. Esau's knife was poised at the throats of each one of his children and their mothers. It was real, as if he could see the knife. He could see the one holding the knife. They were all going to die.

"I fear him, lest he come and slay us all" (32:11 RSV).

Fear was in control. Fear held the keys of death (Heb. 2:14–15; Rev 1:18). Worry was equally present. Worry thrust Jacob into tomorrow, projecting what would happen if God didn't intervene. Worry whispered the inevitable—every detail—and with every horrifying image of their death, fear intensified. Jacob felt it. He admitted it to himself. He confessed it to God. He was not afraid to say to the One he loved that he was afraid.

"I fear him," he confided, his heart raw, honest, and completely exposed.

Jacob did what few of us know how to do. In a prayer, he gave the Lord his scared and anxious heart. The greatest gift anyone can give.

At eleven-thirty at night, my phone rings.

"Hey, sorry about this," Joshua whispers. He doesn't want his family, crammed in the hotel suite, to wake. "It's bad," he tells me, and I know he means his anxieties. "I've got sleeping pills in one hand and antianxiety meds in the other. Best doctors can do for me, at least for now. But to be honest, I don't want to take either. I decided instead to call you. Do you mind?"

"Glad you called." I ask how his day went. He tells me he's already seen the endocrinologist. She couldn't explain all his symptoms, but she was fairly certain something was not right. "Stress is likely compounding it," she added. She ordered a series of tests and said nothing about seeing a psychiatrist—which thrilled him.

But the break-in was still troubling him, causing all kinds of old hurts to resurface. He wanted me to help him with it, but I told him, "I'll do my best keeping your heart and soul focused on Jesus. But for this, you need a good Christian counselor, one who's firmly rooted in the Bible. I think you know that." He told me he did but didn't know of any in his area.[1]

"Find one," I urged. "Even if they're not local, you can do it by phone." He said he would. I told him I'd kindly bother him till he did.

I wonder what worries him most tonight.

He tells me he feels like he's in a prison cell, dark, the walls inching closer, the space shrinking. He bolts from subject to subject—the robbery. The feeling of burnout at church. The health issues—which are worsening, not improving. He says he wants to blame the Devil for all of it but can't. He knows the Lord is standing watch over him. He's sure of it and says it again.

Then he asks, "Why won't He do something?"

I tell him I don't know. Then I ask what scares him most.

"The doctors," he says, and I know tonight he's focused on his health. "What if they can't find anything wrong with me? What if the tests come back normal? Am I supposed to spend the rest of my life feeling like this? Always on a caffeine rush, relying on sleeping pills and antianxiety meds?"

His voice rises, as he momentarily forgets that his family is sleeping. He quickly quiets. And then it begins, all the "what ifs" down the thousand rabbit holes of worry.

"What if they say it's all stress-related, like I can't handle what's happening to me? That makes it worse. Like it's my fault I'm sick, that I'm to blame for feeling like this."

He speaks quickly, his mind racing.

"And what if it gets worse?" he asks, then multiplies it by time. He talks about a month from now, two months, Thanksgiving, Christmas, a year from now. That triggers all kinds of possibilities. He tells me stories of people in his church over the years who've suffered from advanced MS, Parkinson's, ALS, and Huntington's. As their pastor, he knows each story intimately. He's walked with them every step of the way. His mind wanders down each path separately, exhaustively.

"What if that's me?" he says, scared.

"And what if it is?" I shoot back fast. "You were there. Was the Lord with them or not? Did He ever abandon them, really?" It's obvious I'm annoyed. Joshua knows better than anyone that worry never comes with grace. It is utterly and always godless. It thrusts us into tomorrow without God, as if He is not and will not be there.

I know—I'm as much an expert as Joshua is.

"What if I lose my job, my medical benefits?" he says, ignoring me. He wonders how he'll support his family. His mind spins—he thinks about his wife working full time, caring for an invalid husband, and having to raise their boys on her own. "I don't want them seeing me deteriorate like this," he says, horrified. He wants to live his dream and raise Sean and Carson to be men after God's heart.

"It's not going to happen, is it?" he asks.

I'm getting impatient. I want his rantings to stop when I hear him catch himself, quickly repeating over and over, "Casting all your anxiety on Him, because He cares for you" (1 Pet. 5:7).

"That's it," I say, encouraging him.

He then quotes from Matthew 6:34 saying, "So do not worry about tomorrow; for tomorrow will care for itself. Each day has enough trouble of its own."

As he repeats it, I hear him slowing down—his words, his breathing.

"It's just so hard," he admits. "I put my head on the pillow and beg God for sleep, but I can't turn my head off. All I can see is tomorrow—and a world of tomorrows—where there's no change. Everything's getting worse. The prison cell's getting darker and smaller. I'm asking, I'm begging, and all I get back is silence."

I hear him cry. I hear him pray—honest, real, surrendered.

"Lord Jesus, help me. I'm afraid."

I cry to you, LORD; I say, "You are my refuge, my portion in the land of the living." Listen to my cry, for I am in desperate need; rescue me from those who pursue me, for they are too strong for me. Set me free from my prison, that I may praise your name. Then the righteous will gather about me because of your goodness to me.

—PSALM 142:5–7 NIV

QUESTIONS FOR REFLECTION

How aware are you of your emotions? What does it take for you to listen to them, identify them, and confess them to yourself, to others, and then in honesty to the Lord?[2]

When are you most susceptible to worry? How does it exacerbate your fears? Where do you turn to ease or comfort your worries? How has the Lord made a difference?

NOTES

1. See the Christian Counseling and Education Foundation website (www.ccef.org) and their passion in "restoring Christ to counseling and counseling to the church." If you or someone you know needs the guidance of a Christian counselor, this website can help you locate one.

2. Bob Burns, Tasha D. Chapman, and Donald C. Guthrie, *Resilient Ministry* (Downers Grove, IL: InterVarsity Press, 2013), 103. The authors, in discussing "emotional intelligence" reported: "It is hard for any of us (pastors included) to identify our feelings."

21

VACILLATING

*But you promised me, "I will surely treat you kindly,
and I will multiply your descendants until they become as
numerous as the sands along the seashore—too many to count."*

—Genesis 32:12 NLT

What would the Lord do? Would He answer Jacob's prayer?

*Jacob had been honest. Death was near—not just his death,
but the death of his family—and he could do nothing about it. He
was powerless. He couldn't protect them. When the time came,
the forces of evil descended, and his children turned to him and
cried for help—what would Jacob say? What would he do?*

*He was afraid—and fear, like Esau's army, was stronger than
he was.*

*Where was the Lord? Why wouldn't He speak? Why wouldn't
He act? From the beginning of time, hasn't it always been true:
"Those who wait for the Lord will gain new strength" (Isa. 40:31)?
When we make our requests known, won't the "peace of God"
guard our hearts and minds (Phil. 4:7)? Where was that peace
for Jacob? Why didn't God infuse Jacob with the assurance that
He had this covered? He would do what Jacob couldn't do.*

And maybe He did.

*Maybe that's why Jacob ended his prayer, "But you promised
me." Maybe there's hope in his voice because the Lord has given*

him faith to remember His promise at Bethel: "Your descendants will also be like the dust of the earth" (Gen. 28:14). Just as He promised Abraham: "I will multiply your seed as the stars of heaven and as the sand which is on the seashore" (15:5; 22:17). It was, after all, the best possible promise. For Jacob to have descendants "too many to count," they couldn't all die. There had to be survivors.

But maybe—what if—this wasn't the tone in Jacob's voice.

What if God hadn't answered with instant faith? What if faith hadn't come, and here, at the end of Jacob's prayer, his last words were a desperate cry? He was fighting fear with everything in him. For Jacob, right then, fear was stronger than faith. He could admit he was powerless. He could confess his need and his fears, but for how long could he endure? He needed help—now! Where was God?

Jacob said, "But You promised me." Is it possible frustration resonated from his heart, like a child stomping his feet and wagging his finger in protest? All because fear had gripped him and wouldn't let go.

Jacob's last words in prayer aren't easy to understand.

Maybe they came from faith, maybe from fear, or maybe he vacillated between the two. If faith, his prayer was answered. He could rest that night assured the Lord would fight for him and fulfill His promises. But if fear and faith battled inside him, then Jacob would have to choose: Would he trust the Lord and wait for Him to answer? Or would he do the unthinkable and snatch back the reins of control?

The next ten days pass with more frustrations.

Joshua's appointment with the counselor doesn't go well. "We didn't connect," he reports. Irritated, he's decided not to go back. "I scheduled another meeting but cancelled it."

"Then keep looking," I insist.

"I'll think about it," he says curtly.

It bothers him that they still live at the hotel. The insurance company is moving at a snail's pace, which affects how fast the work is getting done. "They keep telling me the check's in the mail, but it never comes." They were promised they'd be back in the house by now. "Two more weeks at least," he groans. He wants his home back. He wants his life back. "I want things normal again."

Making matters worse, the medical tests reveal abnormalities with his thyroid. The doctor orders more tests, schedules a biopsy, and hints at the possibility he might have cancer. "It explains a lot of your symptoms—not all, but most," he is told. The doctor assures him several times, "It's usually very treatable."

One minute, he's thrilled they found something: "You see, I wasn't making it up. I have real symptoms." The next, he's devastated he might have cancer.

Sometimes he calls me. Sometimes I call him.

But every time, Joshua astonishes me. I tell him that often. I hear in his voice the sound of gentle, unshakable faith. He is bound to his Lord, and his Lord is bound to him. Even when his anxieties rage at their worst; when he's barely holding on, his insides convulsing with sobs; his mind imagining the worst-case scenarios, there he is, in prayer, talking to the Lord as a child talks to his father.

He's not angry with Him. He's not running from Him. He never uses words that dishonor Him. It's the exact opposite. He loves Him. He trusts Him.

I hear it when his faith in Jesus remains stronger than his fears. I hear it when his fears prove stronger than his faith—he's consistent, never vacillating. He amazes me.

Until something changes.

I hear a new sound in his voice I don't like. It started when he said he'd cancelled his counseling appointment. Now as I urge him to find someone else, he quickly brushes me aside saying, "It's OK. I'll be fine." And with it comes the perfect excuse: "Plus, I really don't have time." Turns out, he's gone back to work. Full-time, full speed.

"When did you go back?" I ask, surprised.

"I preached last Sunday," he says, and then rambles on a mile a minute telling me all he's done through the week—staff meetings, calls, appointments, pastoral visits. "Payback for all the time I missed," he says, trying to complain. But I don't buy it. I hear the excitement in his voice. He tells me he has speaking engagements coming up, one in Cincinnati and one in Nashville. He says he decided not to cancel.

I wonder what Cindy thinks. They're still at the hotel, still not settled.

"They'll be fine," he assures me.

There it is again—that dreaded word *fine*! I use it all the time when I don't want to talk about something. It's a quick little word that sweeps everything under the rug, gone from sight. But I get it; I understand. Joshua and Cindy have had their lives turned upside down—their work, their home, his health. He's been in control of nothing. Even now, all these weeks later, none of these issues are resolved.

Except this. He's back at work.

I find myself strangely sympathetic. When my life is out of control, nothing normal, nothing in order, I want to do something about it. Let me control something, even small things—clean my desk! Mow the lawn! Pay bills! Eat, fix dinner, then eat some more! Or big things—like what Joshua is doing, plunging head over heels into work.

"What's wrong?" he asks, noting my unexpected silence.

"Just concerned, that's all," I say. He wants to know why. "A few days ago, you were writing your resignation letter," I respond. "You were at the edge of burnout—if not way over the edge. Now you're back like you never left. It doesn't make sense."

"Yeah, I know," he says. "But don't worry. I'll make sure things change at church. I promise."

"Like what?" I prod.

He says he's going to talk to his staff and a few close allies who serve as church elders. "They have my back," he assures me. "Once I get caught up, I'll talk to them about my schedule. They'll keep me accountable."

"Caught up?" I laugh just a little. "Are we ever caught up?"

"Yeah, right?" he says playfully. And I wonder, for now anyway, if he's finally feeling normal again.

That thought pierces my heart. "Is this me, too?" I ask myself. "Am I normal when I'm in charge of my life and not normal when I've lost control and have to rely on the Lord for help? Is that it? Shouldn't normal be the other way around? Shouldn't normal mean He's always in charge— I'm never in control?"

I tell him I'm scared for him.

He then says what none of us should ever say.

"It's OK. I've got this!"

Be anxious for nothing, but in everything by prayer and
supplication with thanksgiving let your requests be made known to
God. And the peace of God, which surpasses all comprehension,
will guard your hearts and your minds in Christ Jesus.

—PHILIPPIANS 4:6–7

QUESTIONS FOR REFLECTION

Have you ever said, "But you promised me?" to the Lord? What difference does it make to remind Him of His promises from a heart of faith versus a heart of fear?

What does it mean for Jesus Christ to be Lord of your life? Is it normal for Him to be in control and not you? When trials come and fears arise, do you easily vacillate?

22

BACK IN CHARGE

For he said, "I will appease him with the present that goes before me. Then afterward I will see his face; perhaps he will accept me."

—GENESIS 32:20

Plan one—already in effect. He'd divided his people into two camps (Gen. 32:7–8). One to go to battle, the other to slip away unnoticed and survive.

Plan two—go to the Lord. He'd prayed the most perfect prayer. In it, he honored the Lord, cried for help, and exposed the terrors of his heart. His faith in God was undeniably real and unshakably firm.

But he still wrestled fear. Where was the help?

The Lord didn't seem to answer. Not right away. Not yet. The silence was deafening. What was he supposed to do—sit still, trust God, do nothing? But how could he when fear was winning, fear was controlling?[1]

Plan three—he could do more. He could send "a present for his brother Esau" (v. 13). A big, extravagant gift: five hundred fifty of his flock, with four hundred ninety being female, able to reproduce, able to make Esau wealthier. It was a simple plan. Bless Esau with the blessing God gave him (33:11).

Just "buy him off."[2]

Jacob was wrestling fear, fear mixed with guilt, for he had to appease his brother. The word used in Hebrew translated to appease more fully understood means to "atone." He knew he'd sinned against Esau. Hopefully, "the present that goes before" him would atone for that sin. How else would Esau accept and forgive him?[3] How else could Jacob and his family survive?

Plan four—send the gift strategically, incrementally, as waves of blessing. Jacob instructed his servants to put "space between droves" (32:16). Let Esau experience the first wave while, on the horizon, he sees a second, followed by a third. Each one purposed to quiet the wild, raging fires in Esau's soul.

Jacob, the wrestler. Fear, his enemy.

Plan five—with each wave, send a message. Esau would undoubtedly ask, "To whom do you belong, and where are you going, and to whom do these animals in front of you belong?" (v. 17). Jacob's servants would say, "These belong to your servant Jacob; it is a present sent to my lord Esau. And behold, he also is behind us" (v. 18). It was the perfect wording. Just like before (vv. 4–5).

With those words, Jacob forced Esau back to the crime scene. From then on, Esau would be the rightful heir of the blessing of Abraham. It didn't matter that God made Jacob "lord" and Esau his "servant." No more. Jacob reversed it. With each gift, Esau would hear again and again, "My lord Esau" from "your servant Jacob."

Jacob was back in charge. The world calls it courage—that indomitable spirit facing insurmountable odds. It never gives up. It always hopes, always believes, and always prevails, no matter what comes. Courageous Jacob—it was deep inside him.

He was a fighter. He had to prevail.

Joshua slips easily into routine.

The next few weeks pass by quickly. We talk less, partly because of his work demands and partly because he feels like himself again. "A comfortable rhythm," he calls it. "And by the way," he exclaims, "we're out of that stupid hotel. There's nothing like being home and sleeping in your own bed!"

The trauma to his family seems nearly over.

The surgery goes remarkably well. He does have cancer of the thyroid. There are "suspicious lymph nodes." But Joshua sounds unaffected by the news. I ask why. He says, "Sometimes I get anxious because I don't understand what's going on. This time, I did my homework, that's all. I read up on it. I talked to a few people at church who've gone through the surgery. They said it's not a big deal."

And it isn't. The final pathology report comes back better than expected.

In coming days, Joshua and I fall into our old rhythm, too, and call each other once every six weeks or so. I stop bothering him about seeing a counselor. I don't want to. Nothing has changed at church. He is busier than ever. But perhaps worse, I know he's stuffing down the violation he felt from the robbery. But every time I mention it, it evokes the same response.

"I think I'm better," he says. "I've given it to the Lord, and He's helped me."

I stay quiet now and don't push. Maybe it's true for him, I don't know. But for me, too often it's not. When I don't want to deal with a painful ache in my heart, I easily make light of it. I convince myself, I convince others, the Lord miraculously stepped in and took the ache, the fear away. When, in fact, it's not true. I am stuffing it down.

Joshua says it with such ease. Just like me.

The last time we spoke about it, it brought my grandmother to mind. She was seventy-one when her daughter, my mother, died. On that day, as we left the hospital, I saw such strength in her. To me, she had an extraordinary ability to rise above her emotions, hold her head high in the face of unspeakable pain, and press into each day determined to make the most of it. Never losing composure. Never looking back.

This, I was taught, is courage. My grandmother didn't have an easy life. Five months before Mom died, her husband, my grandfather, died after eight years of struggle following a debilitating stroke. But she was strong. She took care of him at the house till the day he died.

I wasn't like her, but I wanted to be.

I lost composure a lot. I looked back a lot. But somehow I learned the art of stuffing down. For me, all I had to do was stay incredibly busy, set insanely impossible goals, and continue life pretending an attitude of invincibility.

It's how I learned to avoid matters of the heart.

But my grandmother surprised me. Twenty years later, in her nineties, the pain of losing my mom became too much for her to bear. Her heart couldn't stop the grieving. She didn't have the strength to be strong. Her mind had weakened. Her resilience, her resolve, had lost its rigor and, like a dam collapsing under the weight, it all gushed out with a vengeance. And I learned what I didn't want to learn.

Stuffing doesn't work. The heart always tells its story. And courage is sometimes nothing more than the mask we wear.

But still, knowing this, I kept on doing it. I learned, as a Christian, to use Christian language as a place to hide. It's a simple formula: Stuff it down. Pretend the Lord dealt with it. Tell self, tell others, "I'm miraculously better now."

I rarely get away with it nowadays.

The Lord is simply too persistent. He pokes. He pursues, chasing when I run, tripping me so I'll fall, never tiring, never letting go, always wrestling, always the wrestler.

And, as I walk this journey with Joshua, I find myself jealous of him. Why is he different? Why is he allowed to get away with hiding? Why doesn't the wrestler do with him what He does with me?

Soon enough, he calls.

He tells me Cindy got annoyed that he's never home. Medically, he's fine, the doctors say. But not all the symptoms are gone. His hands still shake. He still experiences the caffeine rush—less in intensity, but still there, and too often late at night.

"But it's the boys," he says. "I can see it in their eyes when tucking them into bed at night. They're scared still—frightened the robbers will come back. I told Cindy I thought maybe we should take them to a family counselor."

"What did she say?" I ask, biting my tongue to keep from saying more.

"She didn't; she just stared at me."

Turns out the stare worked. How could he send the boys to counseling if he wasn't willing to go himself? He called his counselor and got a referral to a partner in the same practice. "A Christian psychiatrist," he muses, after weeks of vehemently refuting his need for one. "It's gone well," he quickly adds. "He's a good fit, and he's giving me space to let the Lord do His work in me—real work."

And I see it, the vision as plain as day. Two figures entangled. Two figures wrestling. Both strangely determined to win.

Yet those who wait for the LORD will gain new strength;
They will mount up *with* wings like eagles, they will run and not get tired, they will walk and not become weary.

—ISAIAH 40:31

QUESTIONS FOR REFLECTION

Can you identify with Jacob? Why was he back in charge? Why couldn't he "trust in the Lord with all" his heart? Why work to save himself in his own strength? Is this you?

How would you describe courage? What do you do to avoid matters of the heart? Do you stuff it down? Pretend it's not there? How well do you know the wrestler?

NOTES

1. Allen P. Ross, *Creation and Blessing: A Guide to the Study and Exposition of the Book of Genesis* (Grand Rapids, MI: Baker Book House, 1988), 543. Ross noted, "In spite of Jacob's dependence on God through prayer, his fear and his guilt appear to have controlled him at this point."

2. Ibid., 544.

3. This word, translated *appease*, in Hebrew is *kippur* (note: Yom Kippur, the Day of Atonement). Also, the word rendered as *accept* or *forgive* has the more literal meaning, "lift up my face." The imagery of the face in this narrative (see also Gen. 32:30; 33:10) is significant. Here, Jacob hopes his atoning gift will cause Esau to lift up his face so that "afterward I will see his face."

PART 4

THE WRESTLER AND ME

23

ALONE

Then Jacob was left alone.

—Genesis 32:24

Night had come.

Jacob was in motion, constant motion. He put others in motion too. The children, their mothers, all crossing the river where it was shallow and safe. Everything he owned moved across the Jabbok with Jacob crossing once, twice, back and forth, crisscrossing the ford of the Jabbok (Gen. 32:22–23).[1]

All under the cover of darkness.

Was that also part of his plan—moving at night? Was he afraid somebody hid out there, lurking in the shadows, mapping their every movement? Spies, perhaps, from Esau? Or was it possible he kept in motion because he had to be in motion? Anxiety always puts us in motion. Jacob was frightened. Esau was near.

Pacing. Crossing, crisscrossing.

Who sleeps the night before his execution? Maybe it is as simple as that: he couldn't sleep. But shouldn't he have stayed with his family? What if they were just as anxious? What if they needed comfort like he needed comfort? At times like this, don't we stay close to those we love? Why separate himself? The Lord

*said from the beginning that it's not good for us to be alone (2:18).
But no, Jacob went back to the river and into the dark of night.[2]*

Alone—pacing, crossing, crisscrossing.

*Is it possible his mind was unsettled too? Was it also pacing
back and forth, analyzing his plan, detail after detail? Was he concerned it wasn't enough: the gift too small, the space too short
between the droves, the message too weak to make a difference?
Was he wishing he could do it over again? Was he scheming to
do more in the little time left?*

He was alone.

*Why was he alone? The Lord said once, twice, "I am with
you" (28:15; 31:3). Jacob knew this promise. He even prayed this
promise. But maybe it reflected how he felt. He had prayed and
nothing seemed to have happened. Silence, that's all he got. The
heavens didn't open. He received no visions, no angelic visita-
tions, no prophetic words, no miraculous interventions.*

He feels alone.

*Pacing. Crossing. Crisscrossing. That night would've been
different had the Lord done something, anything. Why was he
forced to devise his own plan, this multilayered strategy for
appeasing Esau's fury? When do our plans, in our strength, ever
give us the kind of confidence the Lord gives when He steps in
and takes control?*

Jacob at the Jabbok. In Hebrew, the two words sound the same.

*And that night was pitch black. No light gleamed to soften
the dark. No moonlight danced on the water. If someone came,
Jacob would never have seen them. He'd have had to hear them
coming. But how could he? He constantly moved—his feet
splashing in the river; his mind frantic, cluttered with worry; his
heart and soul wrestling fear, battling death, even now.*

Alone, pacing, crossing, crisscrossing.

I stand next to the yellow tape.

It's the kind the police use at a car accident, murder, robbery, or fire—up it goes, defining the perimeter. Lettering black, bold, all in caps, repeats without punctuation: "CRIME SCENE DO NOT CROSS CRIME SCENE . . ."

Outside is safe. Inside isn't. Inside people suffer.

Standing here, strangely, tells my story. Once again, my mind journeys back to the hospital room where my mom died. No, obviously, no literal yellow tape streamed across the door to her room. But in my mind's eye, looking back, I see it there. I was sixteen. I'd never seen yellow tape that close before. I'd been to funerals. I'd seen coffins. But I'd never seen a dead body. I'd never watched someone die, and death scared me. It was my first time to cross the barricade. I ducked under and went to be with her. I didn't stay. I was too afraid. Death hovered near in that room, and I could feel it—cold and dark. I ran out. Back under.

It's odd how the yellow tape tells my story.

But I think it tells a lot of our stories. When Joshua first called me, I pictured that tape. His life was a crime scene. He balanced on the edge of burnout, his health a mess and his home robbed. He didn't ask for it. He didn't choose it. But he was suddenly thrust inside the tape and forced to stay there. When he called, I knew exactly where he was and why he was inviting me in.

And I went, gladly. It's what I've learned to do.

I was with him as he stayed in. I was there when he ran out, and I understood why. It's what most of us do. We want to live our lives on the safe side of the yellow tape.

But Joshua was different. He chose to return for the sake of his boys.

They were still afraid, especially at night—afraid of the dark, afraid of robbers, afraid something might happen. Carson, the youngest, slept most nights between Cindy and Joshua. The boys were still inside that yellow tape. They hadn't come out. It wasn't enough to say, "It'll be all right, you'll see" or "It'll get better over time. God will help us."

That's what Joshua heard growing up. Bad things had happened to him. He got tossed inside the tape. Those who loved him got him out, brushed him off, and told him to get over it as quickly as possible. Pretend it never happened. It's how he lived life. It's how he served as a pastor. Get people out. Brush them off. Help them move on.

But not this time.

The robbery still tormented him. He, too, was scared—like the boys. Old hurts from the past dogged him. What was he supposed to do? Teach the boys his old song from childhood—Avoid! Deny! Pretend!—or could he show them a new way?

He made a choice.

He went back in. In subsequent months he gave brief reports from his time with the counselor. It was difficult for him. It was hard for me listening to the wrestlings of his soul. I didn't tell him this, but it made me anxious.

I'd never do that. I'd never choose to go back in for me.

I easily go in for others. My seminary training taught me to do that. I was required to spend an entire summer—of all places—at a hospital. I had no choice. Over and over, I learned to cross the imaginary yellow tape and be with people suffering in pain, experiencing grief, wrestling with the fear monster, scared to death of death. I struggled all summer. I felt like I was constantly back in that hospital room where my mom died.

Until one day when a pastor whispered a secret in my ear. "Don't make it so hard," he said. "Go inside, just don't take your heart with you." Then he showed me. He took me to the ER one night where a forty-eight-year-old man lay dying of a heart attack. We stayed and watched the doctors violently pound his chest. We went to the family in the waiting room. We were there when the sad news came of his death. I watched the pastor in action—compassionate, sincere, tender, and at times, teary-eyed.

I, on the other hand, was a wreck. Nauseous. My face white as a sheet.

Afterward, we headed to the cafeteria for coffee. The pastor joked, laughed, and told stories as if none of it had ever happened. I asked him how he did it. He said simply, "You'll never make it in this business if you wear your heart on your sleeve."

Stupid me, I took his counsel. I learned to go in but not go in.

Not Joshua. He stepped in, fully in, and chose to do it. I'd never seen that before. Up to that point, the only times I'd crossed that foreboding tape was when I'd been thrust in. Something happened—a trauma of some kind. Or maybe, for no apparent reason at all, when I was alone, really alone—a panic attack. I can feel it even now. Fear comes. Death roars. The wrestler appears out of nowhere.

And I'm suddenly, terrifyingly, back inside the tape.

Therefore humble yourselves under the mighty hand of God,
that He may exalt you at the proper time, casting all your
anxiety on Him, because He cares for you. Be of sober *spirit*,
be on the alert. Your adversary, the devil, prowls around.

—1 PETER 5:6–8

QUESTIONS FOR REFLECTION

Does anxiety keep you awake? What is it like to be in constant motion, pacing, your mind racing, your plans failing? Do you ever feel alone, without God? What is that like?

How often have you been inside the yellow tape? What were the circumstances? Were you thrust in? Were you forced to stay? How do you respond when facing the tape? When have you pretended it's not there? When have you freely chosen to go in?

NOTES

1. Victor P. Hamilton, *The Book of Genesis: Chapters 18–50* (Grand Rapids, MI: Eerdmans Publishing Co., 1995), 329. Hamilton wrote that verses 23–24 together "might suggest that Jacob crisscrossed the Jabbok several times."

2. Ibid., 328. Hamilton wrote, "Distressed at Esau's coming with 400 men, Jacob passes the 'night' (v. 13) to consider strategy. . . . Anxiety may have produced insomnia. He is too afraid to be able to sleep." Also see Acts 12:6 as a comparison.

24

THE MAN

———

And a man wrestled with him until daybreak.

—Genesis 32:24

He couldn't see. Too dark.

But could he hear—was there any forewarning? Maybe the sound of running along the shore, splashing in the water, coming at him fast? Did he have time to brace himself? Or was he completely unaware until impact, their bodies colliding, the attacker's sheer force knocking him back, perhaps throwing him down?

Ambushed.

Jacob—what did he do? Was his assailant too strong at first— overpowering him, taking full advantage of catching him by surprise? How long was Jacob assaulted before he realized he could defend himself—he could loosen the man's grip, push him back, and somehow fight for survival?

He was alive. Yet, why was he alive? This man could've killed him instantly with a knife at his throat, a sword through his stomach, a blow to the head. Why didn't the attacker have weapons? And where were the others? Don't thieves travel in packs? It sounded to Jacob like—it felt like—the man was alone. But Jacob couldn't be sure. He couldn't see. The darkness was too thick.

The man was strong.

But Jacob was also strong. He could fight—fight back and fight hard. He moved to offense. He waged his own assault, and it worked. He bore down on the man, fighting, hurting, immobilizing. Jacob could do more than survive. He could break this man's strength. He could end this battle.

But the man proved stronger still.

He slipped out of Jacob's hold and retook control. Jacob went on defense again. He couldn't see. Predicting the man's next move seemed nearly impossible. The man had Jacob and then he didn't. Jacob had the man and then he didn't. The two of them warred back and forth with Jacob having no idea who the man was or why he was there or what he wanted. If Jacob let go, if he surrendered, what would the man do? Would he kill him? Was that the goal?

Jacob had to fight—with everything in him.

The wrestlers, their bodies interlocked. When did it dawn on Jacob that this man was his equal? Equal in strength, equal in skill. No matter what Jacob did, the man countered with equal finesse, making it impossible to stop him. Jacob tried harder, forcing his adversary down, pinned with all the strength Jacob could muster, but the man kept escaping, just as Jacob did every time the man's power nearly ended him.

And on it went. No end in sight.

Jacob didn't know the man's name.[1] It was too dark to see his face. But he—this man, his equal—had fury inside him. He fought with purpose. Who does that? Was it possible it wasn't a thief? Was it him? Had he come with his four hundred? Attacking at night, fighting to the death? Wrestlers since the days of their mother's womb?

Esau—is it you?

The year 1994 was a hard one.

That January, I remember sitting at Heathrow airport outside London. My wife and I, with two dear friends, were on a mission trip to Uganda—our first time in Africa. We were to land near the capital city of Kampala, drive four hours west to a village called Bulindi, and spend two weeks alongside a pastor and his wife whom we deeply love.

I wanted to go. Only a few times, in the weeks prior to the trip, did I feel a tinge of fear. I'd get anxious about the unknown. I'd think about things my pastor friend had told me: The water wasn't good; electricity wasn't constant; there were no hospitals nearby.

And, of course, the long flights.

I'd flown a lot but never liked it. Too scared. It's too easy to look out the window, see the wing tips bobbing, and imagine the whole thing was about to fall apart. I'd hear the engines make a weird sound and think something was horribly wrong. I hated turbulence. I hated when the "Fasten Seat Belt" sign lit up and the pilot warned of bad weather ahead. The darker the clouds, the bumpier the ride, the worse I got. My palms would sweat. My mouth would go dry. I'd fidget. I'd pray. I'd wrestle with fear.

But not always. I'd known times, many times actually, when the Lord infused me with His grace to fly, grace to go through storms, grace to be tossed about and not fear at all. I had that grace preparing for the African trip.

And then I didn't.

We sat at the gate at Heathrow airport, waiting to board the plane. It was late at night. We were tired, having already flown from the US. We were casually talking. I wasn't expecting it but, out of nowhere, it came—fear struck my heart, struck hard, and grace disappeared, nowhere to be found.

I didn't want anyone to know. I stood up, darted for the huge window overlooking the tarmac, and tried to calm myself. My heart, racing. My breathing, labored. My palms, already sweating. I stood there uncertain what to do. I didn't want to get on that plane, or any plane. Not to Africa. Not back to the US. I didn't want to fly at all, anywhere, which made me stuck, completely stuck, completely out of control.

Panic surged through every cell in my body—I could feel it. I hated it.

My mom experienced this. She had a fear, an irrational fear, of driving on bridges. It made no sense to me whatsoever. Who cares about bridges? Who hears about a bridge collapsing and people plummeting to their deaths?

But I understand it now.

I understand it when an eight-year-old—fully cured of cancer—cries uncontrollably for no reason, with no presenting symptoms, because she thinks it's back. She thinks she's going to die. I understand it when those suffering from anorexia are afraid to eat, or when a friend is terrified of doctors and hospitals, or when our dog trembles at the sound of a coming storm.

Thrust inside the yellow tape.

I heard the announcement. Our plane was boarding. I did what I knew to do. I went to the bathroom, washed my face, took a deep breath, went back out, and played pretend with my wife and friends. A reassuring smile. And then I boarded the plane.

It's a choice. I fight back.

Once in Africa, I realized my fight was nothing compared to what I saw on arrival. In one village, I held a young boy in my arms who was hungry, malnourished, his stomach distended, and his eyes sad and scared. I looked around and saw he was not alone. Other children, too many children, suffered like him. I know the fear in his eyes. But I don't, not really, not like he does. I don't want to let go. I wish I could help.

The monster—he was everywhere. I remember talking to a young mom dying of AIDS. She had other kids. Her husband left her. Her elderly mother cared for her and the children, but she, too, wasn't well. The mom begged the pastor for mercy. She needed the church to do something for her children. She was scared and frail. She was done wrestling the monster for herself. She fought instead for the kids.

The pastor comforted her. He promised her.

Then he drove us to a beaten-down old building outside a nearby town. It was for rent, he told us. Here he'd start an orphanage. The woman's children would have a home. Even if they, too, had AIDS, they'd know Jesus here. They'd know His love and compassion. They'd see His miracles. The pastor assured us.

Because here, he told us, the monster was not welcome.

And I believed him. I don't know how he did it. This pastor—always inside the tape. Always fighting the monster for the well-being of others. It embarrassed me. It made me realize the fight I fight in comparison is nothing but a little skirmish. I can handle it.

I can get back on that plane home to the US. I can face my fears, no problem.

I am strong. I can fight. I can win.

> For it has been granted to you on behalf of Christ not
> only to believe in him, but also to suffer for him, since
> you are going through the same struggle you saw
> I had, and now hear that I still have.
>
> —PHILIPPIANS 1:29–30 NIV

QUESTIONS FOR REFLECTION

An enemy attacked Jacob. He didn't know why. Has that ever happened to you? Have you ever suffered not knowing if it's from God, the Devil, or someone's pride? What were the circumstances?

When suffering comes, what do you do to survive? How do you regain control? Do you ever compare your sufferings with others? Does it comfort or confuse you?

NOTE

1. The biblical text carefully hides the man's identity. Suspense fills the night as the man slowly reveals who he is to Jacob. You are encouraged to experience the same. Enter into the night of suspense as if you've never read the end of the story.

25

ALL NIGHT

And a man wrestled with him until daybreak.

—Genesis 32:24

Why couldn't Jacob end it?

Slam him down, lock his head, pin his arms, press hard against him till he couldn't move, till a limb nearly breaks, till pain steals his breath and makes him beg for his life.

Twenty minutes. Thirty minutes.

He couldn't do it. He couldn't hold him down long enough. The bodies reversed, untangled and tangled again, with the unknown wrestler on top, Jacob crushed down, his body in pain.

Forty minutes. Fifty.

"Evenly matched, even perfectly so."[1] Jacob stayed at full strength. It's an act deep inside the soul to give all, spend all, not let down, not tire out. But for how long? What if it's not physical power or brilliant execution that prevails? What if it's endurance?

Sixty minutes, seventy-five.

Why not pull back, set pace, save strength for a long night? He had to figure it out himself. There was no referee. No time-out. No place to go to regroup, reassess, or catch his breath. No coach whispering secrets in his ear. No trainer tending bleeding cuts or massaging sore, strained muscles. No fans cheering. No stopping. Not till it's over.

Ninety minutes.

Still, no doubt, they were both at full strength. Neither showed signs of weakness. Neither showed mercy. There were no rules. Not when fighting to the death. A quick fist of sand or dirt in the face, the eyes, the mouth. A blow to the head, yanking of hair, kicking, choking, whatever worked. No whistles. No fouls. No penalties. No out of bounds.

Two hours. Three.

Nor do words pass between them. Not now. Not yet. Just the sound of body against body; maybe groans and cries, here and there; probably sounds of bodies, fists, and legs pounding land or slapping water. But no words. No demands. Neither can sustain a death grip long enough to force the other to talk. Negotiate. End it.

Four long hours pass.

How does it end for us? What breaks us? Is it our body? Do we hit a wall when it can't do what we want it to do? Does it turn against us, like a rebellious child, no longer listening to our threats, and suddenly it's over? We completely, terrifyingly, collapse in defeat.

Or is it our mind that breaks us? Without notice, it too can declare mutiny: "You can't win this," it argues. "You've got no strength left. You've tried everything. It hasn't worked." Does the mind then persuade the will to end it and let death come? Is that how the battle is lost?

What kept Jacob going?

Five hours.

Endurance, the two of them, neither broke, neither stopped. Where does this grit come from? What is it inside us that over-powers the mind, the body, and the will, to prevail and survive? The man had it. Jacob had it. They were wrestlers perfectly, evenly, matched.

All night long.

We landed safely back in the US.

I knew myself well enough to know I should call Peter, an older pastor who serves a church a few towns away. I'd gone to him several times over the years. Mostly as a consultant to my work. Occasionally, for myself. He was a mentor more than a friend—wise, helpful, and safe.

But what would I tell him: "I have a fear of flying . . . but only sometimes"? Really, why talk to him? I'd made it home from Africa. I soon would fly to Atlanta for meetings. Then a mission trip to Honduras in May. With the Lord's help, I could fly—no problem. When He didn't help—yes a problem, but not insurmountable. So why see Peter?

I didn't call.

That's the trouble with self-diagnosis. I'd had an episode in Heathrow airport; so what? I dealt with it. I'd handle it again if I had to. But I was blind to a simple fact: I wasn't wrestling a little monster, the fear of flying. I was wrestling the big monster, the one from my childhood, the fear behind all other fears: the "fear of death" and the fear of "him who had the power of death, that is, the devil" (Heb. 2:14–15).

Not seeing, not knowing, made me think I could wrestle and win.

But not this year. Not 1994.

Back from Africa, we learned a colleague was diagnosed with esophageal cancer. I deeply respected this man. He was a few years older than me, physically fit, and pastored a large church in our denomination. We'd meet every couple of months or so. He and his wife rallied their church, friends, and family to pray for him daily. And we did pray, through his surgery and months of treatment.

By Easter, he was in remission, upbeat, and optimistic.

By Pentecost, the cancer returned with a vengeance. He went into treatment again, but this time the chemo knocked him down. Before, he kept up his work schedule at church. Not this time. He was in and out of the hospital with low blood counts, infections, and fevers. Still, the reports were encouraging. The treatment was effectively battling the cancer.

More news came. The pastor we served with in Uganda was e-mailing us almost daily. His home country of Rwanda was in utter chaos. Violence, mass killings, genocide—starting April 6, it would last a hundred days; by the end, a million people would be slaughtered.

"Pray for my people," he wept on the phone.

More news. This time within our family.

In the early morning hours of June 20, my wife's mother— Evelyn Forsberg, a regal, elegant lady—suffered a heart attack and died. People asked us, "How old was she?" We'd say, "She was seventy-nine." They'd nod, like it's expected at her age. But it wasn't to us. When is it ever time to let go of those we love?

More news: in August, a dear friend drowned. Our Old English Sheepdog died. A woman in our church lay in the hospital near death. I visited her most days while, across town, at another hospital, my colleague with esophageal cancer was losing the fight. "He needs strength to endure," one report said. "He needs a miracle."

But a close friend of his told me, "He's ready." I wanted to say back, "I'm not."

In late August, the Ugandan pastor visited us. He brought pictures with him. He had traveled to Rwanda after one hundred days of genocide. The pictures were graphic. Dead bodies strewn everywhere. Mass graves. Survivors with limbs cut off. Little children weeping.

"It's more than the heart can bear," he groaned, his eyes filled with tears.

The monster was everywhere.

The woman from our church died on Saturday, September 3. The wake was held at Wayne Tatalovich's funeral home a few days later. I'd worked with Wayne often over the years. He was a handsome man with a slender build, in his late fifties, who served as county coroner. The funeral went as planned, but it was hard on me. In the days between the woman's death and her funeral, my colleague had died.

His death pushed me over the edge. The panicked episode at Heathrow airport happened again. This time late at night. Twice within three nights. I hated that death took my friend. Why no miracle? Why had the Lord allowed his passing? This man, this great pastor, had died at the age of forty-five. If him, why not me?

I donned the mask and officiated the woman's funeral. I convinced myself that if I'd dealt with fear in the past, I'd deal with fear now. Just fight back, fight hard.

More news. Horrifying news.

Thursday night, September 8, 1994, at 7:03 I was at church with our music team. We were rehearsing for Sunday service.

None of us heard the explosion. Nor did we feel the ground shake from the impact. A dark, black column of smoke gushed into the sky, but we didn't see it. We knew nothing. Not until we heard sirens wail. Everywhere. Fire trucks, ambulances, police cars. Everything in motion, commotion. But we didn't know why. Not until someone ran into the church, crying, telling us a commercial jet had just crashed a mile away.

US Airways Flight 427, we soon learned, was inbound from Chicago. One hundred thirty-two on board.

The monster was everywhere.

Consider it all joy, my brethren, when you encounter various trials, knowing that the testing of your faith produces endurance. And let endurance have *its* perfect result, so that you may be perfect and complete, lacking in nothing.

—James 1:2–4

QUESTIONS FOR REFLECTION

What do you know about endurance? What is your breaking point? When has the wrestling been too long? How have you prevailed? When have you collapsed?

Reflect on Hebrews 2:14–15. What power does the "fear of death" have in your life? Our Lord came because He knew our "slavery." But do we? Do we wrestle with it?

NOTE

1. Leon R. Kass, *The Beginning of Wisdom: Reading Genesis* (New York: Free Press, 2003), 456. Kass wrote, "The match took a long time, the whole night. The opponents were evenly matched, even perfectly so." Allen P. Ross in his book *Creation and Blessing: A Guide to the Study and Exposition of the Book of Genesis* (Grand Rapids, MI: Baker Book House, 1988), 553, said the fact that the "wrestling lasted till the breaking of day suggests a long, indecisive bout."

26
HIS TOUCH

~~~

*When he saw that he had not prevailed against him,
he touched the socket of his thigh; so the socket of
Jacob's thigh was dislocated while he wrestled with him.*

—GENESIS 32:25

Before color touched the sky, they were equals no more.

One prevailed. Perhaps incrementally at first; increasing little by little as he dominated longer, escaped with greater ease, till it was all him in control, till they both knew it was nearly over. Dawn soon would break. They would see each other's faces. And Jacob would finally know why he was attacked in the black of night.

Esau—who else could it be?

All night the unknown wrestler matched Jacob's strength. No matter how long they fought, no matter how much pain he inflicted on Jacob, no matter how close he brought him to the gates of death, Jacob never let go, never surrendered. Jacob's will to survive, his determination to prevail, unyielding. His strength undiminished.

The man saw it all in Jacob.

It appeared, for the moment, it was too much for him. He knew he had not broken Jacob. He had "not prevailed against him." How would a common man react? Would he surrender? Would he negotiate terms? Would he try to free himself and make *a run for it? After all, it seemed he was not Jacob's equal. He was not in control. If anyone was broken, it was him.*

But this man was far from common.

One little touch, that's all it took. There was nothing violent about it. It's not as if the unknown wrestler freed his strong arm and, with all the might left in his weary body, thrust his fist into Jacob's hip socket, dislocating it. That's not what happened. This had nothing to do with human strength. Even Jacob, still fighting blind in the dark, could see that.

A touch—that's all.

That unexpected, altogether surprising touch changed everything. It released power into Jacob's body, power not to heal but to wound, power to dislocate his hip, sending searing pain into his body, rendering half his body below his waist useless. This touch was not a common touch by an ordinary man. So who was he? How did he have this power, this supernatural power?[1] Had he come from heaven above or hell below?

Esau—it wasn't Esau.

But it was confusing. One touch and the man who wasn't prevailing now prevailed, who wasn't in control, now controlled, who was nearly broken, and now was not broken at all. It made no sense. Why would this man with all this power fight Jacob at all? Why didn't he end it before it began? Why wrestle all night, matching Jacob's strength? Why let Jacob dominate him, hurt him, and nearly kill him?

One touch—that's all it was.

And maybe that's all that was needed. Maybe now Jacob would realize he couldn't win. He wasn't in control. It was time to do what he must do and surrender.

Our church is five miles from Pittsburgh International Airport in one direction and a mile from the crash site in another. Four of us hurry into a car, take the back roads, and speed toward the Green Garden Plaza.

"It's not far from there," a friend at US Airways tells us. "A Boeing 737–300 went down. Not sure if anyone survived."

One quick turn in the road and there it is: black smoke from a tree-covered hill opposite us rising straight up into a cloudless twilight sky. Down below at the Plaza, a sea of flashing lights—police cars, ambulances, fire trucks, rescue vehicles everywhere. We get in line, not sure if we can get in.

"Clergy," I inform the policeman at the Plaza entrance.

He lets us through. We head toward the ambulances. Two of our group stay with the car while Ken Ross and I locate a team of doctors. Ken, too, is clergy. We want to know why the ambulances are there, not at the crash site treating people. "County coroner hasn't released us," a doctor explains. "He's up there now, assessing the scene."

It is just past 8:00. An hour after Flight 427 crashed.

Helicopters fly overhead. Some land where we hear there is a makeshift morgue. We go to check it out. Nothing. No bodies. No news of the dead or the living. We also hear there is an area where family members of the passengers are gathering. Nobody there either. Everybody on pause. All these rescue teams poised for action with nowhere to go—just standing, waiting, adrenaline pumping.

We find the command post. At 9:15, still nothing happens. Night falls. Sirens still wail in the distance; media circle with cameras and lights. Still no report.

At 9:30 someone says, "Here comes Wayne." We watch as a car makes its way toward us. I realize it is Wayne Tatalovich, county coroner, the same man I'd done a funeral with just the day before. His car brakes to a stop. I press my way toward him. As he steps out, our eyes meet. All I say is, "Survivors?"

He shakes his head slightly, pained, and mouths back, "Pray for me."

We later learn Flight 427 was on final approach into Pittsburgh, some fifty-six hundred feet in the air, when it jolted left once, then twice, then plunged to the earth with engines at full throttle. Twenty-three seconds—that's all it took. There'd be no rescue. No need for doctors or ambulances or helicopters to fly the wounded to hospitals.

Wayne officially closes the crash site till morning. The "rescue" operation turns to "recovery."

He sends us home.

That night, I drift in and out of sleep. But in a dream, I am there on the plane, flying into Pittsburgh as I've done so many times before. I look out the window at the familiar rolling hills of western Pennsylvania on a perfect cloudless evening in late summer—an easy ride. Close to landing. Almost home. All safe and secure.

Till it's not. Till it's us. Our plane. Our twenty-three seconds.

I shoot out of bed in a sweat, my heart racing. It's a nightmare, but it's not. It's real. It happened. A mile from our home, 132 bodies lay still on a hillside. Dead. This is it. This is exactly why I've been afraid to fly all these years.

Twenty-three seconds. I can't believe it. That's all it took.

Early the next morning, my bishop calls. He's headed to the Plaza and wants Ken and me to meet him.

I'm struck by the change when we arrive. No more ambulances or fire trucks or frenzy. People everywhere, vehicles of all shapes and colors, but everything feels ordered. Out in front, the media has arrived in full force with their huge satellite dishes. A large white trailer serves as the emergency command headquarters.

The bishop spots the Salvation Army truck. It's our first stop. We meet a man named Bob. He tells us the crash site is closed until early afternoon, but it's not hard to get to. The point of impact is near an old logging road. He tells us the Salvation Army already sent a food and supply truck to the site. They've made a dozen or more trips up.

"Bishop," Bob says, "I'll take you there if you want to go."

Next thing I know, we're in a minivan headed to the site. I hate that I got in. We pull out of the Plaza, head up a hill, then veer off onto a dirt road. A few minutes later, the logging road comes into view. Then the food and supply truck. We pull up alongside and there it is, some fifty yards away, stretched across the dirt-and-gravel road.

Yellow tape.

Beyond it is chaos, wreckage, debris everywhere as if a bomb—a huge bomb—had blown everything to bits and pieces. We get out. We walk toward the tape. In the distance, the impact site. A piece of fuselage with the familiar blue and red stripes of US Airways. The trees scorched by fire. We come to the tape. My hands play with the yellow tape. And there, in front of me, I see the remains of a man. Most of him beyond recognition, but enough of him to see that he, like me, is human.

I turn my eyes away. I look ahead, focusing on nothing, trying not to see. The bishop tells us he's concerned for the workers. He doesn't want them inside the tape alone. He wants them to know God is with them in "the valley of the shadow of death" (Ps. 23:4). He looks at Ken and me. He tells us we're to go. And I feel it.

The touch. Pushing me across the tape.

I am the man who has seen affliction under the rod of his wrath. . . . But this I call to mind, and therefore I have hope: The steadfast love of the LORD never ceases; his mercies never come to an end; they are new every morning; great is your faithfulness.

—LAMENTATIONS 3:1, 21–23 ESV

QUESTIONS FOR REFLECTION

Not yet knowing the man's identity, why do you think he, with this power to injure, became Jacob's equal and allowed Jacob to prevail? Why is the mystery of his identity essential to this moment in the story?

Have there been times when you've been touched—wounded—and not known if it was from heaven above or hell below? Are you wounded still?

NOTE

1. Allen P. Ross, *Creation and Blessing: A Guide to the Study and Exposition of the Book of Genesis* (Grand Rapids, MI: Baker Book House, 1988), 553. Ross explained, "The text uses a mild term for it [touch], thereby demonstrating supernatural activity (cf. Isa. 6:7, 'he touched Isaiah's lips')."

27

LET ME GO

Then he said, "Let me go, for the dawn is breaking."
But he said, "I will not let you go."

—Genesis 32:26

Why was there contradiction in the unknown man?

He had power to prevail, yet he chose not to prevail—why? Why not end the fight, state the reason for his attack, then do what he came to do?

There was contradiction in Jacob too.

Half his body was now dead weight. At this point, he knew the man had supernatural power. Why not admit defeat, surrender, and appeal for mercy? Yet still he fought—why? Touch or no touch, his will remained unbroken, his resolve firm. He refused to let go. He would dominate with all his might. He was, after all, by force of nature, the prevailer.

The man, what should he have done? A second touch? A third? Instead, he opted for what neither had yet done. He spoke. All night not a word, but now the sound of his voice filled Jacob's ears. This voice was not his brother's voice. But what was it like? The tone, was it the roar of a lion in pain? Was it the quiet but desperate pleading of a beggar? Did it have power—power like the touch of the man's hand? Power like the voice of God?

Such simple words, yet incomprehensible: "Let me go."[1]

It makes no sense. Why was the stronger abdicating to the weaker? Why give Jacob power and authority to choose to let go or not? Why submit to him? He was Jacob the prevailer. He would not stop. He would beat down. He would kill. It is, after all, the sin of the human race. We take from God only to turn against Him.

"Let me go."

The man didn't say, "Let me go; I surrender!" Nor did he beg for mercy. He was concerned, it seems, about one thing and one thing only: dawn was breaking. The first brush stroke of light had already painted the horizon. Soon day would come, night would flee, and the two men would see each other face-to-face. Why did this concern the man, compelling him to speak? And why tell Jacob? Why would Jacob even care?

But the man cared. He didn't want to be seen.

For Jacob, nothing had changed. Not the touch. Not the sound of the man's voice. Not the plea to let him go or the concern that dawn would somehow change the story. He wouldn't let up. No doubt, he answered the man by pressing in all the more.

First by force. Then by words: "I will not let you go."

This was Jacob the mighty. His name, "Ya'aqob," sounds almost the same as the word for wrestling, ye'abeq, which in turn sounds almost the same as the river Jabbok, Yabboq.[2] It's as if this night was always meant to be—the perfect night, Jacob's night.

Wounded but in control.

Saying no to God is easy.

It's instinctive, inscribed deep in our genetic code. Rebels, all of us. We try to say yes and do what is right, but we fail every time (Rom. 7:18—8:2). It takes an act of God to change our genetic code so that our rebellion stops. But even then, even when we're in Christ, a new creation (2 Cor. 5:17), saying no comes way too easily.

I wasn't going inside that yellow tape.

We return to the minivan and head to the Plaza. The bishop says he can't stay. He has appointments he's got to keep. Again, he insists we go back to the site. He needs to know we're committed. It's what Christians do, he reminds us. "We go. We pray. We tell the workers at the site that comfort is possible in Jesus Christ." I nod my head and say yes.

But my answer is no. I'm not doing it.

Excuse number one: how can I help anyone if I'm the one needing help?

The minivan pulls into the Plaza, and reporters immediately engulf us. The bishop was first. He tells CNN we'd been to the site. Next thing I know I'm up. I'm being asked, "Why did God allow this to happen?" I do my best to explain that God isn't to blame. It's a broken world. Suffering's everywhere. He promises to be with us in it. It's why He came Christmas night—to fix, to heal, not to destroy. A sound bite of it goes over CNN for the next twenty-four hours. The reporters turn to Ken.

My eye catches a friend, also a pastor. I make my way over to him. He informs me that clergy and trained counselors will have a place at the Plaza to help anyone impacted by the crash. He wants me to join him.

Excuse number two: I'm needed at the Plaza.

I'm asked to do another interview, this time with the religion editor at the *Pittsburgh Post-Gazette*. As we talk, I spot a group of men and women bunched together, maybe fifteen of them, mostly young, maybe late twenties, all wearing dark blue jumpsuits with *coroner* written on the back in large yellow lettering. They're waiting to go to the crash site; that's my guess.

I finish the interview, walk over, and introduce myself to two of them. One named Mike, the other Sandy. "What's the plan?" I ask. Mike tells me they're headed to the site at 12:30. Their job is to extricate bodies and get them to the refrigeration trucks so they can be transported to the morgue for identification.

"I didn't see refrigeration trucks up there, at least not yet," I say.

"What's it like?" Sandy asks, surprising me. She looks afraid.

I tell her what the county coroner told us at the site. "He said he's never seen such devastation. He thinks maybe, at best, they'll be able to identify 25 percent of the bodies." Both of them physically react. I learn neither wants to go. Mike says he's seen bodies badly mangled at suicides and car accidents, but nothing like this, not bodies beyond recognition. Not one hundred and thirty-two at once.

"Why were you there?" Sandy asks pointedly, trying to figure me out.

I tell her I'll be working at the counseling center at the Plaza. "We can't help," I say, "if we don't experience it too." I give the false impression that I've been there, really been there, as if I've crossed the yellow tape, walked the entire debris field, and seen it all.

"Why aren't you going back up?" she presses.

"I'm needed here," I say confidently, but it's not true. I'm protecting myself. I have the same fear as she and Mike. They have to go. It's their job. I'm supposed to go. My bishop forced me to commit so that people like Mike and Sandy wouldn't be alone at the site. They'd have Christians alongside them, suffering like they're suffering and bringing the peace of Christ in the midst of chaos.

Excuse number three: I'm too scared to go.

I walk away. My answer is still no, but I'm definitely wavering. I wonder, what if we go up but don't go in? Maybe hang out at the Salvation Army food truck? It's safe. It's not past the tape. We can be there for the workers on their break. I'd be doing what my bishop said to do. Well, close anyway.

An hour, then two pass. The site opens up. Minibuses start transporting workers. Ken and I sign up. Next thing we know we're being dressed in decontamination suits with the word *chaplain* written across the front. It attracts the media and, without our knowing, someone snaps a picture of me and Ken that lands in the *New York Times* and *Newsweek*.

On the bus. The answer is still no. I'm not going in.

Ken and I talk about Psalm 23 on the drive up. It's the yellow tape psalm. When we're in the valley of the shadow of death—on the other side of the tape—there's no need to fear. The Lord is there, inside. He's the Shepherd, and He's staying. He doesn't take us out of it. He keeps us safe in it. Great psalm, great promises. The answer is still no.

No, as the bus lurches to a stop at the Salvation Army truck. No, as I view the hillside covered with people. All of them, inside the tape. The answer is no because saying no to God is easy.

—⁓⁓—

> But my people did not listen to my voice;
> Israel would not submit to me.
> So I gave them over to their stubborn hearts,
> to follow their own counsels.
> Oh, that my people would listen to me,
> that Israel would walk in my ways!
> I would soon subdue their enemies
> and turn my hand against their foes.
>
> —PSALM 81:11–14 ESV

—⁓⁓—

QUESTIONS FOR REFLECTION

Has there ever been a time the Lord has said to you, "Let me go"? Yet you have persisted, resisted, and stayed in control? Why does He give us the choice to say no?

When you do say no, what are your excuses? How do you defend them? Do you ever give others the false impression that you're doing what God wants you to do? Why?

NOTES

1. It is here where we must pause in incredulity. Our Lord, on the night of His capture, with "twelve legions of angels" at His disposal (Matt. 26:53), could easily have freed himself. Yet He allowed himself to be taken by force.

2. Allen P. Ross, *Creation and Blessing: A Guide to the Study and Exposition of the Book of Genesis* (Grand Rapids, MI: Baker Book House, 1988), 549. Ross pointed out that "these similar sounding words attract the reader's attention."

28

TAKEN BY FORCE

I will not let you go unless you bless me.

—Genesis 32:26

Jacob couldn't see his opponent's face. It was still too dark. But that touch, the man's touch, did more than wound him. It gave him insight. He knew something about this man now. He knew he had power beyond human strength. Good power. Odd to say that, since the touch wounded him. But somehow Jacob knew this man wasn't a demon from the pit of hell.

The man was good.

The man had power to bless.

That could mean only one thing: the man was greater than Jacob. The ancient rule states, "Without any dispute the lesser is blessed by the greater" (Heb. 7:7). Abraham, his grandfather, had a similar experience the day he met King Melchizedek, priest of the Most High. This man, greater than Abraham, blessed Abraham (Gen. 14:19). Now Jacob had a man just like King Melchizedek held captive under the force of his mighty grip.

No, he couldn't see his face and he didn't know everything about him.

But this man had what Jacob desperately needed. So why not let him go, ask him for it, and trust he'll give it? Jacob knew how to surrender. He did it in his prayer to God earlier that night. He cried out for rescue. He confessed his fear of Esau. He admitted he was scared for his family. He needed the Lord to do what he couldn't do for himself. Why not surrender now like he surrendered then?

The man was good.

The man had power to bless.

But no, Jacob stayed in control. His physical tenacity, his invincible perseverance, continued to overpower the man who, in fact, had power over him and could help him. Jacob's words are a stunning display of defiance: "I will not let you go unless you bless me." He, the lesser, refused to comply with the greater. Isn't it obvious why? He was driven by urgent need, driven by fear that the need wouldn't be met. He'd do anything to get the blessing.

No, not the blessing of Abraham and Isaac—he had that already. The blessing he needed most right then was rescue from Esau and his four hundred men. Esau was coming. He was near. Jacob was in no condition—not after a night of wrestling, not with his hip dislocated—to face Esau. He had to force the man to save him from Esau's fury.

The man was good.

The man had power to bless.

But Jacob remained defiant. He should have fallen to his knees, confessed his powerlessness and utter dependence on God for help, and fully submitted to the man's choice to bless or not. Isn't that always the right posture when seeking God's blessing? But he couldn't. He had to get his need met. As long as the man allowed himself to be beaten and bruised, Jacob would do what he had to do—storm in and take the blessing by force.[1]

One step off the bus and I realize I was wrong.

Nothing here is safe. Not even the Salvation Army truck. Not some imaginary place close to but outside the tape. In fact, I can't even find the tape. It's gone. Across the logging road, in its place, stands a dark green canvas supply tent with workers going in and out. To my right, a hazmat team strips off decontamination suits from workers who have finished their shift. Behind me, two large refrigeration trucks have bay doors wide open with coroners in their dark blue jumpsuits inside.

The minibus pulls away. No way back, not now.

The place has changed since morning. The site is packed with people, everybody busy and moving. In front of me, two workers pass by, lugging a bin between them. They head to the trucks. They carry the dead. I catch the eye of one worker and see the grief in his soul. He nods; I nod back.

I know this place.

I've been inside the tape enough in my life to know one simple fact: rules change here. We live life differently. All of us do. Whether we like it or not, our hearts get exposed as though someone removed our skin and made us feel everything. A gentle touch, the slightest breeze, a burst of sunshine. We're tender and sensitive; our emotions are raw, right at the surface. Here, non-criers cry. Non-huggers hug. Non-talkers talk.

It's different here. We feel an ounce of the suffering of the people who died—people just like us. They become part of us now. So do the people near us who see what we see and feel what we feel. The suffering unites us. No divisions exist here—not class, color, or prejudice of any kind. Outside the tape yes, but not inside. Here, enemies become friends. People who have never been seen together are strangely inseparable.

I've experienced it in the ER. I've witnessed it at wakes and funerals. I've seen it among veterans who spent years in combat together. They're not just friends; they're family.

I know this place.

I know it's where God is. This is what happens when the heart is exposed. We become aware of Him. People who never gave Him the time of day now talk about Him, even talk to Him. They pray. They allow others to pray. Isn't it shocking? At a time of national crisis, what happens? People pack into places of worship. Politicians talk about God. Reporters interview pastors, filming segments inside the church.

Why? He's here. Inside.

Two state policemen approach us. They see the word *chaplain* written on our decontamination suits and tell us we're the first chaplains at the site. They tell us we're needed out there—past the tent—in the debris field with everyone else.

"That's where we're headed," I say as if I mean it.

Both men tell their stories. At times like this, everybody has a story. Out it comes in precise detail, starting with where they were at the time of the crash. Talking comforts the soul. Listening helps too. As they go on, I can't keep my eyes off the canvas tent. The flaps opening, closing, as the workers go in and out. Inside the tent I think I recognize someone I know.

"Is that Val Tatalovich?" I interrupt.

"The county coroner's wife," one of the police officers says. "She's in charge of the supply tent." Brilliant choice, I think to myself. She's the business face at the funeral home, administratively gifted, and a delightful personality. She knows exactly how to make people feel special and valued, even in the worst situations.

We finish talking to the policemen and head over to the tent. It's dark inside and larger than I imagine. Supply boxes are stacked high on both sides. A man sits by a card table drinking coffee. Workers keep passing through. Val's talking to one of them. Something's wrong with the worker. He's clearly upset. She gives him an old-fashioned pep talk and then, just as quickly, sends him back out to the site.

She sees us and waves.

People swarm her. We watch as she deals with each one. Not surprisingly, she knows most by name. Some need supplies, others direction. But she has that knack for looking them right in the eyes and asking, "You OK?" She means it, she cares, and they know it.

"It's tough out there," she says to us a few minutes later. She'd walked the crash site. She knows what it costs—and what it will cost—the men and women serving out there. "They'll never forget," she tells us and then says bluntly, "That's why you're here."

"Excuse me?" I ask.

Her heart is for the workers. "They need encouragement. They need hope. And who better to help them?" she asks. And then she does the oddest thing. She smiles, opens the flap leading out to the site, and sends us out. My defiance—strong and resilient—where is it? Why can't I say no to her, turn around, and walk away?

But I can't. I am not like Jacob. I can't fight Him anymore.

Therefore I urge you, brethren, by the mercies of God, to present your bodies a living and holy sacrifice, acceptable to God, *which* is your spiritual service of worship. And do not be conformed to this world, but be transformed by the renewing of your mind, so that you may prove what the will of God is, that which is good and acceptable and perfect.

—ROMANS 12:1–2

QUESTIONS FOR REFLECTION

Why not surrender to the man who has power to bless? Is it right, when faced with urgent need, to press in on God, be defiant, and demand our prayers be answered? Why or why not?

Consider Romans 12:1–2. When we present ourselves to the Lord, do we do it on our terms or His? Why do we fight Him? Why are we scared to let go and trust Him?

NOTE

1. In the Gospels, we see Jesus allowing the crowd to press in on Him for healing (see Mark 5:31). We also hear that violent men take the kingdom of heaven by force (see Matt. 11:12; Luke 16:16). Preachers often relate these passages with Genesis 32:26 as positive pictures of perseverance in prayer. But is it? Is this what God wants from us? Thankfully, the story of Jacob's night of wrestling is not yet over.

29

JACOB'S CONFESSION

*So he said to him, "What is your name?"
And he said, "Jacob."*

—Genesis 32:27

Jacob fought. He demanded. He wept (Hos. 12:4). The man fought back. He neither surrendered nor granted Jacob's request. Blessing, if he decided to give it, would not come on Jacob's terms.

The opponent abruptly changed the subject.

"What's your name?" he asked.

The question is shocking. How could he not know Jacob's name? He attacked him in the middle of the night with fury, with purpose, as though he knew him—as an enemy. But if he didn't know him, why was he fighting him? Why wrestle all night?

Did the question confuse Jacob? Did he wonder why the man asked it? Why small talk? Why change the subject? Was Jacob tempted to press down harder and say it stronger: "I will not let you go; I will not answer your question, not until you bless me"? But he didn't. This time Jacob yielded to the request of the man who was greater than him.

"Jacob," he answered.

Their faces were still masked by darkness. In no time at all, the sun would rise and Jacob would see his enemy's face.[1] He may not have understood the significance of this moment, this man, and this question right then. But soon enough, he would.

"Jacob."

It was the perfect answer. His name always had meaning. At birth, he was the baby who held his twin brother's heel. His name simply, delightfully, meant "Heel-catcher." But time changed that. Instead of a positive term, as one who guards, protects, and defends at his brother's heel, it became negative. Jacob wasn't for Esau but against him: always the tripper, the supplanter.

Then it got worse. On the day he stole Esau's blessing, he tricked his father. He came deceitfully, pretending to be Esau, who'd later cry out, "Is he not rightly named Jacob, for he has [cheated me (ESV), taken advantage of me (NIV), and tricked me (MSG)] these two times?" (Gen. 27:35–36). And it stuck.

The mystery man had asked the perfect question: "What's your name?"

Whether Jacob understood it or not, he did more than give his name. He confessed his character. It was who he was. It was what he'd done.[2] And regardless of whether he was Heel-catcher or Tripper or Cheater—every time, the outcome had been the same. He had prevailed. He always prevailed. He was Jacob the prevailer.

And right then, at that moment, that was the only meaning of his name that mattered. When the sun rose, he would have to face Esau and the four hundred. He knew he couldn't win. He was afraid, and that fear drove him. Jacob had to get the man to use his power to help him prevail over Esau. No other blessing would do. How else could Jacob survive?

Oh yes, no question about it. His name was Jacob.

One step and I'm inside. I've crossed the yellow tape. This is it—the crash site, the debris field, "the valley of the shadow of death" (Ps. 23:4).

I'd love to tell you my name is "Courageous." It's not. Call me "Scared," "Anxious," and "Afraid." That's the real me. It's why, in my training as a pastor, I knew I had to do everything I could to conquer my fears. I had to learn to cross the yellow tape, go inside, stay inside, and not run out. And more, to go deep inside where it's not safe—where I've known since the days of my childhood that monsters await.

It's hard for me. I know why. The memory is always with me—standing outside my mother's hospital room as she lay dying, too scared to cross.

I'm scared now.

There's one thing I must do. It comes from the apostle Peter. He was tossing in a boat in the middle of a storm. He saw the Lord walking on the rough sea. With Jesus' permission, he stepped out of the boat and started walking on the water too—the winds were strong, the waves rose high. Call him "Courageous," but it didn't last.

He took his eyes off Jesus.

That's all it takes for the monster to come. The Bible says, "When he saw the wind, he was afraid" (Matt. 14:30 ESV). Because of it, he lost his footing. He began to sink. The sea engulfed him to the point that he feared death and cried out, "Lord, save me."

That's me.

Call me "Courageous" for trying to conquer my fears, but, like Peter, it didn't last. I'd get out of the boat (or cross the yellow tape) and walk miraculously on the raging seas. I, too, knew the secret: Keep my eyes on Jesus. But fear has always been too strong for me. I'd see the storm, the wind, the waves, and the evil lurking "in the valley of the shadow of death," and I'd find myself engulfed in fear, crying for help.

That's what makes the crash site terrifying for me.

I know why I'm here. There are people inside the tape just like me. They're afraid, maybe even traumatized by what they're seeing. They're staying busy, doing their jobs, but inside they're panicked; they're screaming for help. I know my job is to point them to Jesus—eyes on Him— because He alone can make us walk on water in the storm. He's the shepherd in the valley of death who alone comforts the soul.

But I'm scared. I'm not convinced I can keep my eyes on Jesus. What if all of it—the sights, the smells—proves too much for me? What if I collapse into fear and run from the site? What kind of Christian witness is that?

The tent flap closes behind us. We take our first steps, heading slowly up the logging road, carefully navigating where we step and what we're stepping on. Two men approach us and stop.

"You're chaplains," one of them says, reading the front of our decontamination suits. I notice the bin they're holding between them. They are carrying the dead. They set it down, and I choose not to look in. I've got to keep my eyes focused.

"I was watching TV with my kids," one of them says. "My wife heard the explosion from the kitchen and knew something awful had happened. We stepped out the front door and could see black smoke gushing straight into the sky. I told her it was a plane crash. When I got to work this morning, my boss said, 'You're working at the crash site today.' I called my wife. She's pretty upset I'm up here."

Then the other man tells his story.

Soon the conversation takes an abrupt turn. Back and forth, one right after the other, they describe what they've seen: pieces of the plane, mangled bodies, clothing, jewelry, a child's toy—a fellow worker overcome with grief, giving up, and walking out. The more they talk, the more emotional they become.

"Are you Christian men?" I blurt out.

I have to stop them. They are doing what I always do: eyes on the storm. Plus their descriptions—too raw and graphic—are making me anxious.

One of them says, "No, but I need prayer." He shares that he's never given God the time of day. But right here, right now, it's different. He needs God's help. He needs us to pray for him.

"I used to be," the other man says. He tells stories of going to church as a child. "My wife and kids go," he states, "but not me." He looks around, his eyes still captured by the horror around us.

We pray for them. We tell them the secret: eyes on Jesus.

It's what we do "in the valley of the shadow of death." We fear. We turn to God. We beg for His help. There's no other way to handle the shock and the trauma, both now and in times to come. Already in 1994, the medical community had adopted the term "post-traumatic stress disorder" (PTSD). There's no question: doctors and counselors have much to offer in the healing process. But we, in Christ, have always known what to do above all else and what is most essential to dealing with it: we must keep our eyes on the Lord. He stands strong and compassionate in the midst of our darkest valleys and raging storms.

Does it sound too simplistic? It's not. When you're inside the yellow tape, it's a constant choice, minute by minute: eyes on Jesus. For the second I take them off, I know, better than anyone, my real name. Call me "Scared." Call me "Afraid."

Because I know I can't handle the monster on my own.

Jesus saw Nathanael coming to Him, and *said of him,
"Behold, an Israelite indeed, in whom there is no deceit!"
Nathanael said to Him, "How do You know me?"

—JOHN 1:47–48

QUESTIONS FOR REFLECTION

Reflect on John 1:47–48. Both Jacob and Nathanael are known by the Lord. Do you know the same is true for you? How would you confess your name and character to God?

When has Peter's story been your story? When have you had to make the constant choice to get your eyes off the storm and onto Jesus? What difference has it made?

NOTES

1. From Jacob's perspective, the man was his enemy. The attack, the long night of wrestling, the touch to his hip, all point to this conclusion. It begs the question: where else in the Bible, where in the long history of the saints, and in our own life, have we experienced the Lord as our enemy?

2. Leon R. Kass, *The Beginning of Wisdom: Reading Genesis* (New York: Free Press, 2003), 459. Kass wrote, "This act of self-naming is . . . a confession: I am *Ya'aqov*, the heel catcher, the supplanter, the deceiver, the one who prevails over his opponents by means of guile and trickery. Jacob, for the first time, is compelled . . . to describe his character in this act of self-declaration."

PART 5

WHEN COURAGE COMES

30

OLD NAME GONE

He said, "Your name shall no longer be Jacob."

Who was this man?

He spoke like God speaks. Not like us. Only God has the power to change names in this way. Only God could say to Jacob's grandfather, "No longer shall your name be called Abram" (Gen. 17:5). To change a name as Abram's was changed is to change a person entirely. It's transforming who we are, what we've done—right or wrong, good or bad—our reputation, our character.[1]

Did this man really possess that kind of power?

Did he know that to change Jacob's name was to change Jacob? Was he able to blot out Jacob's past? Jacob was supplanter and tripper, deceiver and trickster. These aren't names that can be legally changed at the local courthouse. Jacob earned these names by what he did to his family. These are facts. This is history. Who was this man to say the words, "No longer"? Only God can erase the past as if what happened never happened.

Only God has the authority to forgive sins (Mark 2:5–10).

But for Jacob this moment went much deeper. He was still wrestling, still refusing to release the man until he got his blessing. Why? He was afraid. He needed to survive. He had to protect his family. He must do what he'd always done—prevail! That was Jacob. It had always been Jacob. Deeper than reputation. Deeper than character.

It was his nature.[2]

Even if this man had the power to change Jacob's name, forgive his sins, and rebuild his character, who was he to transform Jacob's nature? Impossible! "Can the Ethiopian change his skin," a prophet would later say, "or the leopard his spots?" (Jer. 13:23). Neither could Jacob stop being Jacob.

Unless . . . it was true. Unless the man did wield power.

And he did. He'd already proved it. With a touch, he wounded Jacob. In that act, Jacob knew this man possessed supernatural power. It was good power, the kind of power that could bless him and deliver him from Esau's hand. It's why Jacob had done everything he could to harness that power for himself.

But what about now?

Is it possible the same thing happened again? Just as power flowed when the man touched Jacob's hip, did power come when the man spoke the words "no longer"? Is it possible, that one by one, each of Jacob's names vanished into the sea of God's eternal forgiveness? Supplanter and tripper "no longer." Deceiver and trickster "no longer."

And deeper still, prevailer "no longer."

No more wrestling, no more fighting in his own strength. Not against God or man. Not against fear. The old name gone. The old nature put to death. The wrestling, the fighting, the prevailing, finally over. And maybe this was it. We're not told when the wrestling stopped, but it's reasonable to assume it happened right there, right then.

The man who spoke like God speaks had won.

Ken and I meet Dan the first day.

He's been assigned to work alongside a pathologist and coroner. Their job is to identify the dead, document what they see, mark the location of the remains, and ready them for transport. Dan is the note taker.

We meet at the worst possible moment. The pathologist and coroner are kneeling down over a body, small and compact. Dan stands by them. Ken and I come alongside at the exact moment one of the men buries his head in his hands and the other looks up at Dan with tears filling his eyes.

"This is a child," he says.

"When he said that, I lost it," Dan tells me weeks later when we meet for coffee. "I was having a hard enough time with men and women my age—but a child?"

"Why'd you stay?" I ask.

"From the moment it happened, I knew I was supposed to be there. My wife and I were a couple of miles away, walking into a mall, when we heard the explosion. A few minutes later, fire trucks, sirens—we knew something terrible had happened. Later that night, a guy at the office called to say we'd lost one of our planes. He said we'd probably be asked to go to the site in the morning."

"You work for US Air?"

"Yeah, in customer service. A few years back I was a mess. I was depressed. My career was going nowhere. I'd applied for a promotion a couple of times, but it never worked out. I didn't know what to do except cry to God for help. I'd given my heart to Christ as a young man, but I'd never suffered with depression, anxiety, hopelessness.

"A friend came alongside and helped. He'd struggled with alcohol. He'd been to AA meetings and learned the hard truth that he wasn't in control of his drinking or his life. When he surrendered control, cried out to God, and said he was powerless over his life, Jesus Christ stepped in. And that's my story, too. The Lord let me come to the end of myself so that I was in control of nothing."

Dan pauses, reaches for his wallet, and pulls out his US Air employment card.

"I know God got me this job. And when that plane crashed, I knew I had to be at the site. Not that I could handle it. I was scared to death to walk down that logging road. In fact, I was given the option to go home. I was supposed to be collecting baggage. We got off the bus and learned we weren't needed yet. I volunteered to stay."

"That's courageous," I offer.

"No, the exact opposite," he states strongly. "I saw men and women break down right in front of me. I watched people walk away and not come back—at the risk of losing their jobs. I'm telling you, I'm no different than them. I was terrified. And you know what I mean. You were there when we saw that sweet little child."

I nod. I felt the same.

"I was able to stay," he admits, "because I knew the secret. Jesus Christ brings us to the end of ourselves. It's what He does. He takes us to places where we're out of control, completely powerless, and all we can do is trust

Him with our lives. You want to know why I stayed? I stayed because He gave me the ability to stay."

As he says it, his voice breaks. He quickly adds, "But it's still hard."

Dan tells me he is forty years old. "There were a lot of people on that plane my age. No different than me," he says, "thinking they have lots of time in front of them. Then boom, just like that, twenty-three seconds later it's over. That scares me. I keep having nightmares I'm going to die soon in some tragic accident. I'm not ready to die."

I see the fear in his eyes. He tries to change the subject, but I interrupt. I tell him it's still hard for me, too. "I think about that little child a lot," I admit.

"I remember as a young boy," I tell him, "being scared something like this might happen to me. I needed to know I was safe, secure, protected. With all my heart, I wanted to believe nothing like this could ever happen. Not to me. So why did it happen to that little child? Why did he have to suffer? That question frightens me—even now."

"But I'd do it again," Dan tells me.

"Would you?" I ask.

"Only because I trust Him," he responds. "I've also had nightmares that I'm on that plane. I'm going down. I'm crying for help. I'm saying all the right things: 'Lord, I give up. I surrender. I need You'; and I'm suddenly awake, sitting up in bed, heart racing, realizing I don't know what happens at the end of my dream. Does the Lord save me, or does He let the plane go down? For the longest time, I didn't know the answer. But I do now. Not that I like it. Not that I want to die."

I look at him puzzled, wondering what he's going to say.

"Either way," he states emphatically. "He wants me to trust Him either way."

That, in reference to your former manner of life, you lay aside the old self, which is being corrupted in accordance with the lusts of deceit, and that you be renewed in the spirit of your mind.

—EPHESIANS 4:22–23

QUESTIONS FOR REFLECTION

How has the Lord spoken the words *no longer* in your life? What names have vanished into the sea of God's forgiveness? How has the wrestler changed you?

What do these words mean to you: "Jesus Christ brings us to the end of ourselves"? Consider Galatians 2:20. Are you able to surrender control to Christ and trust Him?

NOTES

1. It is ironic that the name "Abram," given to a man who in his old age had no children, means "exalted father." The stigma, the shame in his family and community, no doubt shaped his identity and character. Only God had the power to change his name, put to death the stigma, and make a new man, "Abraham."

2. It is vital to reflect on the words *no longer*. In baptism, we celebrate the power of conversion where our Savior first puts to death our old self before He raises us to new life (see Rom. 6:3–4). In the same way, the Christian life is a continual putting off of the old self and putting on of the new (Eph. 4:22–23; Col. 3:5–10).

31

NEW NAME COME

He said, "Your name shall no longer be Jacob,
but Israel; for you have striven with God
and with men and have prevailed."

—GENESIS 32:28

They wrestled all night. The fight ended near dawn. It could be said that Jacob died. The wrestler put an end to him—his past, his sins, his character, his nature, and his name. The wrestler did what only God's power can do: He put to death the old Jacob.

Then, in the same breath, with the same power, he brought him to life again.

Jacob was a new man with a new name.[1]

Jacob knew this story. He knew the principle behind it. The Lord changed his grandparents' names. Abram ("exalted father") became Abraham ("father of a multitude of nations") even though he was childless. With it came the promise of a son and the power to conceive life when their bodies were "as good as dead" (Heb. 11:12). With Isaac's arrival, the Lord revealed His heart for His people. When we finally reach the end of ourselves and are "as good as dead," God does what we can't do.

Jacob knew that principle growing up as a boy.

Now, at the Jabbok, he experienced it himself. His old name, better said, was "Isra-Jacob," meaning "Jacob rules" or "Jacob prevails." That best summed up his life so far. He'd always been the victor—against his father, brother, and uncle. Even here on this night, wrestling with a man greater and more powerful than himself, he prevailed as "Isra-Jacob." But that name and that man, "Isra-Jacob," is "no longer."

He is now "Isra-El."[2]

The Lord put His name into Jacob's new name. He is "El," a shortened version of "Elohim." "Isra-El," in its first meaning, is "El rules" or "El prevails." But given to Jacob, the meaning expanded. The character and nature of El now resided in him. He is "Isra-El." Jacob's reign had ended. El's reign had begun. Jacob no longer had to strive against God or any human being on his own. To say it as the Bible would later say it, he could do all things through El who strengthened him (Phil. 4:13).

The wrestler's blessing had begun. It came first with the touch to Jacob's hip and then with the death of his name, "Isra-Jacob." But now, it came with life. The Lord forever bound His name to Jacob's. "Isra-El" would never go alone. He'd never face fear alone. More urgently, he didn't have to face Esau and his four hundred men alone.

"El prevailed" in him now.

Esau was approaching. Soon the sun would rise and the war with his brother would begin. Jacob, the old Jacob, had no more tricks up his sleeve. He had only the life-giving principle, the ancient principle, taught to his grandparents.

He'd come to the end of himself. He was "as good as dead."

He had to trust that God would do what he couldn't do.

I feel bad for Ken.

He recently graduated from seminary, in June, and has just started his first job as a pastor. Like me, he has no training whatsoever to serve as a chaplain at a catastrophic event like this one. How is he supposed to go home and process it all? How is he going to tell his wife, Sallie, where he's been and what he's seen?

"How was last night?" I ask Ken the day after we stood over the small body.

"Hard," he replies. He tells me the sight of the child's remains has impacted him most. He has two sons: Mark, five; and Will, three. "I went into their room late last night. I knelt down at their beds and hugged them as tightly as I could. I've never felt so helpless as a father. I wept for the child who died. I wept for the father who couldn't do anything about it. I wept for me—feeling like I can't even protect my own boys."

I press in, asking if he'd rather not return to the site.

"I want to be there," he replies.

Right then, I notice something wonderful in Ken. From the moment we first stepped onto the crash site, we had been inseparable. We did everything together. We walked the site. We talked and prayed with people. We took breaks together. But on this, the second day, he rises in stature. I see a confidence about him as though he's been a chaplain all his life. We aren't but a few minutes on the site that day when he spots someone in need and off he goes on his own to care for them.

That confidence—I know where it comes from.

I've seen it in hospitals. I remember watching a woman in her early fifties, scared to death of hospitals, rise to the occasion as her father lay dying. She stayed at his side morning and night. She couldn't imagine being anywhere else. She suddenly knew doctors and nurses, medications and procedures fluently. She became his chief advocate, fighting for him to live with a confidence she knew came from heaven above.

I've seen it countless times at wakes. One woman in particular, I can still see in my mind's eye. There she stood in front of the coffin of her husband of sixty-three years while an endless stream of visitors came by to console her. Her heart was broken. The future scared her. But there and then, she had strength given by God to help her.

A friend of mine calls it "an infusion of grace."

It happens when we find ourselves at the end of ourselves with nothing left and at the verge of collapse. It comes, always surprising, always miraculous, like an IV hooked to our soul. We feel it coursing through our veins, filling our hearts and minds. This gift, this heavenly gift of grace, of confidence and hope.

The Bible calls it courage.

Not the kind the world idolizes—the indomitable spirit. The person who, against all odds, musters superhuman strength from within themselves to face all things, endure all things, and conquer all things—that person demonstrates the world's courage. Such heroes never tire, never give up, never shake from fear, and never run from the face of death. We worship them. We aspire to be like them. We dream we, too, will be courageous in the face of hardship.

But this is not courage. Not real courage. Not the kind that comes from God. He gives it when we don't have it. When there's nothing left to muster from within.

I recognize it in Ken that day. I feel it well up in my own soul. At a certain point, I make the decision to go where I fear most—the place the nose of the plane made impact. It is up a small hill from the logging road with trees surrounding it and open sky above. Debris riddles the fire-scorched trees. The cockpit's remains are beyond recognition to me, but not to the two men I meet there.

Both are pilots. Both on the National Transportation Safety Board (NTSB) investigation team. One from Charlotte. One from Atlanta. Their job is to untangle the maze of metal and wiring and get it to a hangar, so a team can piece it back together and figure out what happened to the aircraft.

"I'm glad there are chaplains here," one of them says to me.

Somehow they already know the angle of the nose as it made near-vertical impact, where the pilot and copilot sat, and how the debris field was created. Both men are matter-of-fact and job-focused. It's the only way, they admit, they can deal with what happened. For still, here, all around us lie remains of the dead.

"I don't know how you do your job," I say. "Putting all these pieces back together."

"It's easier for us than for you," the guy from Charlotte responds. I hadn't thought of it like that, but maybe he is right. Maybe all of us at the crash site feel like this cockpit— a shambles of complicated, twisted mesh.

And then I see it. The oddest thing.

There in the middle of the rubble rests an orange soda can. Unopened. I pick it up and hold it in my hands. It had been on the flight, the pilots say. They can't explain how it survived. But it did. Not one scratch. As if brand new. And I dare to believe this would be my story, too. It would be the story of all who trust Christ. El can do what we can't do. He doesn't just put us back together.

He makes us new again.

I have been crucified with Christ; and it is no longer I who live, but Christ lives in me; and the *life* which I now live in the flesh I live by faith in the Son of God, who loved me and gave Himself up for me.

—GALATIANS 2:20

QUESTIONS FOR REFLECTION

Put your name after "Isra." In what areas of your life do you rule and prevail? How does that change as you confess, "It is no longer I who live, but Christ lives in me"?

When have you felt yourself at the end of yourself and then experienced "an infusion of grace"? Are there times you've felt courage, real courage, rise in times of hardship? What were the circumstances?

NOTES

1. One might argue this was Jacob's conversion. From a New Testament perspective, it has all the marks of baptism. Yet, since his early days, Jacob had known and walked with the Lord. It may be better argued that this night represented a deeper work of God in his soul.

2. Victor P. Hamilton, *The Book of Genesis: Chapters 18–50* (Grand Rapids, MI: Eerdmans Publishing Co., 1995), 334. Hamilton stated, "It seems that in Gen. 32 one must interpret *Israel* as 'El will rule.' . . . Up to this point in Jacob's life Jacob may well have been called 'Israjacob.'"

32

NAME ABOVE ALL NAMES

—✎—

Then Jacob asked him and said,
"Please tell me your name."

—GENESIS 32:29

Jacob's name, seen another way, should have been "Isra-Fear."

All night, fear ruled him. It was why he divided his family into two camps. It was why he sent Esau gifts. He was afraid his brother was about to kill them all. Fear ruled. Fear seized his heart, mind, and soul. When it does, who can think about anything else? Who can do anything else but try to survive? Even if what we do seems crazy to others. And sometimes, it is crazy.

Why does a drowning man try to kill the person rescuing him? It's a natural response. We flail. We grab. We push our rescuer down so we can push ourselves up. It defies all reason. But when is fear reasonable? Don't tell us to let go so the rescuer can do his job. We can't. We won't.

Not when fear rules.

And fear ruled when Jacob said to the unidentified man: "I will not let you go" (Gen. 32:26). It was crazy thinking. He knew the man had power greater than him. Power to bless. Power to save him from Esau. He should have let go and let the man save him. But he couldn't. Like a drowning man, crazy and wild, he grabbed, he flailed, he pushed the man down.

His name, better said, is "Isra-Fear."

Fear was his greatest enemy, not Esau. The unknown man, in response, touched Jacob's hip and broke it. That should've been enough. It wasn't. Jacob fought on. The man did it a second time, another touch. This time he spoke—that's all he did—and power was released to break the hold of fear raging inside Jacob. This time, it worked. Fear subsided.

Jacob let go.

The night of wrestling was over. This was when it ended. What better way for Jacob to demonstrate his surrender than by asking his rescuer's name? If fear still reigned, he'd never have asked. Fear wouldn't care who the man was, but what the man could do for him. For Jacob, this was no small request.

"Please," he said, "tell me your name."

Who was this man who, with a touch of his hand, wounds; then with the touch of his words, heals? Was he human, born of a woman, with father, mother, and genealogy? Was he angelic, a visitor from heaven? Was he something altogether different? If Jacob knew him by sight, he'd never have asked. But perhaps he still couldn't see him. Perhaps the night's shadows still lingered.

Letting go must have felt odd to Jacob. His circumstances hadn't changed. Esau and the four hundred were still approaching. Death was still drawing near. The man had made no promise that he'd do anything about Esau. And yet, he changed Jacob's name. He ended the tyranny of "Isra-Fear" and blessed him with a name like no other: "Isra-El," which best means "El rules!" This man, who was he?

"Please," Jacob said. All he wanted was to hear the sound of his savior's name.

I still hold the soda can in my hand when a loud, angry voice booms behind me.

"Why are you here?"

I turn and see a man inches from my face. He's talking to me—no, yelling. I pick up snippets, phrases: "Get out. . . . You have no business being here. . . . God has nothing to do with this God-forsaken place." People around us stare. I wonder if he's going to hit me.

He points at the word *chaplain* on my decontamination suit and mocks me in a high-pitched child's voice: "God loves you. God's with you. God will help you." His face twists up—red with anger. His voice changes back. He rants in a sound more like a bitter, hurt cry. He's doing what I think all of us want to do—explode and cry and wail.

I stand there quietly.

He grabs my arm, hard and tight, and forces me to walk a few feet to the brow of the hill overlooking the logging road. Down at the bottom—some ten feet away—his team, a coroner and two others, work. He wags his finger, pointing at the ground in front of them. He wants me to see the dead. He wants me to see suffering like he sees suffering. And it's worse today. It's hot like mid-summer. The sun beats down hard, making us sweaty and irritable; making the stench of the remains nearly intolerable. The man still yells. People still watch.

He jerks me down the hill. He wants me to view it up close. His team, frustrated with him, tell him to stop and get back to work. But he can't. He's angry. He has to put my face inches from the remains and make me feel the pain.

"That's not just one body—but three. Can you see it?"

He sees me look. He turns me toward him and releases my arm.

"What kind of God does this?" he mocks. "If God is really God, if He's really up there looking down on us, why didn't He do something about it?" And then he does what I've heard people do all the time. He raises the same old argument: If God's all-knowing, He knew it was going to happen and should've stopped it. If He's all-powerful, He could've stopped it. And if He's all-loving, He would've stopped it.

It's the best we can do when we don't understand why we suffer.

I wish he'd quiet his voice. He's venting his anger at God in front of everybody. I want to speak up and argue back. I want to tell everyone the Lord can be trusted—always. He's faithful, kind, merciful, and compassionate even here amid so much heartache and pain. But I don't. I can't. The man doesn't let me.

"What really ticks me off," he seethes, "where is He? Why isn't He here on His hands and knees digging up these bodies like the rest of us? He has no idea what we're going through. He doesn't get it."

He leans closer, right in my face.

"This is hell on earth. What does He know about my pain, my suffering? I'll tell you what—nothing! Until He sees what I see, smells what I smell, feels what I feel, suffers what I suffer, I want nothing to do with Him. Who worships a God like that?"

He spits on the ground. He walks away.

It's over. People still stare. I try to move, but can't. I feel like the wind has been knocked out of me. Whatever strength I had, whatever grace I felt, whatever courage I'd been granted, is gone. In their place come confusion and fear. I find myself wondering if the man is right. What if God is distant and uncaring? What if He knows nothing about my pain—not intimately, not personally? What if He caused the plane to crash? I feel nauseous.

I look for Ken but can't find him.

The antidote, I tell myself, is to hold fast to what I know. I know the man is wrong. He's confused about God. He doesn't know Him—His name or His character. I know God is not distant and uncaring. Instead, the Lord is our shepherd. He stands with us in "the valley of the shadow of death." He's here. He knows what we're going through. He gets it. It's why I can say, "I fear no evil, for You are with me" (Ps. 23:4).

I say it again, trying to calm my fears. It doesn't work.

The man's voice in my head still echoes too loud. "Until He suffers what I suffer, I want nothing to do with Him." This, too, is an old argument. I've heard it all my life from people who turn away from God when they're in pain. They say, "Did He ever die of cancer? Was He ever raped? Has He ever suffered a broken marriage? If not, what good is He to us? He can't help. He can't empathize. He doesn't get it."

"But He does get it," I want to cry out loud. "I know Him. I know His name. He is Jesus, Lord and Savior. Born in Bethlehem. Lived and died as one of us."

It's no use. Reason isn't commanding the helm right now. Fear is. Confusion is. I place one foot in front of the other and start down the logging road. I need to leave. I need to go home. I can't help anyone right now, not the way I'm feeling, and I don't like it. I don't like feeling scared again. Scared the man might be right.

The Lord knows nothing about our pain and sorrow—nothing.

And His name will be called Wonderful Counselor, Mighty God, Eternal Father, Prince of Peace. There will be no end to the increase of *His* government or of peace.

—ISAIAH 9:6–7

QUESTIONS FOR REFLECTION

What are you like when your name is "Isra-Fear"? What does it take for you to release control? Like Jacob, after being rescued, do you long to hear your Savior's name?

When you're in pain, have you ever been confused about who God is? His name, His character? What are you like when what you feel rules over what you know?

33

DAYBREAK

Then Jacob asked him and said, "Please tell me your name." But he said, "Why is it that you ask my name?" And he blessed him there.

—Genesis 32:29

It was still night back when the man said, "Let me go, for the dawn is breaking." The request made no sense. Why was he concerned about the dawn? Now it made sense. He didn't want Jacob to see his face. Not yet. Not until the work was done. And that was just it. He'd come to perform a work in Jacob. He'd come to put an end to him—his fear, his dominance. He'd come to make a new man who'd no longer strive in his own strength, but in God's.

Jacob was "Isra-El" now.

He could do what "Isra-Jacob" never could have done: He let go. He surrendered.

At dawn, Jacob's hip was still broken. Esau was still coming. Nothing had changed, yet everything had changed. Blessing had come. Blessing had filled his soul. El's name was now bound to Jacob's name, which meant he could do all things, face all things, and endure all things no matter how deep the valley or dark the pit, whether he lived or died. El was in charge now, not him. Not death. Not the fear of death.

This man, who was he? Jacob, now Israel, had to know his name.

"Why is it," the man replied, "that you ask my name?"

The timing must have been perfect. The man never said his name. Perhaps he didn't have to. All he had to do was let the dawn break, which it did, with enough light for "Isra-El" to see his face. One look, that's all it took. "Isra-El" knew him. He knew his name. They were not strangers.

Daybreak!

They'd met twenty years back when Jacob first ran from Esau. At Bethel, at night, Jacob had a dream. He saw a ladder between heaven and earth. Angels ascended and descended and, there as clear as day, he saw the Lord. He saw Him standing, real, alive, in human form. The Lord's voice was unforgettable: "I am the Lord, the God of your father Abraham and the God of Isaac" (Gen. 28:13).

That voice! He knew that voice. Why hadn't he recognized it instantly? That face! He knew that face. It was the same face.

El.

His attacker! His wrestler! Did Jacob now wonder why? Why did El want to fight him? Why allow him to prevail? Why wound him when He could have killed him? Why ask to be released when it was in His power to free himself? This man, that face! He'd come to wound and to bless. He'd come to break the grip of fear in Jacob's soul. But nothing could compare to this moment. Never. El blessed him with the greatest blessing of all.

Daybreak!

"Isra-El" beheld the face of his Savior.

As I walk the logging road I fight to silence the man's voice still screeching in my head: "Until He suffers what I suffer, I want nothing to do with Him." It's not working. I keep searching for Ken.

I'm surprised to see a black lab coming toward me. He's on a leash and happy. I hunch down as he strides up and playfully licks my face. Best distraction ever.

"What's his name?" I ask the man with him.

"Briar," his handler says. "Police dog."

"Police dog?" I answer back, not straightening up. I don't want to. I need more dog time, and Briar seems to appreciate the attention.

"It's what I do. I train police dogs." The man is surprisingly talkative. He's served on the police force nearly forty years. Though retired from active service and in his late sixties, he is still at it. He says precincts all over western Pennsylvania want their dogs trained by him. "But Briar is mine," he tells me. "I trained his daddy, and his daddy before that, back five generations. Briar stays in the house with my wife and me."

He asks if I want to see Briar in action.

"Sure," I say, though unsure what he means.

"I do all kinds of training—mostly narcotics, drugs, explosives—that sort of thing. But I also train dogs to find the dead. They're called cadaver dogs. Briar is here to help with the recovery effort."

I watch as he unlatches the dog's leash and commands him to sit. Briar's response is immediate. He's no longer the playful, happy pet. His body grows tense, rigid; his eyes focus on his trainer, ears up, face cocked.

"You ready?" he asks me. I stand and nod. "When I release Briar," he continues, "he'll head into the woods. Do your best to follow him. The moment he finds something, he'll let you know. He'll sit in front of the remains and bark until I get there. I won't be far behind. I'll ask one of the coroners to come help us. How does that sound to you?"

"I'm ready," I say. But the moment I say it, I regret it. I want to leave. I'm still upset by the man who'd railed against me and God. I want to go home. I try to say something, but it's too late. With a strong voice, he commands Briar, "Go find the dead." The dog dashes off into the woods and disappears.

I decide to follow, but lose him quickly. I pursue, hiking deeper in.

It doesn't take long. His bark signals me. He's somewhere ahead and to the right. There's no one else around. The trees are dense. Debris scattered everywhere. I spot a bit of a clearing ahead with fewer trees and more sunlight. I see Briar there. He's sitting, just like the man said. He barks again. I stride up alongside. He doesn't move.

"Good boy, Briar," I say. I look around, but there's nothing there. No remains. In front of us—maybe ten feet away—stands a young tree, maybe twenty feet tall, its leaves mostly gone, scorched by fire from the plane.

I still can't find anything.

Again Briar barks and I study him. I notice he's not looking at the ground. He's looking up. I do my best to follow his gaze. Still nothing—and then I see it. In the tree. Against the bark of the tree, resting and hanging over one of the limbs. Remains. Partial remains. It's odd, but I notice the jeans first. The person had been wearing blue jeans. No different than what I have on. I feel strangely connected, close and real. Everything else is too disfigured, the body left beyond human recognition. Briar barks again, still calling for his handler. We don't move, either of us, our eyes fixed on the body up in the tree.

That body—I know it. I know what I'm looking at. And I feel it. A calm washes over me. Whatever panic I felt in my soul from the man who yelled at me fades, completely gone, and in its place comes an indescribable rush that makes me shiver inside. I stand in the presence of God.

I can't take my eyes off the body in the tree.

Suddenly Ken is standing next to me. I didn't hear him coming.

No one else is around. Just Ken and me and Briar staring—all staring—at the body in the tree. We say nothing. With all my heart, I don't want the policeman or the coroner or anyone else coming and stealing this moment from us. Not now. Not while the Lord is here. And the Lord is with us. The Lord is answering my heart's cry.

Oh yes, He knows!

He knows our suffering. He knows everything about us. He knows the pain and grief and sorrow we hold in our hearts. He knows our story, the human story, because He knows the agonies of death. He knows that tree. He's been on it, His body "pierced for our transgression"; His body "disfigured beyond that of any human being and his form marred beyond human likeness" (Isa. 53:5; 52:14 NIV). Oh yes, He knows! It's why He can suffer with us. He can weep with us. He can comfort us.

Briar barks again. Ken and I can't move, can't speak. Our eyes stay fixed on the body in the tree.

Therefore, since we have so great a cloud of witnesses surrounding us, let us also lay aside every encumbrance and the sin which so easily entangles us, and let us run with endurance the race that is set before us, fixing our eyes on Jesus, the author and perfecter of faith, who for the joy set before Him endured the cross.

—HEBREWS 12:1–2

QUESTIONS FOR REFLECTION

Has there been a "daybreak" event in your life? When have you experienced the Lord, your Savior, stepping into your story and surprising you?

What does the cross mean to you? How does His suffering for us bring you comfort in the times of your own suffering?

34

THE FACE OF EL

So Jacob named the place Peniel, for he said, *"I have seen God face to face, yet my life has been preserved."*

—GENESIS 32:30

The writer of Genesis didn't tell us when El left or how He left. In times to come, this man—this El-man—would leave in the most surprising ways. He'd simply vanish from sight (Luke 24:31). Or He'd soar into the heavens on clouds (see Acts 1:9). But this time, with Jacob, we're not told. Perhaps it's because Jacob was too overcome by it all. He'd just seen El's face and was shocked he didn't die.

That face.

But why was he so shocked? What happened when he saw the man he clung to so tightly? We know the early morning light hit El's face. We know they'd met before in a dream. Isn't this why El never said His name? He didn't have to. Jacob knew Him.

But this time was different. It wasn't a dream.

Jacob was seeing God face to face. The man was real, physical, the same man he'd wrestled all night. But now he knew this man was God. That face was God's face.[1]

That fact hit Jacob with full force and, because of it, he knew he should be dead. He wasn't. But how did he know that?

What did he see?

Did he simply recognize El? Is that it? Or did something terrifying happen? Is it possible El's face lit up with heaven's glory? In time yet to come, that will be the story. It's not the sun that will hit His face, but His face that will become like the sun. All who'll see the brightness will fall to the ground as though dead—terrified (Matt. 17:2–6; Acts 9:2–5; Rev. 1:16–17).

Is that what happened to Jacob? Is that why he was utterly shocked to be alive?

His life, he declared, had "been preserved." These are the exact words he'd prayed the night before. He'd asked the Lord to preserve him, deliver him—from Esau and his army (Gen. 32:11). He had no concept he'd be confronting a far greater threat to his life.

El! The face of El! "I have seen God face to face," he exclaimed, "yet my life has been spared" (32:30 NLT). He didn't say he'd seen an angel or an archangel or a mighty cherub. He said he'd seen God. This man, fully man, yet God himself.

It was time for Jacob to do again what he'd done before. When El met him in a dream years before, Jacob named the place "Beth-El," the house of God. For, he said, "the Lord is in this place. . . . This is none other than the house of God" (Gen. 28:16–19). It was time to name this place, this holy place, and the name came easily. He called it "Peni-El"—meaning, "the face of El." What better name could there be? For the miraculous had happened here! This was now Jacob's testimony.

He had seen the face of God and lived.

I know I'll never forget this place. Twenty-two years later I would still be able to see us there in the woods— Ken, Briar, and me—lined up side by side under the tree.

Soon enough, the policeman arrives. He pats Briar on the head, tells him to stay, and moves closer to the body. A coroner, photographer, and two others join him. I watch as they talk, their voices barely above a whisper, their mood solemn, as if they instinctively know—it seems we all know—this is hallowed space. We are here to honor the ones who have died as if they were our own.

I watch as two leave. They need a ladder and a receptacle for the body.

My thoughts turn pensive, introspective, as I wait. It feels odd. I am not afraid. I know I should be. This scene, of all scenes, was my worst nightmare growing up. I'd find myself suddenly, painfully alone, in a land dark and filled with shadows. Death would be near. Death so close and there was nothing I could do about it. Nowhere to run. Nowhere to hide.

Three people return. My reverie halts as I hear them approach in the woods behind me. The ladder clanks as they carry it. I turn to watch them approach the tree, hoist the ladder in the air, and slide the extension high enough to reach the body. I hear it gently rest against the bark. They jostle it back and forth to ensure it's secure.

The coroner climbs up first.

It all takes time. She carefully examines the body. As quietly as possible, she dictates her findings to the man below taking notes. No personal effects are found. She makes no mention of age or whether the person was male or female. She calls for the photographer. He climbs up behind her, takes pictures, and carefully goes back. The man with the receptacle steps up next.

I listen to every footstep ring softly on the hollow aluminum ladder. I don't want to miss any detail. Is this it? I wonder. Is this what the moment was like two thousand years ago when our Lord was taken down? Did it take time? Did a ladder hit against the wood of the cross? Did someone carefully climb up to attend to Him? Were they gentle? Was it family? Did they know Him? Did they know they were looking into the face of God?

I wait for anxiety to come. This is usually when it happens—the rapid heartbeat, cold sweat, quick breaths. When it starts, I have to pace or, if I can, if it's possible, I leave. It's a pattern with me. I can face death for a while. I can't face it for long.

But anxiety doesn't come. Not here, not today.

The man with the receptacle climbs as close as he can and holds the bin out. I notice he and the coroner both wear medical gloves. I watch as the coroner, with meticulous precision, extracts the body from the tree. This, too, takes time, but she manages it. She lifts the remains up from the tree and carefully, gently, lowers them into the bin.

With one hand, the man wedges the receptacle against his chest and the ladder as the other hand grips a rung. He moves down slowly, step by step. The men below stand ready to receive it. All is done with utmost care as if crowds were standing around watching them lower the little casket into the safe arms below.

The coroner doesn't move, not yet, not until the man steps off the ladder.

Work remains to be done. The body has to be tagged. The ladder has to come down. The paperwork needs to be finalized.

It's an odd sensation, but I actually feel free. Here I stand in the real "valley of the shadow of death." Fear—that old monster from my past—lurks here, but it doesn't matter. He wields no power over me. I am not afraid of him. I am not afraid of death. "I fear no evil." Here in this wooded sanctuary, I am safe. I am free. And I know why.

Two men now hold the bin. Side by side, they begin their walk through the woods. The policeman calls for Briar, and I watch the dog's ears drop and his face become playful. He runs to the policeman's side for a treat. It's time to go. Ken and I turn to follow the forensic team out of the woods. There's no other place I'd rather be.

It's what we do at times like this. We attend the body. We make the journey as if family and friends walked by our side, step-by-step, in funeral procession. We do all things well to honor their loved one. No words pass between us as we make our way back to the logging road and head to the refrigeration trucks.

Until at last we arrive, and the little casket is safely stowed.

It makes me wonder who made this journey with our Lord? How was His body moved from the cross to the garden tomb? Was He carried by family and friends? Who walked beside Him? Who walked behind? Was it quiet and somber like our walk, or did they wail with loud cries of anguish and sorrow? Did it take time—step by slow step? And who laid His body down? Who clothed Him in linen and last saw His face?

I wonder why no one talks about it.

But I talk about it. That walk. That movement to the grave until at last our Lord was laid to rest and the stone rolled into place. Secure for now until the dawn of the third day. I talk about it because without this story, His story—His death, His burial, His victory over death—I wouldn't have a story.

I'd still be afraid. And I'm not afraid. I am free.

His face was like the sun shining in its strength. When I saw Him, I fell at His feet like a dead man. And He placed His right hand on me, saying, "Do not be afraid; I am the first and the last, and the living One; and I was dead, and behold, I am alive forevermore, and I have the keys of death and of Hades."

—REVELATION 1:16–18

QUESTIONS FOR REFLECTION

Has the presence of our Lord ever overcome you? When have you experienced His glory and majesty? What do you think it will be like to behold His face (Rev. 22:4)?

Why is our Lord's death and resurrection the antidote for fear and anxiety? Have you known it but not experienced it? Or do you know the gift of freedom in Jesus? If so, how would you describe it?

NOTE

1. We are presented here with the mystery of the incarnation in Old Testament Scripture. Inasmuch as no man can see God and live (see the contrast of Ex. 33:20; also 1 Tim. 6:16; John 1:18), we find Jacob seeing God "face to face." It should be noted that Bible translations of Hosea 12:4 render the Hebrew word for *messenger* as "angel." It is common for expositors to say Jacob wrestled with an angel. But the actual text in Genesis 32 indicates that the messenger is both God and man.

35

AND COURAGE CAME

*Now the sun rose upon him just as he crossed over
Penuel, and he was limping on his thigh.[1]*

—GENESIS 32:31

The day had dawned in full strength.

El was gone. It was time for "Isra-El" to rise to his feet and move. He needed to rejoin his family. There were things that had to be done before Esau came. Was it hard to move? After wrestling all night, was Israel tired? Did he need rest? Or is it possible that when he saw El's face his strength revived?

He tried to stand. He felt the break in his hip. He risked a step. He tried to put his full weight on the wounded leg, but pain shot through his body. His good leg would have to compensate. Another tentative step; he limped. Again, he tried. Again, he limped. It was the best he could do.

God did this. Not some devil from hell. Not an enemy of his soul. El left His mark as a sign, a witness, of that unforgettable night. For Noah, He painted the rainbow in the sky. For Abraham, He gave the sign of circumcision. But for Israel, He left a dislocated hip. That would be the mark in his flesh from the night he wrestled God.

He tried again to walk. He couldn't do it. He'd have to limp.

It's odd his hip wasn't healed the moment El blessed Jacob, changed his name to Israel, and allowed him to see the glory of His face. How could Israel be in the presence of God and not be physically healed? But that's the story he'd have to tell.

"Why do you limp?" his children would later ask.

"I fought with God," he would say. "I wrestled all night. He touched my hip. He broke my strength. He changed my name. I am no longer Jacob, able to prevail on my own. I am Israel. I am weak. I rely on God to prevail for me now."

Israel made progress. He could proceed as long as he negotiated the pain by favoring his good leg. He crossed the Jabbok. He headed, step by painful step, closer to his family. This was it—his new life. How would he work again? Being a shepherd required agility and endurance. What shepherd hobbles in pain, resting his leg any chance he gets? What shepherd won't go out in the cold of winter or the hot, humid summer rains because his hip aches unbearably?

Every step, it hurt.

This mark, this gift of God, now tested him. He would have to face his brother in weakness. He would march into battle already wounded. Step-by-step, limp-by-limp. If he and his family died, they died. This was not his war anymore. It was El's war. Israel had to trust Him. This would have terrified the old Jacob. But not now. Not since he'd seen El's face. Not since he'd received His blessing. By the grace of God, fear was gone.

Courage had come.

I want to stay at the site. I know, after the man yelled at me, I was determined to go home. But not now. What happened in the woods changed all that.

The moment the body rests safe on the truck, Ken and I head back.

I am not afraid. It's strange to say that, but it's true. I feel the sun's heat. I know the work is hard and the suffering real as bodies are extracted from the ground. But I want to be there. I want to stand alongside, if for no other reason than to pray for the workers. I am not afraid to meet the man who yelled at me. In fact, I want to see him. If he'd give me a chance, I'd like to talk to him again. I can't find him.

It's the strangest, most beautiful sensation. It's like I've taken the antidote, and it works. Fear is gone! Anxiety is gone! Why didn't anyone tell me about this growing up? I have nothing less than courage flowing in my veins—unexplainable courage—as if I'm suddenly able to do all things and face all things, no matter how terrifying.

Courage! I've been given a gift from God.

Is this what Joshua felt when he faced the giants in the Promised Land?

Or Daniel when he was tossed into a den of lions?

The monster—it's not like he's gone. He's still here. I know that, especially in this place where I am surrounded by death. He's always made me scared of death, my death. Any little pain in my body, any news that a friend my age has died, any little sound in the house when I am alone—countless times, countless ways—he's there tormenting me. The Bible says it's how he torments all of us. He's called the Devil and he uses the "fear of death" to imprison us in "lifelong slavery" (Heb. 2:15 ESV).

I've known that slavery all my days.

Here it is no different. The monster wants me back in prison. He reminds me that what happened here could happen to me. I am not exempt. Christians, he taunts, even Christians with courage die like everyone else. I know that. It's one of the lead stories in the news: a Christian man by the name of Kirk Lynn was on Flight 427. He was twenty-six. In church, eleven days before he died, he sang a song entitled, "As We Sail to Heaven's Shore." It was recorded, and now every radio and TV station is playing it. His voice is everywhere: the sound of a Christian man who died in the crash.

The Devil mocks at this. He tries to make me afraid again.

But thank God for that song! "Storms may rise on seas unknown," it begins, "while we journey towards our home."[2] Death does not have the last say. Storms may rise. Death may come. But Kirk Lynn's voice—a voice silenced by the crash—is the sound of comfort: God has won. Death has lost. Our home is heaven.

I am not afraid.

This faith was also the sound that came out of the mouth of a little boy. The story was also everywhere. He was on the soccer field the night the plane flew overhead. He stood next to his mother. He was too young to play with all the other children. So he saw the plane. He watched its flight while everyone else watched the game. And then it happened. It started with him. He pointed to the sky.

"Mommy, look! Mommy, look! The angels, the angels!"

By the time she looked down at her son and then up to the sky, it was too late. She heard—like everyone heard—the loud explosion. She saw the black smoke. She missed everything. But the boy didn't. He saw the plane, in those terrifying twenty-three seconds, spiral to earth. He saw what few ever see. The angels! They're at work in our time of need. They are, as the Bible says, taking the saints safely to "heaven's shore" (see Luke 16:22).

I am not afraid.

After all was said and done, and our work at the crash site over, I was asked to speak at the memorial service held at the Green Garden Plaza. Governor Bob Casey attended along with a host of dignitaries. I was one of several pastors on the platform. They gave me three minutes.

If I'd not gone into the woods that day, if I'd not seen that body in the tree, I would have spent all my time in Psalm 23. After all, I'd gone to the "valley of the shadow of death." I knew all about fear and our need for comfort. I'd have pointed listeners to the Shepherd and urged them to cling to Him in their grief.

That's all true. But the message has deepened. That same Shepherd knows us. That Shepherd, born in Bethlehem, knows what it means to be us. To live as we live. To suffer as we suffer. To die as we die—His body on that cross. He knows us, yes; He knows us, and He came to do what we could not do in our own strength. He triumphed over death.

He rendered "powerless him who had the power of death, that is the devil" and freed us from the prison of our slavery to the "fear of death" (Heb. 2:14–15).

I had a message inside me. A three-minute message: I know death will come. Death will roar. My body will die and go into the ground. Dust to dust. But I am not afraid. I've been to the tree. I know what happens on the third day.

My Savior lives.

Therefore, since the children share in flesh and blood, He himself likewise also partook of the same, that through death He might render powerless him who had the power of death, that is, the devil, and might free those who through fear of death were subject to slavery all their lives.

—HEBREWS 2:14–15

QUESTIONS FOR REFLECTION

Have you got a limp? Where has God placed a mark in your life as a sign, a witness, that He alone is your strength? How has the limp helped you with fear and anxiety?

Reflecting on Hebrews 2:14–15, how does our Lord's cross become an antidote for our fears? When has the fact of Easter morning impacted how you grieve?

NOTES

1. Bruce K. Waltke, *Genesis: A Commentary* (Grand Rapids, MI: Zondervan, 2001), 448. Waltke stated that *Penuel* is "a variant of Peniel."

2. Phillip McHugh and Greg Nelson, "As We Sail to Heaven's Shore," Sparrow Corporation, 1986.

36

WE NEVER FORGET

*Therefore, to this day the sons of Israel do not eat the
sinew of the hip which is on the socket of the thigh, because he
touched the socket of Jacob's thigh in the sinew of the hip.*

—Genesis 32:32

They remembered.

*Not because God commanded it or because the law of Moses
would later legislate it. The "sons of Israel" just did it. Every time
they sat at a meal with meat, they'd set apart "the sinew of the
hip"—never to be eaten. In that act, they remembered the night
God wrestled with their father, Jacob. God touched "the sinew of
the hip which is on the socket of the thigh." He broke Jacob's
strength. He changed his name to Israel. He caused him to limp so
he'd never again rely on his own strength but on God's alone.*

That's the message of the "sinew of the hip."

*It's also the story of their name, "Isra-El." When did God give
it? On the night Jacob wrestled with God. What does the name
mean? God breaks our strength so we trust in Him alone. Why is
the name important? From that day forth, it would be who they
are. They are the people of Israel. One day they'll live in the land
of Israel. They're a nation dependent on almighty God.*

*King David would say it this way: "Some trust in chariots and
some in horses, but we trust in the name of the Lord our God"*

(Ps. 20:7 ESV). King Jehoshaphat would pray, "We are powerless before this great multitude who are coming against us; nor do we know what to do, but our eyes are on You" (2 Chron. 20:12).

That's what it means to be true Israelites—powerless, dependent.

"Not by might," the Lord would teach His people, "nor by power, but by My Spirit" (Zech. 4:6). This is our God, the wrestler, who breaks our strength and declares for all time, "My grace is all you need. My power works best in weakness" (2 Cor. 12:9 NLT).

It all started here—on this night.

They remember during every meal at which meat is served. It's too easy to forget. When Abraham's name was changed, he was never called Abram again. But not so with Jacob. After that night, he was sometimes called Israel, sometimes Jacob. Back and forth. That back and forth became the nation of Israel's history. Sometimes they were "Isra-El"—powerless, weak, dependent, and trusting God with all their heart. Other times, the nation fell into unbelief and took back the reins of control.

We must never forget.

Or this night will happen again. The wrestler will come. He will touch "the socket of the thigh." He will break our strength. He will cause us to limp again so we can rejoice, with all the saints down through the ages, saying, "I can do all things through Him who strengthens me" (Phil. 4:13).

After all, we're "the Israel of God" (Gal. 6:16), powerless and dependent.[1]

Every time I get on a plane—I remember.

The first time I flew after the crash, I boarded a plane just like the one that crashed, a Boeing 737–300, and didn't know it. Not until we were up in the air and I pulled out the laminated booklet in the seat pocket in front of me. I wish I could say I didn't care. But I did. I wish I could say I wasn't afraid, but I was.

I had a limp in my soul.

I sat there, closed my eyes, and was back at the crash site standing on the logging road next to Ken. I could still see the workers' faces. I could smell death. I could run back into the woods and chase Briar to that tree and remember what it was like to be in God's presence. I wanted that. I needed that. But it was gone, and I was afraid the plane would do what Flight 427 did.[2]

I remembered Kirk Lynn. Was he sitting that day where I was sitting?

My heart raced; my palms sweated. I couldn't stop it. Nor could I stop the guilt. I knew better. Where was my faith in God? Why couldn't I trust Jesus and be calm? What happened to the courage I once knew that would laugh at a time like this, unconcerned? My mind wasn't the problem. I knew the Lord was with me even if the plane crashed. But that, sadly, didn't help my heart.

It's better just to say it: The monster's back in my life. I am afraid again sometimes.

There are things I know to do when the monster comes. The Lord promised that His grace is sufficient for us. His power is made perfect in weakness. Because of it, I can say what the apostle Paul said: "I will rather boast about my weaknesses, so that the power of Christ may dwell in me. . . . For when I am weak, then I am strong" (2 Cor. 12:9–10).

I can push the guilt away.

And rather than beating myself up for the way I feel, I can embrace it. I can boast in it. This is my weakness. This is my limp. Let my heart race. Let my palms sweat. Courage doesn't come from within. It comes from heaven. It's a gift from God. Courage is His power made perfect in my weakness. When it comes, if it comes, then I am strong. And if it doesn't, I am exactly what I feel, weak and afraid.

Oh yes, I have a limp!

I know this word, *Isra-El*. I am dependent on almighty God.

I never want to forget. I've seen people forget. Life becomes hard for them. They suddenly need God. They cry out to Him, confess their sin, admit their weakness, and receive the saving power of Jesus Christ to do for them what they couldn't do for themselves. But the moment the crisis ends, they retake control. There's no sign of a limp. They don't need Him. They don't need the church. It's as if it never happened.

Why do we forget?

Down at the halfway house in town, I regularly have lunch with men who've spent years addicted to alcohol and drugs. They teach me the secret of life—the only way to live sober, drug-free, and pleasing to God—is found in the words, "I can't do this on my own. But 'I can do all things through Christ who strengthens me'" (Phil. 4:13 NKJV). I've seen it happen. I've watched men break free and stay free.

The free ones still limp. They'll tell anyone who'll listen— "Oh yes, we limp!"

And they, like me, have watched men relapse. For some, pride mixed with the Devil's urging takes over. They think they can go back and stay in control. They can't. For others, it's different. The chemical addiction in their bodies is too strong. They know they need Jesus. They know they can't survive without the help of others. They go to programs. They go to meetings. They do everything they know to do.

But sometimes it's too much, and they fall.

Every time I go to a funeral of one of these men, it breaks my heart. I worry for those attending who struggle with addiction. Will despair overcome them? Will they give up? Will they think the same fate awaits them? But I usually see the opposite response. In their sadness, I witness the gift of God come, bringing faith and hope and courage. I see them lock arms and spur each other on.

We don't walk alone. We keep our eyes on Jesus.

We're meant to limp, and limp together.

I am no different. I don't struggle with alcohol or drugs. I struggle with fear. I'm aware of it every time I board a plane, hear the engines roar, watch the plane speed down the runway, and feel the loss of control. I wonder if it will happen again. Will the monster attack in midflight and scare me? Will he bring back memories of Flight 427 and make me fear that what happened to them will happen to me?

Sometimes yes. Sometimes no. But when it's yes, when fear envelops and panic rises in my soul, it's OK. I know the story. This is it—this is my limp.

I never forget. All I have to do is put my eyes on Jesus and wait for courage to come.[3]

"My grace is sufficient for you, for power is perfected in
weakness." Most gladly, therefore, I will rather boast about
my weaknesses, so that the power of Christ may dwell in me.
Therefore I am well content with weaknesses . . .
for when I am weak, then I am strong.

—2 CORINTHIANS 12:9–10

QUESTIONS FOR REFLECTION

When did God break your strength? What do you do to
remember? How often have you gone back and forth,
sometimes trusting Him only, sometimes back in control?

Is it easy for you to boast in your weaknesses and celebrate
your limp? If not, can you explain why?

NOTES

1. Allen P. Ross, *Creation and Blessing: A Guide to the Study
and Exposition of the Book of Genesis* (Grand Rapids, MI: Baker
Book House, 1988), 549. Ross wrote, "Jacob's crippled walk
signified that before God he was powerless and dependent."

2. In March 1999, the NTSB finally concluded that Flight 427
crashed due to mechanical failure—a rudder malfunction.

3. Bruce K. Waltke, *Genesis: A Commentary* (Grand Rapids,
MI: Zondervan, 2001), 450. Waltke said it best, "The limp is the
posture of the saint."

PART 6

FAITH BIGGER THAN FEAR

37

THY WILL BE DONE

———✑———

Then Jacob lifted his eyes and looked, and behold,
Esau was coming, and four hundred men with him.

—Genesis 33:1

There was no time. No time to tell Rachel. No time to shout the news: He'd seen God's face! He'd been in His presence. And what mystery! They'd wrestled all night and, most of the night, God let him prevail. God even cried out, "Let me go!" How was that possible? If only there was time to tell the story from the beginning.

To explain why he was limping.

But there was no time. Esau was near. He could see him in the distance, and with him four hundred men. This was it, what Jacob feared most. Before, he'd panicked. He had divided his family into two camps hoping he could save some. One would go to war while the other escaped (Gen. 32:7--8).[1]

It was different now. He was different.

He was going to trust El. They would meet Esau together—as a united family.

He lined them up. He arranged them in order. But why this order? Was it typical to his culture or unique to Jacob? Was it because his heart belonged to Rachel? Had Laban not deceived *him with Leah; had there been no rivalry between the sisters for children with their maids; his family would have been just Rachel, their son Joseph, and himself.*

But that was not how life played out.

It seems Jacob chose to honor Rachel and Joseph by putting them last; in front of them, Leah and her children; and in front of them, the maids and their children. Jacob took the lead. He didn't know what would happen. Not from the previous night, anyway. El made no mention of Esau. No mention of whether Jacob and his family would survive.

In days before this, Abel faced Cain. Why wasn't Abel protected when his brother rose up to kill him? In years yet to come, the same would happen to Joseph. His brothers would turn against him and sell him into slavery. In even later times, many of the prophets wouldn't survive, perishing at the hands of their fellow Israelites. And, of course, it would happen to the Messiah. He too would head into battle.

And when He did, He taught us how to pray during times like this: "Yet not My will, but Yours be done" (Luke 22:42).

Would Jacob be protected?

He limped toward Esau. And then he bowed. Seven times. It was the perfect picture: he was not in control. He would honor God. He would honor his brother. He had no tricks up his sleeve. No deceptive plans. This was not the old Jacob, but the new. He had seen the face of God, and because of it he was ready to see the face of his enemy.

He had faith now—faith bigger than fear. He had courage now to let the Lord's will be done—no matter what happened next.

I sit across from my friend. He is experiencing a panic attack.

He's convinced he's dying. He has undiagnosed medical issues that won't go away. He describes in detail what he's feeling, what doctors have said, what tests were done, what medications he's on, and how nothing improves. If anything, it's worsened. He doesn't know where else to go, who else to see.

He's wrestles with God. It feels like He doesn't care.

I ask him what scares him most. "Call from a doctor," he blurts quickly, "saying I'm terminal. What I've got is untreatable, maybe a few months to live." He tells me someone at church gave him a book that argues God always cares and God always heals. If we're sick it's not His fault, but ours. If we get right with Him, confess our unconfessed sins, God will heal us.

"That's not true, is it?" he asks. He knows it's not true. But fear does that. It distorts how we see God and how we see ourselves.

"I wish it was that easy," I reply.

He picks up his guitar and strums a contemporary hymn we both know by heart. Then another. It's what we do at times like this—we sing, we pray, we read from Scripture—we do our part to take our eyes off the situation at hand and put them on Jesus Christ our Lord. Just as the Bible says: "Let us run with endurance the race that is set before us, fixing our eyes on Jesus, the author and perfecter of faith" (Heb. 12:1–2).

It's easy to tell someone who's afraid that it's their fault. It's even easier to promise we can fix them with a how-to book.

But there's only one medication for fear: we seek God's face. We come into His presence and trust His promise: "Where two or three have gathered together in My name, I am there in their midst" (Matt. 18:20). Nothing else can satisfy the heart. At times like this, we need Jesus to meet with us. That's the medication we need.

But there's nothing easy about it. It requires we stop wrestling God. Fear never wants to do that. We hold on with white knuckles. We fight. We don't want to release control. We're afraid of what might happen if we do. It's my friend's greatest fear. He might be dying.

He wants the Lord to promise, "If you let go, I'll heal you." He doesn't want to hear, "Let go and trust Me whether I heal you or not." Just like he doesn't want to hear, "He who loves his life loses it, and he who hates his life in this world will keep it to life eternal" (John 12:25). But that's what Jesus says to us, and my friend knows it.

He has to trust Him if the symptoms disappear and he gets a clean bill of health.

He has to trust Him if the doctor calls and his fears come true.

We come to God in worship and prayer. Each time is a little different. Some days I can see my friend wrestling. He says the right things; he prays the right prayer: "Father, I trust You no matter what's going on with me. Your will be done—not mine." But I can tell he's still struggling. He's still afraid—there's panic in his eyes.

Other times, the Helper, the Holy Spirit, washes over him with perfect love that "casts out fear" (1 John 4:18), and with peace from above that passes understanding (John 14:26–27; Phil. 4:7). That is the Lord's doing, and I can see it—my friend is free.

Like Jacob when morning's light came.

The world can't provide this medication. But this is it. This is how the Bible teaches us to negotiate fear, anxiety, and panic attacks. There are times we need the help of doctors, medications, and counselors. But they are never to substitute our need for Jesus. We need to come into His presence and ask Him to do what we can't do for ourselves. This is how we face our "Esau"—whatever our "Esau" might be.

Here's the twist.

That dreaded phone call does come. But it isn't for my friend. It is for me, and it isn't actually a doctor. It is Erilynne, my wife. It's January 2008 and we are living in Connecticut. The snows have come, mixed with rain and sleet during the day, then freezing overnight. By morning, the roads have iced over. I won't be able to go to work till midday. Midafternoon, after I'm at the office, the call comes.

Erilynne has fallen on the ice. Her head hit the pavement hard. She is leaving the doctor's office. He says she'll be fine. No concussion. She'll be sore for a few days. She could take an over-the-counter pain reliever. Which she does.

But her body begins to spiral out of control.

We don't know why, not yet. We have no diagnosis. But wounds begin to appear near her right ankle and calf for no apparent reason. She develops trouble swallowing. The wounds grow. We go to doctors who send us to other doctors.

Our church, our family, and our friends all pray for her. I assume the stress from the fall has caused this reaction and it will soon pass.

It doesn't.

The pain increases. The wounds deepen and spread. She stops eating. She is losing weight. A couple from church, both nurses, dear friends, come to our home, assess her condition, and tell us we need to get to the ER—*now*! I look at Erilynne and watch a gentle calm come over her face. She knows she needs to go.

While inside me—fear rages.

And He went a little beyond *them,* and fell on His face and prayed, saying, "My Father, if it is possible, let this cup pass from Me; yet not as I will, but as You will."

—Matthew 26:39

QUESTIONS FOR REFLECTION

When have you faced an enemy, situation, crisis, or sickness greater than you? Do you know what it's like to pray from the heart, "Not my will, but Yours be done"?

How would you describe what it means to experience the presence of Jesus Christ and know His peace? How do you "fix your eyes on Jesus" in worship and prayer?

NOTE

1. Victor P. Hamilton, *The Book of Genesis: Chapters 18–50* (Grand Rapids, MI: Eerdmans Publishing Co., 1995), 342–343. Hamilton wrote that Jacob's first plan "is purely a military maneuver in an effort to save 50 percent of Jacob's family and herds. . . . No corresponding military strategy is at work in 33:1–2."

38

MIRACULOUS SURPRISE!

*Then Esau ran to meet him and embraced him,
and fell on his neck and kissed him, and they wept.*

—GENESIS 33:4

He was not the same man. Not after seeing the face of God.[1]

With every limp, he was "Isra-El"—off to battle with no strength of his own. He was at God's mercy. With every bow, he put an end to the battle before it even began. He declared his surrender. Esau could do with him and his family as he pleased. Jacob was the weaker, Esau the stronger. He was the servant, Esau his master and lord.

Jacob meant it this time.

He had called Esau "lord" before. But that was because he was trying to win his favor. He was the one in control then. He was no longer in control. He limped, he bowed. He was moving toward Esau, not running from him. Not like twenty years before when Esau, betrayed and angry, vowed to kill him, and Jacob ran. He was not the same man.

Not after being with El.

And so, with every bow, Jacob humbled himself. It was a demonstration of contrition. In part, it was why he sent the gifts. Yes, to win Esau's favor and "appease" his wrath, in an effort to get Esau to accept him. But the desire to "appease" (kippur) went deeper than that (Gen. 32:20). It moved toward forgiveness. It sought reconciliation. It started with an act of confession that admitted wrongdoing. Someone had to own their part to start healing the rift.

And so Jacob bowed.

The figure in the distance, however, didn't bow back.

Jacob saw him. Not his face. But the shape of his body, the way he walked, the way he moved. This was him—his brother, his twin, his oldest friend, his worst enemy. Would Esau be like Cain to him? After what Jacob did to his brother in the past, could he hold the title of "righteous" as Abel did? Esau—he was running.

Jacob bowed again.

It was not hard to do. Not after the previous night. He surrendered himself to El then. He remained surrendered to Him now. If El let him live after seeing His face, would He let him live after seeing Esau's face?

Esau's face. He could see it now. In detail. Why wasn't it the face of Cain, twisted in anger and hatred, bent on killing him? Why wasn't it the face of Laban, disgusted because he, too, wanted to kill him but couldn't—he wasn't allowed—God wouldn't let him? No, those eyes weren't murderous ones filled with vengeance. That face wasn't twisted in fury.

Wait . . . was that joy he saw?

The closer they came to each other, the more Jacob saw it— Esau, wild with delight. His arms open, running at him until their bodies collided in embrace; Esau, wrapped around his neck, kissing him like a brother who'd thought he was dead and just found out he was alive. The surprise—miraculous surprise—they were bound together not like wrestlers, but like brothers.[2]

Weeping.

We are not in the ER long. Erilynne is evaluated then admitted to the hospital, with further tests scheduled for the morning. As for me, I am living Genesis 33:4.

I come to the hospital often in my work as a pastor. People face traumas. They find themselves marching toward their Esau and his four hundred. They don't know what will happen. Neither do I. All we know is to take the right posture. Limp—because that's what we do. The battle belongs to the Lord. If it's won, it's won in His strength, not ours. Then bow—in surrender, in humility—and let the Lord himself decide the outcome.

Will there be a Genesis 33:4 surprise? Or will death come as Esau attacks?

I don't know. Not here, not with my wife.

The next day Erilynne has an endoscopy. The doctor finds ulcers on her esophagus, cause unknown. It appears her body, the hospitalist told me, is fighting itself. The ulcers and the wounds on her legs may be a related condition, requiring more tests. The most important one is sent out of state. Results due back in a couple of days.

"But the weekend's coming," I say urgently. "She needs treatment now."

"We have to wait," I'm told. "Expect the results back Monday or Tuesday. We can't treat what we don't know. Be patient; we'll know soon enough." But how can I be patient? My wife isn't doing well. Whatever is going on inside her is getting worse.

The doctor comes in over the weekend. He is convinced it is an autoimmune condition set off by rheumatoid arthritis. "She's in a flare," he explains. Her joints hurt. Her right arm and right leg have swollen to twice their normal size. She is conscious, awake most of the time, but less aware of what is going on.

The test results don't come back Monday. Or Tuesday.

I need a Genesis 33:4 surprise.

I know they happen. I see it all the time. I remember sitting in a surgical waiting room when the doctor came out and informed my friend his wife had stage four cancer. She'd face rigorous chemo and radiation treatments, more surgeries, and additional chemo after that. She'd have to quit her job and fight for her life.

Then—surprise! The pathology report came back telling a different story altogether. She had stage one cancer— treatable and altogether curable. Oh what joyful news! The big, bad Esau and his mighty army of death weren't so big and bad anymore.

Oh yes, the Lord brings surprise!

At the same time, I've seen when it *was* stage four cancer and, with a limp and a bow, I've walked side by side with people through chemo and radiation, more surgeries, and up days and down days. But we came through. By God's grace, we eventually heard the words—those miraculous words—*Cancer free!*

Surprise—to the Lord's praise!

I also remember being at a fellow pastor's side as his wife lay dying in the hospital. He believed with all his heart he'd experience the Genesis 33:4 miracle. He'd tell me over and over again his wife would recover. He, like Jacob, saw joy in Esau's face—not death. Not death for his wife. Not now.

That was his story, but it wasn't hers.

She knew death was coming, and she wasn't afraid. She'd tell her husband the surprise was this: she had the peace of Christ filling her heart. God granted her grace to face her Esau, and she could do it with conviction because her Lord had already won that battle on the cross. Death could take her body, but it could not have her soul.

She belonged to Jesus.

But her husband couldn't hear it. He refused to hear it.

That's me. I am going to limp and limp well. I am going to bow and bow low. I am going to believe that my story with Erilynne isn't like the pastor's story with his wife, when she was right—not him. She got the surprise of going home to be with Jesus and leaving her husband here, in this life, safely in his Lord's care. He didn't want that surprise. He wanted the Genesis 33:4 surprise.

Just like me.

What scares me most is that I can see in Erilynne what that pastor saw in his wife. She is content. She is at peace. She trusts that Jesus, her Lord, remains in charge either way. Whatever happens is fine with her. But it isn't fine with me. I don't want her to go. Not yet.

Wednesday comes. No test results.

I vacillate between very different emotions. On the one hand, I am back in the night wrestling with God, wrestling fear, trying to retain control. I see it in my attitude toward the doctors and nurses. I want answers—now. I push too hard. I'm neither patient nor kind. But then, at the same time, I keep walking with Jacob toward Esau—with a limp and a bow. Feeling utterly helpless.

And weeping—because I'm not sure which surprise is coming.

Do not fear, for I have redeemed you; I have called
you by name; you are Mine! When you pass through the
waters, I will be with you; And through the rivers, they will
not overflow you. When you walk through the fire, you
will not be scorched, Nor will the flame burn you. For I am
the LORD your God, The Holy One of Israel, your Savior.

—ISAIAH 43:1–3

QUESTIONS FOR REFLECTION

When, in broken relationships, have you taken initiative, confessed your sin, said you're sorry, and made the first move toward forgiveness? Why is humility hard?

Are you surprised by the events of Genesis 33:4? Were you expecting Esau to come in peace? Is it possible, in life or death, that the outcome is always the Isaiah 43:1–3 surprise? If so, why?

NOTES

1. Some expositors believe Jacob's external actions in Genesis 33:1–3 look too much like the old Jacob. They oddly conclude his encounter with El made no lasting change. In this exposition, that change is understood to be both substantive and real.

2. Victor P. Hamilton, *The Book of Genesis: Chapters 18–50* (Grand Rapids, MI: Eerdmans Publishing Co., 1995), 343–344. Hamilton observed the similarity between 33:4 and Luke 15:20. He also called our attention to the "phonetic similarity between 'wrestle' in ch. 32 (*'ābaq*) and 'embrace' of ch. 33 (*ḥābaq*)."

39

POSTURE OF A SERVANT

[Esau] said, "Who are these with you?" So [Jacob] said, "The children whom God has graciously given your servant."

—Genesis 33:5

What happened to Esau?

He'd vowed to kill Jacob. Then here they were, twenty years later, wrapped in each other's arms—weeping. What changed him? When did his fury subside? Did it happen long ago? Was it recent? Had God spoken to his heart as He had Laban's and warned him not to harm his brother? Or did Esau decide by himself?

This change—it's a mystery.

If Esau intended to come in peace, why bring an army of four hundred?

It made no sense. Somehow, at some point, Esau's heart softened. For Jacob it meant the Lord had heard his cry: "Save me, I pray, from the hand of my brother Esau, for I am afraid" (Gen. 32:11 NIV). And God did. He saved him. Jacob and his family were alive! No matter how it happened, he was in Esau's tight embrace. The conflict over.

The hurt—forgiven.

But even so, Jacob had every legal right to change his attitude toward Esau once again. He'd bowed seven times to his brother.

He'd called Esau "lord." But they both knew the covenant's terms: Isaac, their father, had made Jacob "lord" over Esau (27:29, 37). God himself had said, while the two fought in the womb, "The older shall serve the younger" (25:23).

But Jacob no longer wanted first place. His heart had softened too.

All night long he'd fought El. At any point, El could have rightfully assumed His position as Lord over Jacob. He could have dominated him. He could have killed him. But He didn't. For most of the night, El humbled himself by becoming Jacob's equal. Even after touching his hip, El became less than equal. He let Jacob prevail.

This is El.

This is His kingdom.

He willingly took the form of a man. He chose not to "lord it over" Jacob. He made himself of no reputation by taking the posture of a servant (see Mark 10:42; Phil. 2:6–11).

Jacob wouldn't understand this until the sun hit El's face. He had been in God's presence, in God's kingdom—a kingdom marked by the King's humility. This was why Jacob bowed seven times to Esau. It was why he willingly laid aside his legal right of lordship over Esau and took to himself—as El had taken to himself—a servant's posture.

No wonder Jacob's family came and bowed before Esau.

No wonder when Esau asked, "Who are these with you?" Jacob replied humbly, "The children whom God has graciously given your servant." Jacob couldn't help himself. He had to honor God. He had to honor Esau by claiming the title "servant." Of course he did. This was El. This was how El treated him. How could Jacob do anything else?

Thursday morning, still nothing.

The doctor informs me something went wrong at the lab. She has to reorder the test and send it overnight. She promises results back sometime Friday. Saturday at the latest. It's the worst possible news. I tell her I'm not sure we have that much time.

She examines Erilynne. She sees her condition worsening; her joints bloated and hot to the touch. The doctor asks simple questions—what day is it? Who's the president of the United States? What are your daughters' names? Erilynne is pleasant but agitated. She can't answer every question. She says she's in pain.

"Can't you just start the medication?" I ask, pleading.

"I'd prefer not to," the doctor says, after considering it. "But for now, let's get the test ordered and sent out. I'll come back this afternoon and we can decide then."

I want to explode in anger and cry out, "The lab's mistake is unacceptable. Erilynne's life is in danger. Do something! Make it right."

Surprisingly, the doctor beats me to it. "I'm calling the lab myself," she jumps in, irritated. "I'll make sure we get results by noon tomorrow. For now, sit tight. We're not letting anything happen to your wife."

It's nice to hear but not enough. Erilynne needs medicine—now. What am I supposed to do—stand by and watch the disease ravage her body? How am I supposed to tell our daughters—our family, our church—the lab made a mistake?

I am despairing.

The day drags on. We don't see the doctor until late afternoon. She examines Erilynne. Again, she tells me we need to wait. "The lab promised we'll know by noon."

Again, I plead for her to start the medication. I tell her I'm scared of the long night ahead. She assures me, "This time tomorrow, it'll all be different."

Evening comes. Our daughters circle their mom's bed with their husbands and kids filling the little hospital room. We pray. We quietly sing Erilynne's favorite hymns. We pry our focus off what went wrong and onto Him who can make it right. They try not to show their tears. Not to me, not to Mom—but I know they're as scared as I am. After they leave, I try to stay busy. I keep watching the clock: 10:13; 11:36. Long night ahead.

The lounge chair in the room becomes my bed. I don't sleep well in hospitals. Who does? Nurses come in at 1:23, 3:05, 4:52, and that's it. I'm up. I get some instant coffee at the nurses' station and go back to the room. Enough light glows above Erilynne's bed to read. I pull out my Bible and some notes. I'm scheduled to preach Sunday.

It's Palm Sunday.

I read the familiar story: "The crowds going ahead of Him, and those who followed, were shouting, 'Hosanna to the Son of David! Blessed is He who comes in the name of the LORD! Hosanna in the highest!'" (Matt. 21:9). In my tired state the word *hosanna* is more than I can handle. I know what it means:

"Save us, we pray."

It comes from Psalm 118:25. It is, perhaps, the most comprehensive summary of all prayers ever spoken for all time.

Just one simple word. One loud cry from the heart poured out in utter desperation—we need Him. We need the Lord to save us. We need Him to do what we can't do for ourselves. It always grows louder and rises from deeper within as the powers of darkness surround us—as death draws near. Why doesn't it happen sooner? Why don't we reach the end of ourselves more easily?

"Save us, we pray."

Tears fall. I look at Erilynne, sleeping, and the cry—the prayer—becomes a deep groan. "Lord Jesus, hosanna, save us."

The night shift ends, day shift starts. Doctors make their early morning rounds. The rheumatologist tells me she ordered Erilynne's medication. They'll treat her the second the lab calls in the results. My cell phone rings a little past eight. It's an old friend—Chip Edgar, senior pastor of a church in Columbia, South Carolina. His voice is comforting, concerned. He wants to hear about Erilynne. I slip out of the room and find a private little corner window at the end of the hall.

I try to tell the story, but my voice breaks. His kindness, his caring—I wasn't prepared for it. It seems all I can do is cry.

"Let me get on a plane and fly to New York," he says. "I can be in Connecticut by tonight. Let me help. Let me serve you and Erilynne. I can even take the church service Sunday if you want."

"It's Palm Sunday," I manage to say. "You have to be at your church."

He tells me not to worry. He talks to me for a bit and then prays for Erilynne. The love in his voice, the concern in his heart, the soothing sound of compassion and mercy in his tone wash over me. This, I know, is a gift from God. It is El. It is His kingdom. It is what His people do. They take a servant's posture and then they serve.

I try to speak more with Chip, but can't. Words elude me; emotion swallows them. His call, his offer to come, means everything to me. No matter how the morning turns out with Erilynne, he is an answer to my prayer. For now I know, and I know with certainty, the Lord is here. The Lord has heard.

My hosanna has reached His heart.

But whoever would be great among you must be your servant, and whoever would be first among you must be slave of all. For even the Son of Man came not to be served but to serve, and to give his life as a ransom for many.

—MARK 10:43–45 ESV

QUESTIONS FOR REFLECTION

How did Jacob's encounter with El shape his response to Esau? How does your encounter with Jesus, who came to serve you, shape how you respond to others?

Why is being served sometimes hard to receive? As we grow in knowing Jesus our Lord, does it become easier to serve and be served? How does living out Mark 10:43–45 impact your life?

40

THE ENEMY'S FACE

*Jacob said, "No, please, if now I have found favor
in your sight, then take my present from my hand,
for I see your face as one sees the face of God,
and you have received me favorably."*

—GENESIS 33:10

Esau asked why Jacob sent gifts (Gen. 33:8).

*In truth, Jacob could have answered, "Because I was afraid of
you." And he had been. On the night he sent the gifts, in his mind's
eye, he saw Esau's face through the lens of fear. He thought Esau
was coming to kill him as he'd once vowed (27:41). Without military
strength to stop him, the best Jacob could do was send gifts.*

Waves and waves of gifts.

*Jacob reasoned it might "soften him up" (32:20 MSG). It might
"wipe [the anger from] the face" of his brother so he would accept
him.[1] It's why Jacob could have said, with all honesty, "I saw you
as one sees their enemy, and I was afraid." And it would have
been the right answer had the wrestler not come.*

The wrestler changed all that.

*He rules a kingdom like no other. In centuries yet to come, He'd
describe His kingdom's people as those who love their enemies
(Matt. 5:44). He'd demonstrate that love on the day He'd be thrust
on the cross to die. He'd show us what kingdom people do. He'd
pray for His enemies, saying, "Father, forgive them" (Luke 23:34).*

His kingdom is altogether different.

That kingdom, that love, most certainly transformed Jacob. There's no other way to explain it. Fear no longer ruled Jacob's heart. Seeing Esau and the four hundred coming at him should have terrified him. It didn't. Jacob said it didn't. Seeing God's face made the difference. It gave him the grace, the power, to see his enemy's face with kingdom eyes and kingdom love.

"For I see your face," Jacob testified to Esau, "as one sees the face of God."

His heart had changed.

He could love his enemy—not fear his enemy—because the wrestler had given him the ability to see the face of God ("Peni-El") in the face of Esau ("Peni-Esau").[2] The two interchangeable. This was El's gift to Jacob. This is what made the difference. Not the gifts Jacob sent—the waves and waves of gifts. Esau didn't even understand why Jacob had sent them. In fact, he tried to return them to Jacob, saying, "I have plenty, my brother; let what you have be your own" (Gen. 33:9).

But Jacob urged Esau to keep them (v. 11). And why not? He'd sent them "to find favor in the sight of my lord" (v. 8) and he found favor. It's not clear what had moved Esau to receive his brother. But what is clear is the Lord let Jacob experience the wonder of His kingdom. Look at Jacob! He can love his enemy.

And more. With new eyes, he can see El like he's never seen Him before.

The clock marks 3:00 on Friday afternoon. Lab results are still not in. No sign of the doctor. No suggestion that medication will ever begin to be administered.

I head to the nursing station. "Still nothing?" I ask. I'm told they've paged the doctor again. I need to stay patient. As soon as they hear anything, they'll tell me. I head back to Erilynne's room. Just outside her door, I see two nurses. One is Haley. She's been on the day shift. The other I don't recognize.

Neither sees me as I step closer.

Just as I'm about to say something, I overhear Haley. Her voice sounds sad. She likes Erilynne. She laments, "I'm not back till Monday. I doubt she'll be here then."

It took my breath away.

I pass by. I make sure they don't see me. Haley would be horrified to know I heard her. Soon enough, I circle back and slip into the room. I pull up the chair and sit next to Erilynne. She is asleep. I look close. It's the first time I see her face as the nurses see her. I don't want to—but I do.

And I understand. I recognize that look.

It's one of the hardest parts of my job. Being a pastor, attending a family at the bedside of a dying loved one, is what I do. Often I can see the signs as death comes near. The face once full of color turns pale and ashen. I know the look. It can frighten family members, for they can see the face behind their loved one's face is the face of death himself, our "last enemy" (1 Cor. 15:26).

We do everything we can to stop death from coming. We'd turn heaven and earth upside down if we could for our loved ones. But there comes a time when we can do nothing more. Helpless, we keep vigil. We watch, we pray.

I know my job.

I am there to help the family see the face of God in the face of death. I can do this only because it's the gift our Lord gives. He has promised He is able "by the power that enables him to bring everything under his control" to "transform our lowly bodies so that they will be like his glorious body" (Phil. 3:21 NIV).

Our Lord said in no uncertain terms, "I am the resurrection and the life; he who believes in Me will live even if he dies" (John 11:25). This promise, this hope, is only possible in Jesus Christ. The reason is obvious: He's the only One to defeat death. Death was never in God's plan. At the beginning of time, sin came into the world and death through sin (Rom. 5:12). But the Lord's plan has always been life—eternal life.

I get to tell families His story.

Death lost.

He rose—bodily, physically.

The pale, ashen face before them isn't the whole story. If our Lord did not die on the cross for our sin, if He didn't rise on the third day, we have no hope. But with kingdom eyes, we get to see the face of Jesus in the face of death. We have what the world can never have—hope, real substantive hope.

This is what we as believers turn to at Christian funerals. That occasion is never first about the eulogy of our loved one who died. Rather, it tells the epic story of Him who destroyed death and triumphed.

These eyes, these kingdom eyes, I need them now. I don't have them. All I see is the color of my wife's face nearly gone. All I hear is Haley's voice speaking out my deepest fears.

It's just the two of us now.

With everything in me, I want to storm back to the nurses' station, stomp my feet, and demand something be done. All day, I've done that. All day, nothing I've tried has worked. And now here I sit bereft. I am heartbroken. I don't want to put on kingdom eyes. Not now. I want my wife to get well again.

By late afternoon, the workday over, our family starts arriving. Our girls look at me in confusion. They don't understand the change in their mother. The medication was supposed to start no later than noon. They head to the nurses' station. They try to move the same mountain I tried to move.

An hour passes, and then another.

We stay with Erilynne. None of us are ready to let her go. We start doing what we have to do. We recite the promises our Lord gave us. We help each other put on kingdom glasses so we can see with kingdom eyes. It's the only way to find comfort. How else can we see Jesus' face in Erilynne's as death approaches?

And then it happened. About 8:30 that night. Two doctors burst into the room followed by a medical team. "She's going to be fine," a doctor assures us. "I'm furious at the lab. But we're ready. We can start the meds. She should respond quickly."

I watch them hook up the IV. We can't believe it—none of us can. I see the commotion confuses Erilynne. I draw

THE ENEMY'S FACE   283

close and quiet her. As I gaze into her beautiful face, I realize, suddenly, almost miraculously, I can see.

Even now—with death so near—her face is like the face of God to me.

> But being full of the Holy Spirit, he gazed intently into heaven and saw the glory of God, and Jesus standing at the right hand of God. . . . They went on stoning Stephen as he called on *the Lord* and said, "Lord Jesus, receive my spirit!" Then falling on his knees, he cried out with a loud voice, "Lord, do not hold this sin against them!"
>
> —ACTS 7:55, 59–60

QUESTIONS FOR REFLECTION

What has it been like to face your enemies? How do you love your enemy? As you consider Jacob and Stephen, how does seeing the face of Jesus make a difference?

As we face our last enemy, what does the hope of the resurrection mean to you? With kingdom eyes, can you see the face of God in the face of death? If so, what is that like?

NOTES

1. Victor P. Hamilton, *The Book of Genesis: Chapters 18–50* (Grand Rapids, MI: Eerdmans Publishing Co., 1995), 326. This is Hamilton's translation of 32:20. In Hebrew, the imagery captures Jacob "wiping off" anger from Esau's face so Esau might "lift up" Jacob's face in acceptance and pardon.

2. Ibid., 346. Hamilton translated 33:10 as: "Just to see your face is like seeing God's face." Hamilton commented, "'Peni-el' (face of God) has been followed by 'Peni-esau' (face of Esau)."

41

TENTATIVE TRUST

—⁓⁓—

*Then Esau said, "Let us take our journey
and go, and I will go before you."*

—Genesis 33:12

Was their relationship back to the way it had been?

*Esau thought so. He was ready to head home together.
After all, they were family. They'd embraced, a sign that past
issues were behind them. All seemed well. All was reconciled.
The future awaited them as Esau said to Jacob, "Let us take our
journey and go."*

It appears he used the word us *quite naturally.*

*But what about Jacob? Why did he refuse his brother's offer
to head home together? He told Esau to go on ahead without
him because "the children [were] frail" and his nursing flocks
needed extra care. He said he had to proceed slowly. "Please,"
Jacob told Esau, "let my lord pass on before his servant, and
I will proceed at my leisure" (Gen. 33:13–14).*

*Esau tried again, saying, "Please, let me leave with you some
of the people who are with me." But Jacob again gently, graciously,
refused, "What need is there?" he asked. "Let me find favor in
the sight of my lord" (v. 15). He then quickly assured Esau he
would come to him in his homeland of Seir.*

There was no question that as Esau left that day, there was peace between them.

But were they reconciled? Could Jacob trust him?

Jacob did everything he could to own his part in causing the break between them. He took the posture of a servant. He bowed before Esau seven times. He sent an abundance of gifts. He spoke openly of God in his life. Esau did none of these things in return.

He embraced Jacob—that's what he did. Passionately, with kisses and tears.

Was that enough? Was Jacob to assume the past was now past with no conversation, no confession of wrongdoing, and no exchange of forgiveness between them? Was the fury that once filled Esau's soul really gone? Was Esau right with God? Had he dealt with the reality that Jacob received the blessing of Abraham and Isaac—not him? Did he care? Had he changed as Jacob had changed, or was he still volatile?

Esau's embrace—was it enough?

Perhaps Jacob's responses to Esau should be taken at face value. He rightly told him it was easier to travel home at a slower pace without Esau and his men. But it may also be possible that Jacob was demonstrating wisdom. He needed to affirm Esau. At the very least, it provided a start. There was peace—real peace— between them. But trust, was it there?

He knew reconciliation had begun.

Trust had begun. And with every embrace to come, every conversation ahead, it could build. But for now, Jacob remained tentative. The best he could do was promise to meet Esau in Seir. It offered a next step. It recognized what Esau had done. It also bought Jacob time.[1]

For only time would tell if the embrace between them could last.

Haley gasps when she walks in the room.

It is Monday morning. Erilynne rises early. She wants me to get her a good, strong cup of coffee down in the hospital lobby. While I am gone, she gets ready as if she has places to go, people to see, and appointments packing her day. When I return, she is sitting up in bed, nearly glowing.

"I can't believe it!" Haley exclaims. "You look beautiful."

"Thank you," Erilynne says. "We had a really good weekend."

"I can see that," Haley replies. She tells Erilynne quite honestly, as a nurse, it was hard watching her go downhill so quickly. "When I left here Friday, I didn't think you'd be here this morning."

"That's what I hear," Erilynne says with a nod and a smile. She has no memory of Friday or the few days before it. Once the medication got into her system, everything changed. By Saturday morning, she was alert and responsive. By Sunday afternoon, she looked like she had no business being in a hospital bed.

"In my opinion," Haley comments, "you're a miracle!"

She is to me, too. Throughout the morning, doctors stream in, as surprised, I think, as Haley is. The rheumatologist, when she comes by, announces, "We have good news. The flare has subsided, and you're in remission. You should be able to go home on the weekend."

While we delight in the news, I can't hide my disappointment. "We have to stay here the whole week?"

"That's right," the doctor says firmly. "She needs IV treatment. We will slowly wean her off, monitor her wounds, and make sure she stays in remission. You've got to remember how sick she was last week. It's going to take time for her to get well and regain her strength."

It makes sense.

But I amaze myself at how fast I want all this behind us. I've immersed myself in understanding as much as I can about this disease. But the gap between my mind and my heart is light-years apart. To me, she looks healthy again. Last week is over. From a completely emotional perspective, it feels like she had the flu. It nearly killed her. She got medication. Flu is gone, end of story.

It's all behind us. I live in that little bubble for two days.

Wednesday midmorning, the rheumatologist pops my bubble. The doctor feels it is time for us to face the reality of this disease. I write down snippets from our conversation.

"The disease is chronic. . . . She will have flares again. Stress plays a big part, but the disease is fickle. It can happen at any time. . . . As far as we can tell, Erilynne is an autoimmune nightmare. . . . The road ahead will be hard at times. You're going to need to pay attention to symptoms so we can stay ahead of the game. . . . Don't trust this disease. Read up on it. Adjust your lifestyle accordingly."

I don't want to believe the doctor—at all.

Erilynne asks some questions. She seems far more accepting than me. I, on the other hand, want a second opinion immediately. I want this disease gone. Neat and tidy. Buried in the past, so she never has to suffer like that again.

It can happen at any time? Chronic . . . autoimmune nightmare?

I don't like stories like this. The ones I prefer have wonderful, happy endings. The Lord steps in. He performs miracles. The sick are healed. The dead are raised. Sins are forgiven. Enemies are reconciled. All is well. Faith fills our hearts with songs of praise to God. The future awaits bright, blessed, and filled with hope.

I don't like stories that begin, "The road ahead will be hard at times."

After the doctor leaves, we don't talk about it much. Not yet. How could we discuss future battles while we are still recovering from the most recent one? We simply agree together that the Lord who was faithful this time will be just as faithful next time. And that, for now, must be enough.

Still, everything inside me longs to rewrite the doctor's narrative. I desperately want Erilynne's story to be different than anybody else's with this disease.

But that's me. I like to rewrite endings. If I could, I'd make sure Jacob and Esau's reconciliation ended on a peaceful note. I'd have them travel home together—friends, brothers, happy, like old times. I'd probably even add the news that God wondrously and miraculously healed Jacob's hip. Wouldn't that be perfect? Everything neat and tidy. But that's not how stories go sometimes in real life.

It's not our story.

And it's not the story of this week. Friday is coming—Good Friday, the stark reminder that the only way to celebrate our Lord's resurrection is through suffering.

Something I am not exactly in the mood to hear.

And I am certain that God, who began the good
work within you, will continue his work until it is finally
finished on the day when Christ Jesus returns.

—PHILIPPIANS 1:6 NLT

QUESTIONS FOR REFLECTION

What is required in biblical reconciliation? Where do repentance and forgiveness fit in? When have you experienced godly reconciliation? What about tentative trust?

Do you need everything neat and tidy? What is it like for you to believe Philippians 1:6, that God who is faithful will continue the good work He began in you?

NOTE

1. Bruce K. Waltke, *Genesis: A Commentary* (Grand Rapids, MI: Zondervan, 2001), 451. Does Jacob ever go to Seir? We're not told. Did Jacob deceive his brother with this promise? Waltke wisely stated that the writer of Genesis allows us "to live with ambiguity regarding Jacob's motives" for not going directly to Seir.

42

MAGNIFICENT PROMISES

*Jacob journeyed to Succoth, and built for
himself a house and made booths for his livestock.*

—Genesis 33:17

It was over. Esau was gone.

Jacob could journey home now. Just not fast. Not like twenty years before when he ran from Esau in the first place. This time, he had to move slowly—for the sake of his family and flocks, not to mention his limp. But back when Jacob wasn't yet far from home, the Lord met him in a dream at Bethel and promised him, "I . . . will bring you back to this land" (Gen. 28:15).

Each step closer to home—that promise was coming true.

Jacob never forgot that. Nor the fact that at the end of his time with Laban, El spoke to him, saying, "Return to the land of your fathers . . . and I will be with you" (31:3). El said it not once but twice: "I am the God of Bethel . . . arise, leave this land, and return to the land of your birth" (v. 13).

The Lord, in charge, determined the time of his leaving—not Jacob.

These two facts: El's promise to bring him home, and His prompting about when to leave Laban, meant everything to Jacob. The moment he heard Esau was approaching with four

hundred men and fear seized his heart, he needed those prom-
ises. He depended on them. He begged the Lord in prayer to
remember them. Twice he prayed, "You said" (32:9, 12).

That's what fear does. It scares the heart. It shakes every
confidence that what God said must come true. It sends doubt
and panic to the soul. But now Jacob could rest easy. The Lord
had fulfilled His promise. Esau was gone. Jacob's prayers had
been answered. El had been faithful to His word.

Jacob was nearly home.

This could mean only one thing: all the promises yet to come
true would come true. The promise concerning the Promised
Land: "I will give it to you and to your descendants" (28:13). The
promise about Jacob's family: "I will make your offspring as the
dust of the earth, so that if one can count the dust of the earth,
your offspring also can be counted" (13:16; 22:17; 28:14 ESV).
And of course the special promise: "In you all the families of the
earth will be blessed" (12:3; 28:14; Gal. 3:8).

When Jacob first heard these words, he responded with a
vow to the Lord: "If God will be with me and will keep me on this
journey that I take . . . and I return to my father's house in safety,
then the Lord will be my God" (Gen. 28:20–21). Now it was true!
Now, as he limped toward home, that "if" was behind him. He
was returning "safely" (33:18). The Lord was indeed his God. All
these years, El remained with him.

Of all God's promises none compared to this: "Behold, I am
with you and will keep you wherever you go" (28:15; 31:3).

All perfectly spoken. All magnificently true.

Friday morning in the hospital is no different for us than
any other day in the hospital. The night shift left, the morning

shift took over. The doctors make their rounds. The doctor in charge says Erilynne will be going home soon. We're not sure when.

Midmorning, we are alone. No nurses. No visitors.

Erilynne and I are both profoundly aware this is not a typical Friday. It is Good Friday. Neither of us can remember, in all our married years, missing a Good Friday service at church. We decided to do our own.

"Why not read the story from Luke's gospel?" Erilynne suggests. I get my Bible and slide my chair closer to her bed. Just as I am about to start reading, she rests her hand on mine, looks into my eyes—sad, and says, "I'm sorry."

I offer a reassuring smile and brush the apology quietly aside.

She squeezes my hand to get my attention. I've been avoiding this conversation. Even now, I don't want to think about what's ahead for us. Every time I do, I find myself entangled in worry—and worry isn't my friend. Worry always fuels the fire of fear and anxiety in me. But I can see in Erilynne's face that she's already looking forward, already anticipating what's coming.

"Me too," I say.

"I keep thinking," she starts, "about how many times we've been here before. We've gone through some pretty hard times together. But no matter what's happened, it never separated the two of us. If anything, it brought us closer together. And always, the Lord was good to us. He saw us through."

We reminisce back as far as our honeymoon. While in St. Thomas, I accidentally stepped on sea urchins. Who knew I was deathly allergic? I was sick for the first three months of our marriage. Then we remember another story, and one after that. No matter what we suffered, no matter what we went through—we did it together. And with every story we see the real story behind it.

The Lord had been with us.

From my earliest days as a Christian, the Lord had placed a promise deep into my soul: "I am with you always, even to the end of the age" (Matt. 28:20). He'd given Erilynne Isaiah 26:3: "Thou wilt keep him in perfect peace, whose mind is stayed on thee" (KJV). It seemed as though every heartache from our past came with a promise from God to strengthen us—comfort us.

And every time, He got us through.

He'd done it again, we realized, right here in the hospital. He hadn't left us. His promises of the past remained just as real in the present. That realization alone makes it possible for us to talk about the doctor's words: "The road ahead will be hard at times."

Erilynne picks up the Bible. She flips the pages and begins to read. "Jesus said, 'I have told you these things, so that in me you may have peace. In this world you will have trouble. But take heart! I have overcome the world'" (John 16:33 NIV).

"We're promised trouble," she observes. "But Jesus promises peace. He told us to 'take heart.'"

She hands the Bible back to me. I slowly read the Passion narrative out loud, from the time of our Lord's arrest to His crucifixion, death, and burial. We both know this is how

He overcame the world. This is how He saved us—through suffering, through bearing our sin, our shame, on the cross.

So why, I ask—after His suffering—do we have to suffer too?

In my perfect little world, I'd make Christians exempt. I turn to another passage and read it to her: "For to you it has been granted for Christ's sake, not only to believe in Him, but also to suffer for His sake" (Phil. 1:29). I look at Erilynne and find her gently smiling.

"How does that sound to you?" she asks.

"I'd rather He grant suffering to somebody else." I smile back, but I'm honest. I tell her I don't want to think about what this disease will do to her—or to us. "The Lord gives grace for today's battles, not tomorrow's," I state.

"I agree," she responds. "But what we have today is all we need for tomorrow. We have each other. We have the Lord. We have a long history together—one in which He has never failed us. He has always been faithful. He tells us to 'take heart,' and He promises that whatever happens—as long as we keep our eyes on Him—He gives peace. He gives grace."

Her voice trails off.

She sees right through me. She knows I vacillate too much. Her faith is bigger than mine, stronger than mine. She has an assurance her Lord will take her safely into tomorrow. It makes her courageous. I see it in her. And I, too, have it—or at least a portion of it, sometimes. And then other times, I don't. The monster of my past roars, and I get scared just thinking about what lies ahead.

It's my limp—my Jacob's limp.

I look down at our hands clasped together. I tell her I'm willing to say yes to God, to her, to whatever He has planned for us.

She nods. "I say yes, too."

And just for a minute, I feel strong again—even courageous.

And you know in all your hearts and in all your souls
that not one word of all the good words which the
LORD your God spoke concerning you has failed; all
have been fulfilled for you, not one of them has failed.

—JOSHUA 23:14–15

QUESTIONS FOR REFLECTION

Why do fear and anxiety make us quickly doubt the promises of God in our life? When have His promises been most real to you? Are you confident in them now?

Are you confident Joshua 23:14–15 is true, and will be true, for you? Why or why not? Do you have assurance the Lord will take you safely into the future? Has He given you courage? If so, what does that courage look like?

43

EL, THE EL OF "ISRA-EL"

*Then he erected there an altar and
called it El-Elohe-Israel.*

—Genesis 33:20

It was first, always first.

*Jacob arrived home, found a place to settle, bought land,
and then did what God's people always do. He came before the
Lord in worship.*

*He built an altar—like Noah (Gen. 8:20), Abraham (12:7; 13:18;
22:9), and Isaac (26:25) all did. No doubt, he brought an offering
from his flock as the Lord taught Abel (4:4) and all subsequent
generations. No doubt he also did what his grandfather and father
had done: he called on the name of the Lord. He proclaimed His
greatness (12:8; 26:25).[1]*

Jacob, following ancient traditions, prepared to worship God.

*Like his forefathers, he erected an altar at an epic moment in
his life. El had promised to bring him home safely—He did! Jacob
was finally home. El protected him on the journey. He rescued
him from danger. El had been with him. There's no greater
response than Jacob's. It was his first act. He worshiped the Lord
with adoration and praise.*

That praise was captured in what he named the altar.

El—that first syllable proclaimed God's name. This alone was no minor thing. Jacob and his company were surrounded by pagan nations who worshiped multiple gods. Not Jacob. Not at this altar. El is a singular term. God in the singular! God who himself declared, "For I am [El] and there is no other" (Isa. 45:22).

El—His name means "strong" and "mighty."[2]

El—He's the "Creator of heaven and earth" (Gen. 14:19 NIV); He's the "Everlasting God" (21:33); He's the "God of Bethel" (31:13) who met Jacob in a dream and proved himself real, alive, and near. This is El—the personal God; the God who entered into covenant with Jacob and made promises to him. Promises He kept.

El—He is faithful to His word.

At just the sound of His name, Jacob worshiped Him.

But Jacob was not done naming the altar. After speaking El's name, he proclaimed El was his God. Not just his father's and grandfather's. He was the God of Jacob. Twenty years prior, Jacob had vowed that if El fulfilled the promises made to him, "then the Lord will be my God" (28:21). On this day, at this altar, Jacob fulfilled that vow. He declared his allegiance to El.

And he said it with his new name—not Jacob, but Israel. The name El gave him at the Jabbok River after wrestling all night (32:28). From that point on, his name was forever bound to El's, and El's name forever bound to his. He was "Isra-El," and he declared it as he, in worshiping God, named the altar.

The altar! It had a name like no other. All who would see it, for generations to come, would know El is God. El is the God of Jacob. El is the El of "Isra-El."

I sleep each night in a hospital chair that converts into a bed. This morning, a little past 4:00, a nurse steps in to check on Erilynne. I wake. It is Easter morning.

I'll leave for church a little past seven. But for now I get up, get some instant coffee at the nurses' station, head back to the room, and continue preparing for the morning. I have the rare privilege of being a pastor. I get to stand in the pulpit today and declare the greatest news the world will ever hear: Jesus Christ is alive—risen from the dead! By His death, He defeated death. By His cross, He forgave our sins. The reign and tyranny of the Devil are over. The entrance into the kingdom of God is now open. Eternal life is possible. We can, by believing, "have life in His name" (John 20:31).

This is the heart of the Easter message—every Easter message.

But sitting here in the hospital room as Erilynne sleeps, I hear it differently. I suddenly realize these words are the same words shared at every funeral sermon I've ever given. We always bury our Christians with the sounds of Easter. We stand "in the sure and certain hope of the resurrection to eternal life through our Lord Jesus Christ."[3]

We're not like the world clinging to superstitions of the afterlife.

There is a real heaven. We have a Savior there, seated on His throne, who has triumphed. He has ascended into the eternal heavens and made a way for us to be with Him forever. He has promised us life, eternal life, beyond this earthly one. This is the comfort we bring to those who grieve. This is our "sure and certain hope."

But I find my heart strangely pierced.

I study Erilynne as she sleeps peacefully. There is no sign of sickness on her face. Not like ten days ago. I remember what she looked like then. I remember how close we came—she nearly died. We almost lost her, and if she had died, we'd have held her funeral this week. Some pastor would have stepped into the pulpit and given us these words, these Easter words.

I hear them differently now.

Not as a pastor preparing to preach on Easter Sunday but as a grieving husband whose wife has been wrenched from his side. I allow myself to feel what I would feel, had that happened. I imagine myself desperate for these words—needing to hear the story again. Needing to know I have a risen Savior who is real, who is here, who knows my broken heart—what else, who else, can comfort me?

Don't give me the line, "She's in a better place." And don't tell me that all religions are alike. Not now, not here, not at the grave. I need a Savior who has conquered death. I need to hear the Easter sound: "Death is swallowed up in victory. . . . Thanks be to God, who gives us the victory through our Lord Jesus Christ" (1 Cor. 15:54, 57).

Without Easter morning, how else will I know she's safe?

Erilynne wakes. I break from my reverie. It's nearing 7:00. Our Krissy is coming at 8:00 to spend Easter morning with her mom while I go to church. Before I leave, Erilynne admits she wishes she was going to the Easter service with me. "But who knows," she adds, with a playful tease, "maybe you'll find me at home after church."

"An Easter surprise," I say and smile back.

From the moment the church service begins, my heart fills with praise and worship. The Lord, in His mercy, kindness, goodness, and love has spared my wife. He's given us a little glimpse of Easter by raising Erilynne out of her sickness and allowing us more time together. I am overcome with joy. And yet, even then, I know if He had taken her, I'd still be worshiping Him—because I know, I really know:

Jesus Christ is alive. He alone has triumphed over death.

I cry as I give the sermon. Can't help it.

I tear up again after service when somebody tells me Erilynne was released from the hospital midmorning. She is already home! Plans for family and friends to stop by the hospital are scrapped and effortlessly turn into a celebration at our home with tons of food.

"We won't stay long; we don't want to tire her out," everyone says.

"I bet we'll tire before her!" I reply with a laugh. And it is true. She lasts all afternoon and into the early evening. None of us can believe it. She is home! She looks beautiful, and on Easter Sunday, of all days.

As we gather around the buffet table to eat, we join hands in prayer. We give thanks, one voice after the other, for Erilynne being safely home. And then we worship Jesus our Lord, our risen Savior. "Because He lives," we begin to sing, "I can face tomorrow. Because He lives, all fear is gone. Because I know He holds the future. And life is worth the living just because He lives."[4]

And, not surprisingly, I cry again.

Then the LORD came down in the cloud and stood
there with him and proclaimed his name, the LORD.
And he passed in front of Moses, proclaiming, "The LORD,
the LORD, the compassionate and gracious God,
slow to anger, abounding in love and faithfulness."

—EXODUS 34:5–6 NIV

QUESTIONS FOR REFLECTION

What does worship mean to you? When have you praised God for who He is, for what He has done for you, and then recommitted your life to Him?

How does the fact of our Lord's death and resurrection impact your worship of God? Does the phrase "because He lives" comfort you when you're most afraid? If so, how and why?

NOTES

1. Allen P. Ross, *Recalling the Hope of Glory: Biblical Worship from the Garden to the New Creation* (Grand Rapids, MI: Kregel, 2006), 142–145. Ross translated "He . . . called upon the name of the Lord" (Gen. 12:8) as "He made proclamation of Yahweh by name"; that is, he proclaimed God's nature—"Who he was, what he was like, what he had done, and what he had promised."

2. Allen P. Ross, *Creation and Blessing: A Guide to the Study and Exposition of the Book of Genesis* (Grand Rapids, MI: Baker Book House, 1988), 566. Ross stated, "The name given to the altar says, in effect, 'the God of Israel' is an '*ēl*,' that is, a strong God, a mighty one—a God who keeps his promises."

3. *The Book of Common Prayer* (New York: Church Publishing, 1979), 501.

4. Bill and Gloria Gaither, "Because He Lives" (Alexandria, IN: William J. Gaither, Inc., 1971).

PART 7

BE STRONG
AND
COURAGEOUS

44

FULL CIRCLE

Then God said to Jacob, "Arise, go up to Bethel and live there, and make an altar there to God, who appeared to you when you fled from your brother Esau."

—GENESIS 35:1

Sometimes God takes us back in time.

It's not always a pleasant journey. We can find that painful memories long since forgotten seem as vivid again as though time never passed. And with them, emotions tightly boxed and buried in the dark catacombs of our soul suddenly come alive, overwhelming our heart. Perhaps it's why we don't take the journey often.

But sometimes it's God's plan for us.

It was God's plan for Jacob. He sent him back to Bethel where it all began. In particular, Bethel sparked two dominant memories. The first was the hardest. There was a reason Jacob first came to Luz (which he later named Bethel). As God told him, it was where "you fled from your brother" (Gen. 35:1).

At Bethel, Jacob feared Esau.

Jacob had deceived his father. He'd stolen the blessing God gave to Abraham and then Isaac. A blessing that was due Esau. Once done, it was irreversible. Esau hated him for it and planned to kill him. When Jacob heard this news, he ran in fear. Twenty years later, at the Jabbok River, he still felt afraid.

That fear—it was time to remember where it all started.

There was a second memory in this place: Bethel was also where God met him in his fears. It's where "El" first appeared to Jacob in a dream—the ladder, the angels of God ascending and descending, El at the top of the ladder and yet near—so close Jacob would exclaim, "Surely the Lord is in this place" (Gen. 28:16).

That dream—it happened in Bethel.

There Jacob, in response, made a vow to El. He was so overcome by El's presence ("How awesome is this place!") that he named the city Bethel because, he proclaimed, "This is none other than the house of God [beth-El], and this is the gate of heaven" (v. 17).

It was time to remember.

God was sending him back. First, to recall the time the fear began. Second, to remember how God remedied that fear. For there is no greater antidote for fear than this: God! He met Jacob. He entered into relationship—real and personal—allowing Jacob to see His face, hear His voice, and receive His promises.

Promises He'd now fulfilled in Jacob's life.

It was time for Jacob to head to Bethel and "make an altar there to God." The moment had come to stand where he once made his vow and declare that vow was forever true: the Lord was his God. In the place where his heart once knew terrifying fear, the Lord wanted him to build an altar and fill that heart with worship and praise.

Everything was about to come full circle.

I have longed to write this book.

Times are changing. Everything around us seems to be falling apart. The basic family unit isn't stable. The morality of the Bible no longer guides the morality of our first-world culture. Job security and financial security can't be trusted. The speed at which we live—always too busy, never enough time—has no end in sight. We're stressed. We struggle with health issues, relationship issues, and personal issues.

Add to that images of terrorism throughout the world today—every day.

Many of us aren't afraid to admit we suffer from fear and anxiety.

It isn't a hard story to tell. It's been this way since the beginning of time. In the garden of Eden, the first sound out of Adam's mouth after he sinned against God was "I was afraid" (3:10). Fear—it's our soul's natural condition when we're separated from God. It always has been. It takes the hardest heart not to feel it, not to know it.

To find comfort, we seek the Lord. Fear's power over us diminishes when we do that.

But the more we deny Him and walk in the ways of the world, the more God steps back. Fear then steps up. It's true for us individually. It's true in our relationships. It's a governing principle in business, school, church, government, and culture. When we make decisions independent of God, darkness prevails—injustice rules. The Bible explains it this way: "For even though they knew God, they did not honor Him as God or give thanks. . . . Therefore God gave them over in the lusts of their hearts" (Rom. 1:21, 24). It's an accurate description of the world we live in today.

God steps back.

And every time He does, we sense it. It's like the second we don't feel well. We know something's wrong. The first sign—the first symptom—appears. It's the same when God steps back. The first sign is fear—just like the days of Eden. We become afraid. We feel insecure and anxious. We do our best to handle it, stay in control, up our game, and pretend it'll be over soon. But it's there. And it's real.

Or rather, he's real—I've always called him the fear monster.

He's everywhere today. He's like a rogue cancer cell running free through the body, pouncing wherever he pleases. He frightens us. He frightens our children. They're growing up more scared, more unsafe, in a world filled with violence and corruption. The monster—he's here. He's an epidemic.

What do we do about it?

We who know Jesus Christ have the antidote—do we not? It's Him. He's not some dry, empty religion. He's not a list of rules to follow. He's God. He came to right the wrong, our wrong, done in Eden—to deal with our sin on the cross, to defeat the power of death. And He did. His Father raised Him on the third day. He's alive. He possesses the power to deal with the grip of fear in our lives.

No one else can. Not like Him.

It takes courage to face our fears. In the world's view, courage describes those who face insurmountable odds and do everything in their power to overcome it. Not so in Christ. Real courage admits we are powerless to overcome. Like David, we look at our Goliath and say, "You come to me with a sword, a spear, and a javelin, but I come to you in the name of the LORD of hosts" (1 Sam. 17:45).

The courageous say: we can't, but You, Lord, can.

This is why I longed to write this book. I wanted, with you, to run to the Jabbok River and begin wrestling with God. He knows our fears. He knows we struggle to give up control and surrender. The wrestling can be long. The wrestler can sometimes hurt. But the Lord knows how to bring us to the end of ourselves and then surprise us. Come morning's light, He lets us behold His face.

We have an antidote for fear in Jesus Christ.

But soon after I started writing this book, the monster roared again. Our life turned upside down. Erilynne and I were preaching in Jackson, Mississippi, when we learned that a water pipe had burst in our home in Connecticut. It was winter and had been too cold for too long. The house was deluged. Everything recoverable went into storage. We moved into a hotel for nearly three months.

Add to that, we were experiencing a job change.

In the years leading up to this, Erilynne had been doing well health-wise. Her rheumatoid condition, however, reacts to stress; and we had no control over the stress we were in. Her condition worsened. Add to that, I'd thought the Lord was establishing my next job in Connecticut— near family and dear friends. Soon that changed. Every-thing was changing.

I found myself up late at night, scared and anxious, doing what I always do—running to the Jabbok. Wrestling with the wrestler. Hating that I wasn't in control. Hating that the monster was back—tormenting me like he did when I was a child.

Full circle.

And, for a while, all I could hear was him laughing at me.

This day the LORD will deliver you up into my hands. . . .
That all this assembly may know that the LORD
does not deliver by sword or by spear; for the battle is
the LORD'S and He will give you into our hands.

—1 SAMUEL 17:46–47

QUESTIONS FOR REFLECTION

Do you have "Bethel" stories in your life? Has the Lord ever taken you back in time to remember how He met you in your fears? Did you find fear replaced by praise? What was that like?

What does the concept "God steps back, fear steps up" mean to you? Have you received real courage in times of overwhelming trial to say, "I can't, but You, Lord, can"? How would you describe that courage that comes from God?

45

BREAKING FREE OF IDOLS

*So Jacob said to his household and to all who
were with him, "Put away the foreign gods which
are among you, and purify yourselves and change your
garments; and let us arise and go up to Bethel."*

—Genesis 35:2–3

*Where did Jacob get these words? They belong to the prophets
yet to come.*

*Joshua would later urge Israel, "Now therefore, put away the
foreign gods which are in your midst, and incline your hearts to the
Lord, the God of Israel" (Josh. 24:23). Samuel would preach,
"Return to the Lord with all your heart, remove the foreign gods . . .
from among you and direct your hearts to the Lord and serve Him
alone; and He will deliver you from the hand of the Philistines"
(1 Sam. 7:3).*

But Jacob was the first.

*He lived centuries before the Lord issued His command at
Mount Sinai: "You shall have no other gods before Me" (Ex. 20:3).
And yet he already knew it.*

*He also knew the cautionary tales of his grandfather Abraham
whose family "served other gods" (Josh. 24:2). He experienced it
personally with his uncle Laban who worshiped idols and raised his
daughters to do the same (Gen. 31:30–32). Even at that moment,
nations worshiping foreign gods occupied the Promised Land.*

Idolatry was everywhere.

Even his family "and all who were with him" had somehow slipped casually into the rhythms of the culture. They, too, acquired physical idols along the way. Even though Jacob had already set up an altar and worshiped God, the only God (Gen. 33:20), they worshiped the gods of the surrounding nations at the same time. This sin would plague Israel for generations to come. And every time it happened, the Lord would send His prophets with the same message: "Repent and turn away from your idols" (Ezek. 14:6).

But Jacob was the first to say it.

And with the command, Jacob added, "purify yourselves and change your garments" (Gen. 35:2). These words, too, belong to a generation centuries later. The Lord himself would say to Moses, "Go to the people and consecrate them today and tomorrow, and let them wash their garments" (Ex. 19:10). Before the Lord descended on Mount Sinai in power and glory, He required the people to be clean in body and soul.

They were about to "meet God" (Ex. 19:17).

Jacob's family was no different. They were travelling to Bethel to worship the Lord, who, as Jacob said, "answered me in the day of my distress and has been with me wherever I have gone" (Gen. 35:3). Though it's not recorded in the Bible, at some point, God must have revealed His eternal gospel to Jacob's heart so he'd know exactly how to prepare them.

And that's what the prophet Jacob did.

In response, his family surrendered and broke free from their idols so they could "serve a living and true God" (1 Thess. 1:9) who never changes—not in Jacob's day. Not in any day.

Fact: We're without our home. Our daughter Jill discovered the flood when it first happened. She'd gone to the house to collect the mail while we were gone. She called family and friends to come help. One friend in particular happens to run a business specializing in residential water damage. Another friend is a building contractor. Within days, a team assembled to repair the house. Our daughters are constant encouragers. They keep assuring us the Lord is in charge and everything is under control.

Fact: My job is changing. I've been the senior pastor of a church in Connecticut for eleven years. Recently, after months in prayer and conversation with our church leaders, we all agreed the Lord was calling Erilynne and me to a new ministry focused on caring for pastors. All of us sensed the Lord was in charge. He was leading the change.

But why both big events at the same time?

Just two weeks after our home floods, I stand in front of our church family on a Sunday morning and announce my resignation.

I try to stay objective.

Routine helps. Erilynne and I both know how to stay busy. We plan our days and weeks. We keep people around us who keep us focused on Jesus. We are not alone. Long before, we'd learned a simple lesson: in times of change, don't make quick decisions. Ask for prayer. Get wise, godly counsel. Emotions can be deceiving. It can be too easy to think we have perspective when we don't.

One day at a time, one foot in front of the other; that is how we cope.

Fact: A month later, Erilynne's body reacts. She experiences a rheumatoid flare. The oddity with her condition is that it manifests in two ways. One, her joints hurt. Two, slow-healing wounds develop near her ankles. The skin breaks and the wound begins. Her doctor immediately increases her medication hoping to knock the flare back into remission.

Every night before dinner I change the dressing around her ankles. Every night I watch the wound get bigger. Two weeks later, a second wound appears. Then a third.

I am not in control here. I can't do anything for her.

We pray. We ask the Lord for help. We say to each other, "God is our refuge and strength, a very present help in trouble. Therefore we will not fear though the earth gives way" (Ps. 46:1–2 ESV). These words have proven true in our past. The Lord has always been with us no matter what we've gone through. We trust Him now.

But I'm still scared. I can't tell her though. I don't want to add to her stress.

I say to the Lord, "Take our home. Toss our stuff in storage. Put us in a hotel room. End my work. Don't tell us exactly where or when we'll start the new work. But not this. Please, not Erilynne's health." I feel so helpless.

Every night as I change her dressing, I am face-to-face with my utter inability as a husband to do something about it. I wish I had stronger faith. I wish I could say with the psalmist, "We stand fearless at the cliff-edge of doom, courageous in sea storm and earthquake" (Ps. 46:2 MSG). But I can't. I am not fearless. I am not courageous. Not right now anyway.

I muddle through the days. But not the nights. The early-morning hours seem the hardest. I get out of bed. I head to the desk in our hotel room and use a little lamp from home for light so I don't wake up Erilynne. I pray— no, I beg. I need the flare to stop. I need the wounds to stop growing. I need Him to answer my prayers.

But I'm afraid—panicked even—His answer will be no.

It's not uncommon. He has said no to me many times before. I've gone to Him in prayer with specific requests for me, my family, and our church, and sometimes my desire is His will, sometimes it's not. And when it's not, I've asked Him for the grace to accept it. But not here. Not now. I need Him to help us. I need Him to say yes.

There are too many changes going on.

I know the monster plays with my mind. He makes me feel worthless. Even guilty, as though it's my fault everything's falling apart around us. Is that true? Is there something I've done to deserve what's happening here? Have I sinned and I'm too blind to see it or too arrogant to confess it? Is that why He's not answering my prayers?

And He's not. At least, that's how it feels as I watch my wife's wounds grow. It feels like He's left us. I know He hasn't. I know He won't. But the fear I feel, the anxiety pressing in on me, tells a different story. Where is He? Why won't He help? Why can't we have what the psalmist says we can have in Psalm 46:3 (MSG):"Jacob-wrestling God fights for us, GOD-of-Angel-Armies protects us"?

I hate the early morning hours. I hate that I am wrestling with the "Jacob-wrestling God." But I am. Wrestling for control. If I have an idol, and I do, this is it. I need Him to be for me, not against me. And I'm afraid, desperately afraid, if I let go, if I break free from this idol of control, I'll do just that—break. Into tiny little pieces.

God is a safe place to hide, ready to help when we need him.
We stand fearless at the cliff-edge of doom, courageous
in seastorm and earthquake, before the rush and roar of
oceans, the tremors that shift mountains. Jacob-wrestling
God fights for us, GOD-of-Angel-Armies protects us.

—PSALM 46:1–3 MSG

QUESTIONS FOR REFLECTION

Can you name the idols of our culture? When has it been easy to step into the rhythms of culture and worship those gods while also worshiping the Lord?

What are you like when you've lost control of what's going on in your life? Do you get anxious? Can you release control to the Lord? When has that been hardest to do?

46

IN REMEMBRANCE OF ME

He built an altar there, and called the place
El-bethel, because there God had revealed Himself
to him when he fled from his brother.

—GENESIS 35:7

Was it still there after twenty-plus years?

Jacob had taken the stone he'd used as a pillow and "set it up as a pillar" (Gen. 28:18). It marked the spot where the ladder from heaven touched earth. "This stone," he declared, "will be God's house" (v. 22). For Jacob knew his dream was real. The place he slept was "none other than . . . the gate of heaven" (28:17). That pillar, was it still there?

That night, so long ago.

He was alone then. He wasn't now. He had family and a host of people with him (35:6). Even Deborah, his mother's nurse, was there—a woman he'd known all his life. And his children came with him. He could show them the exact spot where God—the God of Abraham and Isaac—had appeared to him. And then, as they looked on, he did what God commanded him to do.

He built an altar. Together, as a family, they worshiped in the familiar traditions passed down to each generation. And if one of the children asked, "Why are we doing this?" (Ex. 12:26 MSG), Jacob would have told them the magnificent story of Bethel.

It was here he slept at night.

He was running from his brother, their uncle, Esau. It was, he would have explained, "the day of my distress" (Gen. 35:3). He had few possessions. He came to Bethel "with my staff only" (32:10). And that night, as he laid his head on the stone, God came to him in a vision. Jacob saw a ladder with angels on it. Atop the ladder, the Lord "appeared" (35:1).

Jacob saw His face. He heard His voice.

On this sacred ground, God confirmed the promise to give Jacob and his children the land, to make his offspring as numerous as "the dust of the earth," and that through them "shall all the families of the earth be blessed" (28:14).

God was worthy to be worshiped and praised.

For He was the One who said, "I am with you and will keep you wherever you go" (28:15). He was the One, Jacob declared to his family, "who answered me . . . and has been with me wherever I have gone" (35:3).

He is faithful. He is true to His word.

Faithful even at that moment, as news came that Deborah, Rebekah's nurse, had died. The family must gather in sorrow at the "Oak of Weeping" to bury her (v. 8).[1] Still, it's no wonder Jacob did what he did. He changed the name of "Beth-El" to "El-Beth-El." He added El's name again—accenting an even deeper devotion to Him. In sorrow and joy, in worship and weeping, El was God of the House of God. El was everything to him.

And for Jacob, all things, always, were to be done in remembrance of Him.

It's odd, at times like this, how little things become big things.

We've been invited to a dinner party. It's late Friday afternoon and Erilynne tells me we somehow got the date wrong and the dinner is tonight. We need to get ready to go.

"We really should," she says. "They'll be disappointed if we don't. It'll only be a couple of hours." I know that and agree with her. I try to take it in stride—like I could be spontaneous and "go with the flow." I start getting ready but stop. Too much anxiety. One more thing—not planned, not in my control, pushing me to perform, demanding I find emotional strength to cope, strength I don't have.

Over a dinner party with friends? Really?

I tell Erilynne I am sorry. I call our friends and apologize. This little thing, somehow such a big thing, has surprised me. I'm not as strong as I'd hoped.

A few weeks later, we drive to a pastors' conference near Ithaca, New York. I've been invited to be one of three speakers. Our job is to encourage pastors in their daily walk with Jesus Christ, providing every opportunity for Bible teaching, personal sharing, and prayer.

My talk comes after lunch.

As I near the end of it, I admit to the pastors I am going through a difficult time. I give them a brief glimpse and say, "What I've learned most in recent months is this: never go alone. Ask for help. Be surrounded by people who keep you focused on Jesus—who He is, His goodness and mercy—and who remind you that He who has been faithful in the past is faithful now in the present."

My voice breaks. I'm not expecting it. I quickly recover, finish the talk, and send them to their small groups for reflection and prayer.

"Can we talk for a few minutes?" a pastor asks a few moments later.

We find a quiet spot in the auditorium. After introducing himself, he says, "When you mentioned your personal suffering, I knew the Lord wanted me to come and encourage you. There's a Bible verse He wants you to hold on to that says, 'My grace is sufficient for you, for my power is made perfect in weakness' [2 Cor. 12:9 ESV].

"I know how hard that is to hear," he continues. "When I was in my midthirties, I lost everything. I was a Christian. I was a pastor. I had a good church, a beautiful wife, and three incredible kids. But when nobody was looking, I drank. I couldn't get through the day without it. I convinced myself I wasn't an alcoholic and that I was in control of how much I drank. I thought no one knew.

"But everyone knew. Rather than getting help, like they encouraged, I tried to keep up the image at church and at home. But it only got worse. I lost my job, my wife and kids, my dignity. I lost everything.

"Months passed before I attended an Alcoholics Anonymous meeting. They gave me a mentor whom the Lord used powerfully in my life. Our first meeting, that man looked me right in the eyes and said, 'My grace is sufficient for you, for my power is made perfect in weakness.' And then he sang a verse from an old Christian hymn:

Did we in our own strength confide,
Our striving would be losing;
Were not the right Man on our side,
The Man of God's own choosing. . . .
And He must win the battle.[2]

"That man taught me the secret of God's grace. It comes when I'm powerless, when I have no control over my life, when I can say with the apostle Paul, 'I will rather boast about my weaknesses, so that the power of Christ may dwell in me.'

"It's hard to hear, isn't it?" he asks.

I nod. "Hard, but true," I say.

"I hope it encourages you," he states. "Don't be afraid to give up control. Confess your weakness to Jesus. Tell Him you're powerless over the situation you're in. He will give you all the grace you need for today."

He reaches for my hand, grabs it, and prays for me. Before he leaves, I am gratified to hear that the Lord has restored his marriage, given him back his children, and allowed him, these past twelve years, to return to pastoring a church.

I thank him for talking to me. He has given me a gift. He makes me remember all the times I've battled fear. I seem to go through the same cycles. I fight. I wrestle. I do what I can to end the monster's tyranny in my life until, at last, I come to my senses. Then I realize that everything this pastor said to me is true. I can't depend on my own strength. I must rely wholly on the "Man of God's own choosing. . . . He must win the battle."

How many times has the Lord brought to my mind the first three steps of the twelve steps of AA: "I am powerless. I am dependent. I am surrendered to His will, not mine"?

But it's harder this time. More than losing our home, my job, and any sense of what the future holds, my problem is that I can't do anything to stop the growth of Erilynne's wounds. Nothing. And I am afraid—I am! I don't know what else to do but confess it to the Lord and say, "I am weak. I need Your grace. I am scared. Help my wife."

And so I do, with all my heart. I yield control to my Savior and Lord.

"This is My body, which is for you; do this in remembrance of Me." In the same way *He took* the cup also after supper, saying, "This cup is the new covenant in My blood; do this, as often as you drink *it*, in remembrance of Me."

—1 CORINTHIANS 11:24–25

QUESTIONS FOR REFLECTION

Why does the Lord emphasize that we remember? How does it affect your reading of the Bible, your worship of the Lord, and the understanding of your past?

When, during your most anxious times, have little things become big things? How has the Lord used others, as they remember His faithfulness, to strengthen your own faith?

NOTES

1. Victor P. Hamilton, *The Book of Genesis: Chapters 18–50* (Grand Rapids, MI: Eerdmans Publishing Co., 1995), 373. Hamilton pointed out that sadly "there is no reference to Jacob being reunited with Rebekah" upon his return. "Presumably," he wrote, "she died and was buried before Jacob returned" from exile.

2. Martin Luther, "A Mighty Fortress," 1529, public domain.

47

THE WONDER OF HIS APPEARINGS

*Then God appeared to Jacob again . . .
and He blessed him.*

—Genesis 35:9

Jacob was a blessed man.

The Lord brought him back to Bethel. He'd told him to return, build an altar, and remember the day He first appeared to him (Gen. 35:1). In that appearing, Jacob met El. He had a real, personal encounter with the living God. He'd grown up knowing it was possible. He'd heard the stories of how the Lord appeared to Abraham (12:7; 17:1; 18:1) and Isaac (26:2, 24). Here, in Bethel, it happened for him.

Jacob was a blessed man.

So many years later, he got to do what his father and grandfather did for him. He got to tell his children the story of the Lord's appearing—all God did that day, all God said—so they'd know that an encounter with the Lord was possible for them, too. And he could tell them not just one story, but two.

Because the Lord had appeared to Jacob a second time.

The second story was altogether different, though. Jacob wasn't running from Esau that time. Esau was coming at him with an army too big and too strong for him. In his distress, when he felt most afraid, God came in the night, not as a vision, but as a man, as though Jacob's equal. And because it was dark, Jacob didn't know it was Him. He couldn't see His face. All he knew was that the man had not come in peace.

He'd come to fight.

It took everything Jacob had to wrestle Him. He couldn't beat Him. Not at first. The man fought as hard as Jacob fought. Who does that? Who fights all night long? And why—knowing now the man's identity—did He let Jacob prevail at the end? But He did. And that's when it happened. The man broke Jacob's hip.

It was why, even now at Bethel, Jacob still limped.

But after wounding Jacob, the man was not done. He spoke a blessing over Jacob. And then, as the sun rose in the sky, He let His glory appear. The man allowed Jacob to glimpse the radiance of His face and the wonder of His splendor.

This—the second appearing!

Here, in Bethel again, Jacob could step back in time and remember it all. As he did, something surprising—something miraculous—happened. A day came when Jacob, it seems, was alone once again. Was he standing near where he'd built the altar? Is it possible he was still grieving Deborah's death? Did he have any expectation, in his wildest imaginings, that what happened before would happen again?

The Bible simply says, "God appeared to Jacob again . . . and He blessed him." Not in a dream at the top of a ladder. Not after a night of wrestling. But here, in the perfect place, where it all began, for the third time, Jacob received the greatest blessing of all.

He got to see El's face, hear His voice, and behold His glory.

Why is it so hard to say, "I need help; I can't do this on my own"? I think about the pastor I met near Ithaca.

I wonder what it was like for him to lose everything. What made him go to an AA meeting? What helped him most? What made the difference?

I get his phone number to ask.

"The drinking got worse," he shares when we finally talk. "I got a job so I could pay the bills but kept to myself. I played right into the Devil's hand. His strategy is always to make sure we isolate, withdraw—become loners convinced we can handle all our problems on our own. And it generally works. Even if we do need help, we're too proud to ask, too much in control to release control.

"That's why AA is so effective. It counters the Devil's attack," he says.

"How?" I ask.

"It's all about meetings and mentors. If you want to get well, if you're serious about being sober and staying sober, you attend meetings. You get a mentor who keeps you accountable, asks hard questions, makes sure you've stopped drinking. If the Devil's message is 'Walk alone,' AA's message is 'Never walk alone.'

"But it's funny how it happened for me," he continues. "I got overcome by guilt. After Christ came into my life, I never missed church. Even when we went on vacations as a family, we found a church on Sunday morning. But after my wife and kids left, after I lost my job, I stopped going. I hated myself for it."

"Guilt can be a good thing," I muse.

"Yes, it can! The Lord used it in my life. It took a few months, but I finally went. I was real particular. I needed a gospel-preaching church with a pastor as good as or better than me." He stops and laughs at himself. "How's that for being a snob! But it's true. I went there as a critic and judge. But the moment the music started, I couldn't believe it—I began to weep uncontrollably. I tried to stop, but I couldn't. I almost ran out of the church. I wanted to, but chose not to.

"You see, I knew the Lord was there. This was Jesus touching my heart. He'd come to this stubborn, rebellious drunk and let me feel the wonder of His presence again. It was more than I could bear. I couldn't stop crying. I felt like such a failure."

He pauses a minute to collect himself.

"In the church bulletin, I saw they hosted AA meetings, and I figured this was it. It was decision time. Was I going to leave that church and drink myself into oblivion or recommit myself to Christ and His people? Does that sound like an easy choice to you? It wasn't for me. I didn't want to admit to anyone, let alone myself, that I needed help.

"But for reasons I can't explain, the Lord didn't let go of me. That Sunday morning, He was there when the congregation began singing His praise. He was there when the preacher opened the Bible to us, when we prayed, and when we took Communion together. You see it, don't you? AA got its secret of meetings and mentors from the Bible. The Lord wants us to be in His church, no matter what we're going through. And it's such a simple message: We stay together. We never walk alone."

"You see, this is where victory over the Devil begins. When we commit to a church that preaches the Bible and believes in Jesus, something happens. And I'll tell you what it is. Jesus said, 'Where two or three have gathered together in My name, I am in their midst' (Matt. 18:20). That's it! Our Lord is there. He meets with us. He takes control of every aspect of our lives.

"You believe me, don't you?" he asks.

I tell him I do.

"Well, that's my story," he says. "I went to my first AA meeting that night. I asked for help. I admitted I was scared to face my failures as a pastor, husband, and father. But I made the decision. I told them that night, 'I'm not walking alone ever again. I need these meetings. I need Jesus. I need His church. I need His blessing.'"

He tells me he's been sober since that Sunday twelve years ago.

"You're right," I say, "it does sound so simple."

"But it's true," he responds. "Meetings and mentors, that's all."

I realize he doesn't know much of my story—not really. He knows the last few months have been hard on us. He knows I'm scared for Erilynne's health. But that's about it. Still, talking to him helps. He reminds me that the Devil torments us all in different ways. But no matter how he torments, the treatment is always the same: Don't go alone; get involved at church. Ask for help. Surround yourself with people who keep your focus on God—Father, Son, and Holy Spirit.

But I'd forgotten the mystery of it all.

I'd forgotten that when we meet together in Jesus' name, He appears! Just like He promised. There's no greater antidote when the monster roars, when I get most afraid and the panic wells up, especially now, with my life so out of control. This promise, this magnificent promise, means everything. It's what I want most.

Just to experience the wonder of His presence.

And though you have not seen Him, you love Him, and though you do not see Him now, but believe in Him, you greatly rejoice with joy inexpressible and full of glory, obtaining as the outcome of your faith the salvation of your souls.

—1 PETER 1:8–9

QUESTIONS FOR REFLECTION

When have you experienced a real, personal encounter with the Lord? How do you describe the wonder of His appearings to you? How does 1 Peter 1:8–9 affect you?

Are there times you isolate, withdraw, and stay away from meeting with brothers and sisters in Christ? When have you experienced the wonder of Matthew 18:20?

48

THE WONDER OF HIS PROMISES

*God said to him, "Your name is Jacob; You shall
no longer be called Jacob, but Israel shall be
your name." Thus He called him Israel.*

—GENESIS 35:10

It was the wrestler—same face.

*It was El—the One who appeared to him at Bethel the first
time (Gen. 35:1); the same One who attacked and fought him all
night at the river Jabbok. When morning's light came—same
face, this face!*

There—real and alive. No dream, no vision.

*It all happened fast. There's no indication He lingered. No
eating of a meal (Ex. 24:11; Luke 24:30). No conversation
between them, not this time. No sense of how near He came or
how bright His glory shone. All that's said is that God appeared.
God blessed. God spoke.*

That voice—the same voice.

*The Lord's first words were no different than before. That
night when they wrestled, while it was still dark, He'd said, "Your
name shall no longer be Jacob" (Gen. 32:28). His name meant
"heel-catcher." But in time, his behavior had shifted the meaning
to "heel-tripper" . . . "supplanter" . . . "deceiver." Eventually, it
became "prevailer"—always controlling, always dominating.*

It was evident in how he fought God.

With a broken hip, Jacob still tried to overpower Him, saying, "I will not let you go unless you bless me" (v. 26). But El did more than break his hip. He did what only God can do: He put to death Jacob's sinful, self-driven nature. No more deceiving. No more prevailing in his own strength. No more Jacob as Jacob. El was making a new man with a new nature and a new name—a name like no other.

"But Israel shall be your name" (35:10).

God bestowed on him the honor of bearing His name, "El." "Isra" meant he'd rule, he'd prevail, but not in his strength, nor for his own fleshly desire. He was "Isra-El" now, forever dependent on God, surrendered to Him and His will. This name, bestowed that night at the Jabbok, would pass on for all generations. His children would be called "Israel"—a people who can do all things through El who strengthens them (Phil. 4:13).

Here, now, the wrestler said it again.

Though Jacob had wanted to know the wrestler's name years before at the Jabbok (Gen. 32:29), the wrestler now finally told him openly, "I am God Almighty [El-Shaddai]" (35:11). And then, with words that went back to the earliest days in Eden, He instructed Israel to "be fruitful and multiply" (1:28). He promised what He'd promised before to him and his fathers: nations and kings would come from them (17:4–6), and they'd possess the Promised Land (12:1–8; 28:13).

The wrestler said nothing new.

The promises He'd made in the past, He repeated. For reasons not revealed, He knew Israel needed to hear them again and to know, by His personal appearing, the greatest of promises was forever true: "Do not fear, for I am with you" (26:24; 28:15; 31:3).

And with that, the wrestler was gone.

I have taken risks in writing this book.

Admitting "I'm afraid" isn't easy. Even when life is hard, when the ground beneath us shakes, we do everything we can to stay in control. And life does get hard. Who wants to hear, "You have cancer"? Or worse, "Your child has cancer"? Who needs the stress of another broken relationship, one more negative pregnancy test, bills that can't be paid, someone close to our heart dying, or a teenage daughter whacked-out on drugs?

Maybe, for a while, we admit our fear. But soon, we rally. We fight. We survive.

It's why I come to the Jabbok. Jacob found the courage to admit to God in prayer that he was afraid (32:11). Then, in a moment unparalleled in Scripture, God came to him. God fought with him, and Jacob fought back because that's what we do when we're frightened. We fight. We battle to stay in control. We demand that God answer our prayers. We say as Jacob said, "I will not let You go unless You bless me."

Surrender is hard. It's easier, even with a broken hip, to fight.

But this is where the gospel begins. Jesus said, "If anyone wishes to come after Me, he must deny himself, and take up his cross and follow Me" (Mark 8:34). At some point, we've got to let go, trust God—put all things under His control no matter what He decides—and stop fighting Him.

It's here, and only here, we find the real antidote to fear.

Jacob saw the face of God. He saw Jesus.[1]

That's what I want for you. That's why I started writing this book in the first place. I've been to the Jabbok before.

I've been a night wrestler. I know what it's like to be afraid, to feel my life out of control, and to beg God—to demand He do what I need Him to do. I know how hard it is to surrender and trust Him with my life, my circumstances.

But unexpectedly—not far into my writing this book—our life turned upside down again, and I need to journey back here, to the Jabbok, for myself.

I hate feeling afraid like this.

Too many changes all at once. Job uncertainty. The house floods. A month passes, then two, then six—and rather than things improving, they grow worse. It's a summer morning, before dawn, and I inscribe my heart's cry to the Lord in my journal: "When will we have a home again? What job is next? Will You heal Erilynne's wounds? Will You help us with our finances? Will You calm my fears? I'm feeling so lost."

Midafternoon that same day, an insurance adjuster calls to say they aren't going to cover twenty thousand dollars for repairs that have already been made to our home. We'll have to pay it ourselves, and soon. Three days later he calls back. He'd made a mistake. We actually owe only three hundred and fifty dollars.

But during those three days in between, the monster roars.

My pastor friend from Ithaca says it perfectly: never go alone. All of us, no matter what we're going through, need meetings and mentors. Erilynne and I have no problem with the meeting part. We have a strong church family that meets, not just on Sundays, but often, and gives us the gift of joining together in prayer and worship.

But the surprise comes with the mentors.

One man, Paul—a dear friend, strong in Christ—asks if he can come alongside me. Not to fix me or our situation; but simply to listen, pray, offer counsel and perspective, and do the one thing I've forgotten I need most: remind me of the promises of God, those "precious and magnificent promises" (2 Pet. 1:4) that tell me who I am in Christ and keep me grounded in Him in the fiercest storm (Matt. 7:25).

There are others—David, Steve, Quigg, Ken—friends, colleagues in ministry. They and their wives become a great help to us. Ken actually flies from Colorado to spend a few days with us as we vacation in Maine. The time together is etched in my memory. One day in particular, we go out for a long walk. I take him to a favorite spot of ours—to a house friends of ours own and a most beautiful porch, set on a hill overlooking the ocean. It is cold and windy, and rain falls on and off. We sit bundled up in sweaters and rain gear and talk for the longest time.

He knows me. We walked the crash site of Flight 427 together. I don't have to pretend I'm better than I am. Nor am I afraid to tell him I'm afraid.

He, too, speaks the promises of God to my heart. I find comfort here. He tells me again of the wonder of the Father's love—perfect love, which "casts out fear" (1 John 4:18). We are, he says, to "wait for the Lord." Not to answer our prayers. Not to fix our upside-down life. But to fill us with a love for Him that we've never known before.

And then it happens. We both see it at the same time.

Up in the sky, directly overhead, floating just above the tree line—close, maybe fifty feet away—a bald eagle soars in flight. The winds still strong, he hovers there—just above us, stationary in the sky, riding the winds effortlessly, allowing us the best view possible, and then turning and shooting downwind and circling back around.

In thirty plus summers in Maine, Erilynne and I have never seen the bald eagle in flight.

When he comes back, he doesn't return alone. Two eagles fly overhead now, both commanding the stormy winds with ease and confidence. Both testifying to the wonder of God's promise: "Those who wait for the LORD will gain new strength. They will mount up with wings like eagles" (Is. 40:31).

And I feel it, we both do, like an infusion straight to the heart—"new strength" arrives, real and alive. Just as He promised.

Yet those who wait for the LORD will gain new strength;
They will mount up *with* wings like eagles, they will run
and not get tired, they will walk and not become weary.

—Isaiah 40:31

QUESTIONS FOR REFLECTION

When has the Lord repeated His promises to you? How has it impacted your faith in Christ? When has it given you courage to face the future? Who are the mentors in your life? When have those mature in Christ stood with you in times of fear and confusion? In what ways have you been a mentor to others?

NOTE

1. Bruce K. Waltke, *Genesis: A Commentary* (Grand Rapids, MI: Zondervan, 2001), 470. It is hard for many biblical scholars to say explicitly that Jacob wrestled with the pre-incarnate Jesus. It's unclear why. Waltke speaks of Jacob's "encounter with the God-man," for Jacob wrestled with a man and said, "I have seen God face to face" (Gen. 32:30). Why, then, shall we too not say it explicitly?

49

MARKERS AND MONSTERS

—✎—

*Jacob set up a pillar in the place where
He had spoken with him.*

—Genesis 35:14

Twice the Lord appeared to Jacob in Bethel.

Twice he responded by setting up a stone pillar to mark the spot where God came, God met, God spoke to Jacob. These pillars declared a historical event had happened, never to be forgotten. At the first pillar, angels came, a ladder from heaven touched earth, and God spoke promises to him. Jacob saw all that in a dream. He knew he was standing in "Beth-El"—the "house of God"— and at the very "gate of heaven" (Gen. 28:17).

That pillar told a story.

It stood as a testimony to all God promised Jacob in the dream. More than twenty years later, the Lord instructed Jacob to return to Bethel and build an altar. It, too, told a story: the altar testified that God is good. He is faithful to His word, and His word is true. The Lord had fulfilled and was fulfilling all He said He'd do.

But God came, God met, God spoke to Jacob yet again. This third time, He blessed him, confirming all He'd said both in the dream and at the Jabbok River. He repeated His promise that Jacob's offspring would bring forth nations and kings and possess *the Promised Land. Their future was secure, for God said it. He promised it.*

This event, this third appearing, required another pillar.

For generations to come, the children of Israel would stand at these three historical markers in Bethel—the two pillars and the altar—and learn their stories. And if they had ears to hear, they'd know that the promises the Lord, the God of Israel, made to Jacob were meant for them, too. It would strengthen them in faith and give God-infused hope for their future.

It's why markers are gifts from God.

It's why, after the flood, God placed a rainbow in the sky. Every time it appears, the Lord assured Noah, "I will see it and remember the everlasting covenant" (9:16 ESV). In the same way, He gave the mark of circumcision so every time a child is circumcised the people of Israel would hear again the promises of the "everlasting covenant" (17:13).

Markers tell a story.

We are prone to forget. Too often, present circumstances shut out any memory of the past. Trials come, storms rage, the monster roars, and fear floods the soul. We have no sense that God is near, that God cares, and that God never abandons those who seek Him. We need markers. We need them to tell us God is good. He is faithful to His word, and His word is true. He always does what He says He'll do.

The three markers in Bethel had stories to share and courage to give. Little did Jacob know how much he'd need them soon. Trials were coming, storms—fierce and strong. The monster was about to roar again.

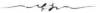

Ever so slowly, the Lord begins to piece our life back together.

Blessings come. Soon we know where we'll relocate to and what I'll be doing in my job. We're profoundly grateful the new job provides temporary housing until we get settled—much-needed relief after months in and out of hotels and furnished rentals. Better still, Erilynne's wounds calm and even begin to heal.

Setbacks still come. Our house in Connecticut goes under contract for sale, and the day before closing, the buyers back out for no apparent reason. The house goes back on the market right at the moment home sales slump. Months pass, a year, and still, as I write this, the house remains on the market.

There's no question about it: I have a limp.

It's hard not being in control.

Every night before bed, I take the dog out for her evening walk. She takes off to explore as I pray, and every time my prayers turn to tears, she comes up alongside to cheer me up. My dear L'Oréal, our beautiful Old English Sheepdog. And tears come frequently, as does my prayer night after night: "Lord Jesus, I am powerless here. I surrender to You, no matter what happens."

The eagle helped. I'd snapped a picture of it with my phone. I printed it and pasted it in my journal with a caption underneath Isaiah 40:31. That way, I can see it often and remember the day the Lord encouraged us. I don't want to forget.

I also take a friend's advice. He gets me an appointment with a licensed counselor, and I know I need it. Before my first appointment, I write the counselor a two-page letter describing the previous couple months. I think it might help him as he prays and prepares for our time together. But, in fact, it helps me. As I write, what I am experiencing sounds all too familiar. Our present story feels like stories from my past. Stories of the monster and me.

Oh how I wish I tucked Bible promises in my heart as a boy or established stone pillars I could run to that marked times when God had revealed himself to me, but I didn't know Him then. I didn't know what to do when the monster came and scared me. I remember how much I needed the bathroom light on for comfort at night as I lay in bed, frightened of the dark. I remember how scared I felt standing outside my mother's hospital room as she lay dying. I was terrified. Scared of death. Scared of her death.

I chose to stay on the safe side of the yellow tape.

But eventually, God used that tape in my life. He gave me strength I didn't have on my own; courage I'd never known before. He took me by the hand and led me into that dark kingdom inside the yellow tape.

The Bible calls it the "valley of the shadow of death" where evil reigns, and the monster runs wild (Ps. 23:4).

But I had to learn the hard way. I eventually discovered that I can go inside anytime I want as long as I put my trust in Jesus. If I confess my inability to handle things and rely on His ability, it's possible to enter that place. But the moment I take back control, the monsters descend.

And I, even as a Christian, get afraid again.

This, as I've said, is my limp. I want to retain control even inside the tape where I have no control—absolutely none. Saying the words is easy: "Father, I trust You. I need Your help." But the act of surrender is hard. Even now, with all we're going through at the present time, I'm struggling to open my hands, lift them to the Lord, and give myself to Him.

That's what I write to the counselor.

And then I remember. I do have a marker in my life. It stands on a hillside near an old logging road in western Pennsylvania. I can close my eyes, and I return again to the crash site of Flight 427. It was there the Lord gave me strength to cross the yellow tape day after day to be part of the recovery effort.

I had courage in those days, courage that came from heaven above.

In my mind, I go there again. Briar waits by my side, attention focused. Ken stays there too. Just the three of us standing in front of the tree with the dead body—that tree! It's everything; I knew it that day. I don't have to be afraid. The monster wields no power over me. Because that tree pointed me back to *the* tree, the only tree—the cross.

And that cross tells a story, loud and clear.

It proclaims God's power to rescue me from fear. There, Jesus Christ took on the monster of old and won. He won for all time, defeating the Devil and death. My Lord won! I don't have to fear the monster anymore. I don't have to fight for control when I know—no matter what happens to me— the Lord is in command.

Just the memory of that tree in western Pennsylvania strengthens me. I open my eyes again. I hate what Erilynne and I are going through. I finish the letter to my counselor and tell him what I need most—I "just want courage that is not overcome by fear." I tell him that some days I get a taste of it and other days, not at all. I share what the tree— that marker in my life—taught me years ago.

Courage, real courage, is possible.

Only be strong and very courageous; be careful to do according to all the law which Moses My servant commanded you; do not turn from it to the right or to the left, so that you may have success wherever you go. . . . Have I not commanded you? Be strong and courageous! Do not tremble or be dismayed, for the LORD your God is with you wherever you go.

—JOSHUA 1:7, 9

QUESTIONS FOR REFLECTION

What markers has the Lord given His church down through the ages? How do they strengthen Christians in faith and you in particular? Do they help calm your fears?

Name markers in your life where the Lord came and spoke His promises to you. When has courage, His courage, filled you? How can you experience that courage today?

50

ON THE WAY TO BETHLEHEM

*So Rachel died and was buried on the way to Ephrath
(that is, Bethlehem). Jacob set up a pillar over her grave; that is the
pillar of Rachel's grave to this day. Then Israel journeyed on.*

—GENESIS 35:19–21

He'd seen God face-to-face three times, and his life had been "preserved" (Gen. 32:30). Why didn't that guarantee happiness? Why couldn't he live out his days in peace—unencumbered by trouble and sorrow? He'd gone through the dark night of wrestling. He had a limp that would never leave him. Wasn't that enough?

Why did all the trials come?

Twice the Lord changed his name. The first time happened the night they wrestled. His name—still held by his offspring to this day—had special meaning: Jacob would no longer rule ("Isra") in his own strength. He had, in his very name, the name of God ("El"). Nothing could separate them. All things were possible. He could conquer; he could prevail, as he relied on God's power working through him.

This is the secret of God's kingdom.

This is the place where courage is found. "In this world you will have trouble," El would warn centuries later. "But take courage; I have overcome the world" (John 16:33 NIV). It's a fact of life. Troubles come. But the Lord's promises never fail. Perhaps that's why He appeared to Jacob at Bethel a second time and restated His promises when He did—before sorrow came.

Rachel.

She had been everything to Jacob. He worked seven years—then another seven years—so he could marry her—and those years "seemed to him but a few days because of his love for her" (Gen. 29:20). Yet soon after God appeared at Bethel the second time, as the caravan left Bethel and travelled toward Bethlehem, Rachel went into labor with her second child. But what was meant for joy turned to bitter pain.

Rachel—Jacob's beloved Rachel—died in childbirth.

He had to bury her there, at that place, on the way to Bethlehem. He decided to build a pillar over her grave to forever proclaim his deep sorrow (48:7 MSG). And then more trouble hit as his eldest son committed an indecent, unthinkable sin against his family (35:22). Then more sorrow fell when Jacob's father died. And still further heartache came when, years later, Israel held in his hands the blood-soaked, multicolored coat of his seventeen-year-old son, Joseph—the cherished firstborn child of his love, his heart, his Rachel (37:3, 33). How could his soul bear all that grief?

The secret was in his name.

He could rely on "El" for help and comfort. He could face sorrow as he faced fear, for the Lord was with him. The Lord gave strength and courage beyond measure, for nothing—not even the weight of all this sorrow—could separate Jacob from El. But did he receive it? Did he let the love of God fill his soul?

Or did he make sorrow his constant companion? Did he, in mind and heart, get stuck on the way to Bethlehem—at Rachel's grave—and never journey on?

Tears come easily these days.

We think the storms this past year are nearly over when we learn of the death of our sister-in-law Rosemary, who brought contagious cheer into our lives. In the week around her funeral, we notice our Sheepdog, L'Oréal, isn't feeling well. Erilynne and I are not ready to hear she has untreatable lymphatic cancer. I can't explain how this little "baby girl" of ours had stolen our hearts—but she had.

We have her only a little while longer.

I miss her. I miss our nightly walks.

And I, again, must face my limp. I am not in control—Jesus is.

As I finish writing this book, I'm profoundly sensitive to people in my life who suffer from panic attacks, paralyzing anxiety, and debilitating fear. They want answers. Simple. Quick. Effective. It's why how-to books sell. It's why masses of people take antianxiety medication. And I know, for some, it's needed. But for others, it's because we want relief. We want it now. Who wants to take the time or spend the energy to find out what's really going on?

A friend of mine expressed it so well: "In my case, anxiety is a medical issue. I went to a doctor, got diagnosed, and I'm on meds. They help—big time. But I'm afraid to talk about it. At work, in the media, with my friends—it's all a joke. If you're on Prozac or Zoloft, it means you're weak. You can't handle stress. I know that's not true. I also know that without the Lord and Christian friends around me, I'd be a mess."

Me too, I tell him. And it makes me wonder how secular people cope. I get the fact that we're survivors. We prevail by mustering the strength to overcome from within ourselves. This, we're told, is real courage. Our indomitable spirit perseveres. We endure. We triumph.

Well done, us.

But that's not me. I've known it since I was a little boy: the monster is bigger, louder, and stronger than me. Ever since we, as the human race, separated ourselves from almighty God—fear has reigned (Gen. 3:10; Heb. 2:14–15). It doesn't take a thousand scholars to figure it out. If we want to deal with our panic attacks, our paralyzing anxiety, our debilitating fear—we need to return to God.

He's the answer. Plain and simple.

For this reason, I do what the Lord has taught us to do. When people get afraid, when the monster rises up and roars with everything he's got, and life suddenly falls apart—way, way beyond their control—I bring them here.

To the Jabbok.

I wish it were easier. I wish I could wave my magic wand and give simple how-to steps to a stress-free life. But that's not our God. He has a work to do that pierces the heart. He changes us not just for the present life but also for the life to come.

He wrestles.

He demands we relinquish control and trust Him. "He who loves his life loses it," Jesus said, "and he who hates his life in this world will keep it to life eternal" (John 12:25).

He wounds.

He brings us to that place where we, like Mary, our Lord's mother, say, "Behold, I am the servant of the Lord;

let it be to me according to your word" (Luke 1:38 ESV). And then He does what He came to do: He puts our old selves to death—by His cross, by His blood shed for the forgiveness of our sins. And then He breathes His resurrected life into our mortal bodies and makes us new (Rom. 8:11).

Is He safe? No, said C. S. Lewis in *The Lion, the Witch, and the Wardrobe*, "'Course he isn't safe. But he's good. He's the King, I tell you."[1]

And the King issues His promise: "For if we died with Him, we will also live with Him; if we endure, we will also reign ['Isra'] with Him ['El']" (2 Tim. 2:11–12). We are "Isra-El" too—a people utterly and completely dependent on Jesus. For this reason, we can "do all things through Christ who strengthens" us (Phil. 4:13 NKJV) and nothing—not even the powers of hell—"will be able to separate us from the love of God, which is in Christ Jesus our Lord" (Rom. 8:39).

Let the monster roar.

We have a promise like no other. Jacob's story is our story. The Lord is with us. He has promised He will never leave us (Matt. 28:20; Heb. 13:5–6). No matter what we must go through, no matter how dark the night becomes, even when evil and death surround us—the Lord has promised us morning's light. The sun will rise! We will behold our Savior. We will "see His face" (Rev. 22:4) and "death shall be no more, neither shall there be mourning, nor crying, nor pain" (21:4 ESV). The monster has lost.

Our Lord Jesus Christ has won—to the glory of God the Father!

Courage, real courage, is possible in this life.

It's why I come running—despite my limp—to the Jabbok with you. I know it's hard. I know fear is real. I know the night of wrestling can be long. But thank God you're not wrestling with the Devil or death or cancer or all the evil and injustice of the world against you. You are in the grip of God himself—your wrestler.

Trust Him.

And you are here with His people. We don't journey through the night alone. We don't let anyone travel through the darkness alone. We who belong to Jesus go together to the Jabbok and let the wrestler perform the work He has come to do. For soon enough, His promise will come true. Fear will fade away. Blessing will come. Morning will dawn.

And together, forever, we will see Jesus.

But in all these things we overwhelmingly conquer through Him who loved us. For I am convinced that neither death, nor life, nor angels, nor principalities, nor things present, nor things to come, nor powers, nor height, nor depth, nor any other created thing, will be able to separate us from the love of God, which is in Christ Jesus our Lord.

—Romans 8:37–39

QUESTIONS FOR REFLECTION

Why do trials, sorrows, and heartaches come? What does it mean to "take courage" (John 16:33)?

Have you been able, in the past, to trust the wrestler? What have you learned from Him? When has He given you confidence to believe His promises for you are true?

NOTE

1. C. S. Lewis, *The Lion, the Witch, and the Wardrobe* (New York: Macmillan Publishing Co., 1950), 76.

Where Bible and Life Meet
DEEPER DEVOTIONS FROM THADDEUS BARNUM

FREE Shepherding RESOURCES AVAILABLE

For those tired of wading in superficial faith, author Thaddeus Barnum's Deeper Devotion series reaches far into the spiritually real depths of lives defined by God's mercy. Barnum's writing is not for the spiritually timid. His poignantly transparent storytelling joins arm-in-arm with readers, leading them deeper into authentic discipleship where Bible and life meet.

Real Love
978-0-89827-914-6
978-0-89827-915-3 (e-book)

Real Mercy
978-0-89827-916-0
978-0-89827-917-7 (e-book)

Real Identity
978-0-89827-755-5
978-0-89827-756-2 (e-book)